DANIEL MORGAN SOUTHERN INVESTIGATION

A First-Person account of Life and Death at Southern Investigations

David Bray

DANIEL MORGAN SOUTHERN INVESTIGATION

DANIEL MORGAN SOUTHERN INVESTIGATION

DANIEL MORGAN SOUTHERN INVESTIGATION

About the Author

David Bray met Daniel Morgan in 1984 and worked at Southern Investigations from early 1986 until September of 1988. He became best friends with Daniel and remained so until his tragic murder.

In June 1987 David joined the Territorial Army, passing out as a trained soldier in November 1987 attaining the rank of Fusilier; whilst still working at Southern Investigations.

In the 1988 New Year's Honours list David was awarded a General Officer Commanding Commendation for highly meritorious service in the London district awarded by Major General Avery (Lifeguards) presented at Horse guards' parade, Whitehall, London, SW1 for saving the life of a road traffic accident victim.

David remains a consulting detective on a case to case basis in the investigation industry. He lives in London.

CONTENTS

Author's Note

Daniel Morgan Inquest Legal Representatives

Foreword

Chapter 1: The 10th of March 1987   2
Chapter 2: The Beginning   12
Chapter 3: Danny   19
Chapter 4: Misconceptions   29
Chapter 5: The Offices of Southern Investigations   32
Chapter 6: The Hostelries   38
Chapter 7: The Motor Vehicles   44
Chapter 8: The Irony of an Axe   49
Chapter 9: Repo Man   55
Chapter 10: Process Server   66
Chapter 11: Quarter Days – The Bailiff is Coming   72
Chapter 12: The Best Thing about the Police was Sting   78
Chapter 13: Where is Danny's Rolex?   83
Chapter 14: The Algarve Trip   88
Chapter 15: The Elnathan Mews Possession   93
Chapter 16: The Malta Repossession   99
Chapter 17: The Office Burglary   114
Chapter 18: Sir Monty and the Inquisition   118
Chapter 19: Belmont Car Auctions Robberies   131
Chapter 20: Something Doesn't Add Up   143
Chapter 21: Daniel's Desk Diary   154
Chapter 22: Ladies Man   166
Chapter 23: Conflict of Evidence   175
Chapter 24: Morgan Rees & Co.   200

Chapter 25: The Teflon Trail   203
Chapter 26: Was Danny Afraid   237
Chapter 27: The Winds of Change   244
Chapter 28: Detective Constable Alan 'Taffy' Holmes   249
Chapter 29: Read All About It   256
Chapter 30: My 10th of March 1987   259
Chapter 31: The Dark Side   263
Chapter 32: The Daniel Morgan Independent Panel   280
Chapter 33: It's About Time   296

In Closing   303

Acknowledgements   306

Glossary   308

This book is dedicated to the memory of my friend,
Daniel Morgan.

DANIEL MORGAN SOUTHERN INVESTIGATION

Author's Note

This book contains actual witness testimony taken from the transcript of the Inquest into the death of Daniel Morgan; as transcribed by the court reporter.

I was a witness involved at the inquest into the murder of Daniel Morgan. I was granted the status of a properly interested person by the Coroner and as such I received an official copy of the inquest transcript.

It is not permitted to make changes, corrections or otherwise to the official court document so misspelled names and titles, typographical errors and pauses in speech appear exactly as transcribed.

There is occasional repetition of testimony from one chapter to another. This is done for ease of reading and understanding how the testimony is relevant to that chapter.

Information is also taken from the UK National Archives and Government Databases under licence.

I have utilised certain media sources that, over the years, I believe have been reliable in reporting the murder investigations and full attribution has been given under licence. Again, occasional repetition of a news article is used for understanding and emphasis of what took place.

Every reasonable effort has been made to attribute and identify source material reproduced in this publication. However, if any error has occurred and/or any attribution has been missed this was completely unintentional and I would appreciate hearing from those concerned.

DANIEL MORGAN SOUTHERN INVESTIGATION

Daniel Morgan Inquest Legal Representatives

SIR MONTAGUE B. LEVINE – The Coroner

MISS J. TWEEDIE (instructed by Messrs Gagg & Co., Crickhowell) Appeared for Mrs. Isobel Mary Hulsmann and Mr. Alastair Morgan.

MR. J. NUTTER (instructed by Messrs Coffey Whittey, Thornton Heath) appeared for Mr. John Rees.

MR. I. GOLDSWORTHY (instructed by Messrs Russell Jones & Walker, WC1) appeared for Detective Sergeant Fillery, Detective Constable Foley and Detective Constable Purvis.

MR. J. GOMPERTZ Q.C. AND MR. J. NORRIS (instructed by The Solicitor to the Commissioner of Police) appeared for the Commissioner of Police.

(Transcript of the Shorthand Notes of Marten Walsh Cherer Ltd., Pemberton House, East Harding Street, London EC4A 3AS. Telephone Number: 01-583-0889)

DANIEL MORGAN SOUTHERN INVESTIGATION

Foreword

D aniel and I worked together as Private Investigators but first and foremost we were close friends. Danny was most human, he was far from perfect and none of us are. I will share with you all of his fantastic qualities and his terrible imperfections in a true account of the man he really was; many accounts which are fully supported by actual witness testimony.

A tremendous amount of the details reported are shocking and scandalous, some of you may not like or believe what you read, however as Daniel would say, *"the truth never lies"*. My friend absolutely did not deserve to be executed and his life taken in such a horrific manner.

Daniel was murdered on the 10th of March 1987 in the car park of the Golden Lion Public House in Sydenham, South London; Daniel was 37 years of age. He was found with an axe embedded in his face and if that is not shocking enough; after 31 years, five police investigations and the Daniel Morgan Independent Panel inquiry no one has ever been convicted of this crime. This unsolved murder is one of the most expensive criminal investigations in UK history.

Since the 10th of March 1987, I have remained a witness and assisted the authorities in the police investigations. I have stayed patient with an open mind in the hope that one-day true justice might be found.

Every day that I knew Daniel I learned something from him and what I learnt I carry through to this day and that is knowledge, life experience and an understanding of human nature both good and bad.

Over the last 34 years I spent a large part of my life as a consulting detective undertaking investigative research in all areas of civil and criminal investigation. On leaving Southern Investigations in September 1988 I had no further contact with any of my previous work colleagues.

DANIEL MORGAN SOUTHERN INVESTIGATION

The internet and the media are powerful tools that supply us tremendous resources in reporting and recording information however that recorded information is not always accurate or true and can be sensationalized or watered down.

Over the decades I have had numerous opportunities from the media and broadcasting companies to be interviewed and to tell my story; however, I chose to remain silent until now. In writing this book, I believe I have expressed a fair assessment of these experiences from 34 plus years ago. I know that Daniel would not wish me to remain in the wings as an onlooker any longer; he would be demanding and egging me on to write this book which, includes my recollections of the day to day investigative operations and events that transpired at Southern Investigations along with our experiences involving family and interaction with the public and the police.

As I write these memoirs, I think back to days gone by. At times I struggle with my thoughts and emotions of sadness but I know the reason why I am writing this; you never forget tragedy.

Let me introduce you to my friend, Danny Morgan....

Chapter 1
The 10th of March 1987

March 10th 1987 was a day that changed a nation's history; the events and the repercussions which have continued and are still ongoing to this day. A period of time, in excess of 31 years, that a tragedy has brought to the attention of the world a story so unfathomable it beggars belief.

Daniel Morgan had been killed. Dr Michael Heath the forensic pathologist who performed the autopsy gives evidence.

This is an excerpt from Day 4, page 29 of the Daniel Morgan Inquest. Dr Michael Heath is being examined by the Coroner.

----*I found that there were a number of injuries to the head which in my opinion would cause death. There were five lacerations over the scalp. There were two on the back of the scalp, one over the right side of the ear which had a surrounding rim of abrasion, one over the left side of the back of the scalp and the most important was the one over the right side of the scalp in the temple region. This contained an axe. The axe had actually penetrated the skull to a depth of four inches and in so doing had actually cut part of the vital structure of the brain. Three of the other wounds to the skull have actually penetrated through the skull, one of which had also damaged the back of the brain.*

Injuries such as these would have rendered Daniel senseless and unconscious before he hit the ground leaving no chance whatsoever for him to call out for help. (See Chapter The Irony of an Axe)

This was a particularly vicious and cowardly assault; clearly the assailant came at Danny from behind.

This was not a mugging or a robbery gone wrong. Daniel still had his Rolex watch on his wrist and nearly £1100 in his pocket. The murder weapon had been methodically prepared for the attack as the assailant used fabric tape on the handle

2

to mask the weapon from finger prints and to aid in grip. Daniels death was an execution.

An unsolved killing so horrific and catastrophic that the snowball effect of the ensuing investigations has lead this country into one of the darkest periods in police law enforcement; which segued into the unravelling of a sensational media scandal (Hackgate) that is unprecedented in modern times.

Let's pause for a moment to remember what was happening in 1987.

On the 6th of March whilst leaving Zeebrugge harbour in Belgium, the British ferry, MS Herald of Free Enterprise capsized killing 193 on board.

The 19th of March saw Winston Silcott sentenced to life imprisonment for the murder of PC Keith Blakelock in the Broadwater Farm estate riots in Tottenham, London. Silcott was later acquitted of the murder on the 25th of November 1991.

On April the 1st The House of Commons voted against the restoration of the Death penalty by 342-230. (What a shame)

Margaret Thatcher became the longest serving Prime Minister since Lord Liverpool when she was re-elected in June.

On the 10th of March the number one music single on the UK pop charts, was "Stand by Me" by Ben E. King.

The motion picture "Evil Dead II" directed by Sam Raimi was one of the most viewed movies of the year.

"The Last Emperor", directed by Bernardo Bertolucci won the Oscar for best picture that year.

Around the time of Daniel's murder at 9:30 pm BBC1 was showing Tutti Frutti, episode two of a six-part miniseries by John Byrne; at 9:00 pm BBC 2 was showing the movie, "Two of a Kind", starring George Burns and Cliff Robertson.

The weather in London for the 10th of March 1987 was similar to the earlier days of the month. It was cold with frosty nights with high temperatures of only around 3° or 4° Celsius (around 36° Fahrenheit) with lows as much as minus 4° Celsius. The beginning of March there was occasional light snowfall, however no measurable rain fell between the 9th and 17th.

I remember the night of the murder well. It was cold with light wind-chill in the air; the type of weather that brings a painful coldness to your lungs as you breathe and on exhaling you can see your breath. The roads and pavements were clear however the cold weather saw a lot of people stay at home and not venture out that night.

Daniel began his day at home with his family in South Norwood. He contacted me at home by telephone around 7:45 am and told me that he had something important to talk to me about and that he was preparing to go to the office. He asked me to attend his home and pick up the children and take them to school and then get to the office as quickly as I could.

I did as requested arriving at the office around 8:45 am where I found Danny doing a bit of hoovering clearing up after a carpenter who he had come in to put some shelves up the previous evening. As he finished the hoovering the phones started to ring; Peter Newby arrived then other staff showed up, the office started becoming very busy so we got on with our daily routines.

It was around midmorning on the 10th of March 1987, that I last saw Daniel. He was in his office and was preparing to attend a very important meeting with the Cooperative Wholesale Society in Slough, Berkshire. Danny informed me that he was driving to Slough with Tony Pearce. This was a big meeting for Daniel as CWS was a large land owner and existing client of the business and he was hoping to cultivate even more bailiff related work from them.

Daniel was busy that morning and seemed a little rushed, he had his desk diary open which he was referring to and making notes; he was talking back and forth with Tony. Danny never did get around to telling me what he wanted to talk to me about so urgently. I could see that he had a great deal on his mind but his overall demeanour was nothing out of the ordinary. He did not seem worried about anything and was his usual self. I had seen Daniel prepare for meetings like this many times before. He changed his clothes in the office and was tidy, suited and looked the consummate business man.

I was preparing to leave the office and said to Danny: *"Hey, Dan, I am off"*. Danny replied: *"Okay, Dave, see you later"*. Unaware that these were the last words he would ever speak to me.

After the murder Tony Pearce told me the meeting that he and Daniel had, in Slough, was with Mike Fairhurst and it had gone well and the business was looking forward to a lot more bailiff work from CWS.

This is an excerpt of Day 3, page 82 of the Daniel Morgan Inquest. Anthony Pearce is being examined by the Coroner.

Q -------- A. -----. *I can remember 10th March because I was with him all day. We went to Slough.*

Q. *You went to Slough. – A. We went to Slough, we took our clients out, we had a very pleasant luncheon, Daniel was very happy, we came back to the office, booked in the new cases and at about 6 o'clock or thereabouts, John Rees was still in the office and he just said: "I will see you later in the Golden Lion" and that is it.*

Tony Pearce mentioned that Danny was very happy that day suggesting his persona to be normal without any undue concerns. Pearce also recalls around 6:00 pm John Rees saying to Daniel, *"I will see you later in the Golden Lion"*. From his evidence it would seem that there was no indication of anything untoward or any concerns in Daniel's behaviour. This is further clarified by Daniel's wife Iris who said when he left for work and when she spoke to him on the telephone during the day Danny seemed really happy.

This is an excerpt of Day 1, page 45 of the Daniel Morgan Inquest. Iris Morgan is being examined by the Coroner.

Q. Do you know what he did that day? – A. He had a meeting. He was going to Slough.

Q. Did, he at any time on that day, the 10th March -----? – A. He seemed really happy. From the weekend he seemed as if he had brightened up.

Q. Did he at any time on that day, the 10th March, say to you that on that particular night he was going to have a meeting with his partner? – A. Yes. He 'phoned me at 7:30.

Q. 7:30 that night. – A. He did not say who he was meeting. He said that he had a meeting.

Q. Where was he until 7:30? – A. I spoke to him in the afternoon. Brian Crush mechanic had come to the house and he was not sure how to use his car phone. He said that the only person whom he knew had a car phone was Daniel. He guessed that I would know how to work it. I phoned Daniel from Brian Crush's car to Daniel's car. Daniel phoned Brian back on the car phone.

Q. What time would that be? – A. 3:30/4 o'clock.

Q. You said he had a meeting at 7:30. – A. No. He called me at 7:30 on his car phone to say that he was going to a meeting and he would be in at 8:15.

Work colleagues clarified with me and it was later reported that Daniel arrived back at the offices of Southern Investigations at approximately 5:00 pm that evening. Malcolm Webb said that when he got back to Thornton Heath, from a Bailiff job he was doing in Dorset, the banks were already closed and he was therefore unable to bank any cash. Malcolm had collected £1100 in cash from his work that day and left it in the office. Peter Newby reported that Daniel picked up the £1100 and put it in his coat pocket. Daniel then left the office and met up with a lady friend, Margaret Harrison and proceeded to Regan's Wine Bar in Thornton Heath.

This is an excerpt of Day 4, page 21 of the Daniel Morgan Inquest. Malcolm Webb is being examined by the Coroner.

Q. Did you go back to the office? – A. It would have taken about two hours or 2 ½ hours to get to Poole by car. I had to collect the money down there and I got back to the office about 3:20 or 3:30 in the afternoon.

Q. When you got back to the office what did you do with the money? – A. I gave the money to Peter Newby.

Malcolm said that he returned to the office around 3:30 pm. In those days the high street banks closed at 3:30 pm and therefore he was unable to bank the cash that he had collected.

In the days after the murder it was insinuated from talk within the office that Daniel had put off a meeting on the 10th of March in which he was to pay a large bill in cash.

This is an excerpt of Day 3, page 19 of the Daniel Morgan Inquest. Peter Newby is being examined by the Coroner

Q. *"At approximately 4.40 p.m. Daniel Morgan returned to the office as the banks had already closed when I received the cash from Malcolm Webb I went to his office and handed over -----£1100----*

Peter goes on to clarify that Daniel placed the cash in his left inside jacket pocket. I believe Danny had very little cash on him that day until he picked up the £1100 from the office and I have good reason in saying this. Daniel then left the office walked along the high street and met Margaret Harrison at her office.

This is an excerpt of Day 2, pages 6 and 7 of the Daniel Morgan Inquest. Margaret Harrison is being examined by the Coroner.

Q. *"He rang me in the office at about 6 PM he asked me what I was doing. I explained I had some cleaning up to do and if he wanted a cup of coffee to pop over. ------*

Q. *"When he arrived, he asked me if I wanted a drink and suggested going to Regan's Wine bar which is just down the road from our premises. --- I agreed and we walked to the wine bar arriving at 6:20 PM."*

Q. *"We left Regan's together about 7:15 PM ......" Did you have any more to drink? – A. No. I went straight home.*

Daniel left Regan's with Margaret Harrison probably around 7:15 pm passing the Victoria Wine off license on Thornton Heath high street; a journey on foot of around five minutes to get to his car that would have been parked on or around Gillette Road. This concurs with reports that the last time Daniel was seen, in the Thornton Heath area, was around 7:15 pm by the manageress of Victoria Wine whom he assisted by bringing in the shop's advertising billboard.

I knew the manageress and had spoken to her after the murder and she said she remembered that night and recalled Daniel was carrying some file folders. This would not be out of the ordinary for Daniel to be walking around with files as he did this every day.

On arrival at his car Daniel would have undertaken the short drive (no more than 15 minutes) to the pre-arranged meeting with John Rees at the Golden Lion Public House in Sydenham. John Rees has said they were to meet Paul Goodridge for the purpose of obtaining a loan to fund Southern Investigations civil defence of the Belmont Car Auctions court action. (See Chapter Belmont Car Auctions Robberies) This would concur with the time John has said Danny arrived at the pub shortly after 7:30 pm.

Iris Morgan has confirmed that she received a call from Daniel at around 7:30 pm telling her that he expected to be home at 8:15 pm. Danny probably made this call as he approached or parked at the Golden Lion Public House. Iris's evidence tells us that Daniel did not expect his meeting to last more than 30 minutes taking into account a period of 15 minutes driving time from the Golden Lion to Daniel's home. The significance being how important is a meeting that is only expected to last 30 minutes.

On the morning of the 10th Daniel did not mention to me he had any plans to meet with anyone that day other than CWS. He made no mention about paying any outstanding bills.

Iris Morgan confirms that Daniel did have a conversation with Brian Crush between 3:30 – 4:00 pm that day. I had met Brian Crush on numerous occasions through Daniel when visiting his garage at Albion Place or when he visited Daniel's home. Brian was a skilled motor repairer someone Daniel gave work to because he was good at his job. I found Brian to be a likeable and knowledgeable fellow. Daniel would often speak at great length with Brian and they seemed to get on very well. Brian had undertaken a vast amount of the restoration work on Danny's classic car collection. Daniel would normally make payment to Brian for his work in increments of £1000.

Daniel had previously told me that Brian Crush had been requesting for some time a payment on account for restoration work. Daniel said he had been putting off paying any large bills and that car restoration costs were not a priority as he was budgeting because of concerns of the upcoming court case relating to Belmont Car Auctions. Daniel was blowing off anyone who wanted large sums of money at this time and would find any excuse to avoid paying them.

When Daniel arrived back in the office from his meeting in Slough, he barely had any cash on him. Daniel would have been unaware that Malcolm Webb had left £1100 with Peter Newby until he returned to the office around 5:00 pm when the banks were already closed. If Daniel had made any plans of paying a bill in cash he would have already gone to the bank and had this cash in his possession.

Even after 5:00 pm and armed with £1100 Danny did not spend the money other than for drinks; a sum around £35; the balance of the £1100 being found on his person at the scene of his murder. This clarifies what I allude to that he had no other cash on him prior to picking up the £1100.

If Daniel had so desired he could have dropped off the money at his home, (and given his wife instructions what to do with it) which would have easily formed part of the route on his way to the meeting with John Rees at the Golden Lion.

I remember I said to Dan, a few days earlier, that if he was strapped for cash he need not pay me my wages and I would work on expenses until the situation sorted itself out. He appreciated my sentiment and said to me, "*That it hadn't come to that just yet*".

John Rees told me after the murder that he arrived at the Golden Lion Pub at around 7:30 pm and he parked his BMW 5 series outside on the main Sydenham road. Daniel got there a few minutes later.

Daniel arrived in his BMW 3 series. His car was found at the back of the pub in the darkest area of the car park. John Rees has stated that he and Daniel were supposed to be meeting Paul Goodridge however, he never showed up. Daniel and John sat together drinking and Daniel is said to have made some notes on scrap paper using his Parker pen.

This is an excerpt of Day 8, pages 25, 26, 30, 31 of the Daniel Morgan Inquest. John Rees is being examined by the Coroner.

Q. You got to the Golden Lion at 7.30pm. Did you go into the pub on your own straight away or did you wait outside? – A. I went straight in.

Q. So you sat there, it is now 7:30pm and you ordered yourself a drink, did you? – A. Yes, I did.

Q. What time did Daniel Morgan arrive? – A. Shortly afterwards.

Q Would you agree? Give or take a few minutes. – A. Sometime between 7.45 and 8.15 certainly.

Q. Had it bothered either you or Daniel Morgan that Paul Goodridge had not turned up? – A. It didn't bother me.

Q. Did it bother Daniel Morgan? – A. I think Daniel expected Paul not to turn up that night.

Q. You did mention earlier on Mr Rees that one of the reasons the Golden Lion was chosen was because Daniel liked or was attracted to the barmaid. – A. Yes.

Q. You left first and you think it was 9 o'clock? – A. Yes.

The Golden Lion public house was not a known Hostelry that Daniel had frequented or was known to have ever drunk at before. Apart from the time Daniel was looking for John (See Chapter Ladies Man) with me and we sat opposite the venue. It is only known that he actually visited the Golden Lion as a patron on two separate occasions being the 9th and 10th of March 1987.

What I have always struggled to understand is why Daniel would park his car in an almost pitch black public car park. For me this would be the last place in the world that he would ever park his car especially in an area of almost complete darkness. I would have given you odds of 1000/1 that he would never do that. I do not believe the murderer could guarantee that Daniel and/or his car would ever have found their way into that dark car park.

This is an excerpt of Day 2, pages 68 and 69 of the Daniel Morgan Inquest. Amada O'Brien is being examined by the Coroner.

Q. You say, "My mother and father are the tenants of the ----- public house." What is the name of the public house – A. The Golden Lion.

Q. I was shown where the lights were at the time. It appears to me that one part of that car park at night is virtually in total darkness at that particular time. – A. Yes.

Q. You were living there at the time. As a young lady would you have considered walking across that dark patch of that car park on your own at night? – A. No way.

Q. And you live there? – A. Yes.

Q. I think it will surprise lots of us here later on in this inquest to find out that Daniel Morgan's car, the BMW was parked in this dark area.

This is an excerpt of Day 3, page 38 of the Daniel Morgan Inquest. Peter Newby is being examined by the Coroner.

Q. *You were surprised that Daniel had put this car in the car park.* – A. Yes.

Q. *Why?* – A. *My desk used to be littered with car park tickets given to him by traffic wardens because Daniel would leave his car anywhere normally other than in a car park.*

Q. *So he would rather leave his car on a main road outside.* – A. *For Daniel to leave his car in a car park was completely out of character.*

Q. *Completely?* – A. Yes.

Q. *Would you be surprised if I told you that that car park was in the rear of a pub at night, almost in the dark?* – A. *Yes, I would.*

Around 9:00 pm John Rees left the Golden Lion and a few minutes later about 9:20 pm the barmaid Deborah Armstrong stated she believed Danny came up to the bar and purchased a drink and two packets of crisps. Danny was not seen leaving the pub however, Danny's tragedy was just about to unfold.

This is an excerpt of Day 2, page 77 of the Daniel Morgan Inquest. Deborah Armstrong is being examined by the Coroner.

Q. *"On Tuesday evening (10th March) I started work in the pub at 7pm as usual.*

"Again, I remember the time being about 9:20 pm, because we were quite slack up until 9 pm and it was after this that I served. I remember he was a white man he was slightly taller than me, about 5'7" or 5'8". He was in his late 30s to 40s. He was wearing a suit; I think it may have been dark grey. He wore a shirt. He had a beard, -----. He ordered a brandy and lemonade, I think, and a bitter from a pump and two packets of ready salted crisps.

It would seem that it was Daniel who Deborah Armstrong served at around 9.20 pm. The time it took Daniel to finish his drink and to leave the pub he likely left around 9.30 pm and it is the witness testimony of Thomas Terry that is most significant, he may have missed witnessing the murder by a couple of minutes maybe even seconds.

On Tuesday the 10th of March 1987 at 9:40 pm Thomas Terry, a BBC sound producer, pulled into the car park of the Golden Lion. He saw something on the ground, parked his car and took a closer look. He saw the body of Danny laying there and then rushed into the pub to raise the alarm. One of the first police officers on the scene was DC Noel Cosgrave and it was he who witnessed Thomas Terry's statement.

This is an excerpt of Day 3, pages 13 and 14 of the Daniel Morgan Inquest. Thomas Terry is being examined by the Coroner.

Q. *This is a statement you made on the 10th of March 1987. Again, I remind you that it was the day of the killing of Daniel Morgan. "On Tuesday 10th March 1987 at about 9:40pm I had just finished work at the BBC. At 9:05pm. I drove into the car park at the Golden Lion public house, Sydenham Road, SE26. I stopped my car, a Vauxhall Cavalier, index A334 RGW in the car park and in the headlights, I saw what I took to be a dummy lying on the ground. I pulled my car up to the body and went to have a look. I saw that he had an axe in the right of his neck. I also saw two packets of crisps by his left hand and that his trousers were ripped on the right side. He* *was wearing a grey striped suit. He was dressed quite smartly. I then went into the saloon bar and told the barman, Mr. Joe O'Brien. We both went into the car park where I showed Mr. O'Brien the body. I touched the body with my right hand on the back of his left hand just to make sure it was real. We both then returned to the pub and Mr. O'Brien called the police."* That is signed *"T.D. Terry."* It was witnessed by Noel Cosgrave.

Daniel was almost always rushed going from one case to another; constantly busy with outstanding work never having much time to himself as there were not enough hours in his working day. Ultimately, I believe this made Daniel an easy target as he paid more attention to his assignments than his own safety; and in my opinion, this could well have been a contributory factor in any planning of his murder. I do not believe that Daniel fell upon his murder by chance as premeditation was clearly present in the preparation of the murder weapon; this much cannot be in question.

The Golden Lion was very busy on the night of the murder. Detective Superintendent Campbell said at the inquest, *"There were 84 people in that public house that we interviewed."* The entire building was being used including the upstairs function room. A large number of patrons spent time in the saloon bar that evening during the peak hours until closing time; however not one of the witnesses gave any evidence at the inquest seeing anything regarding Danny's murder.

At 9:40 pm on the 10th of March 1987, the events pertaining to the Daniel Morgan murder began.

Chapter 2
The Beginning

shall never forget my first encounter with Daniel Morgan. The thoughts live with me fondly as I write these over 34 years later. It still brings a smile to my face however my eyes swell as I hold back the tears.

It was around April of 1984. I was a mere 19 years of age and working as a motorcycle messenger for Carlton Flyers of Selhurst; my radio call sign was One One. I had undertaken this work since I was 16 and accumulated an extensive geographical knowledge of London and the Home Counties.

I recall it was a late Friday afternoon, the sky was almost dark from the cloud cover, the weather was miserable as it had been bucketing down rain all day. I was wet, cold and standing at my regular spot at the motorcycle bays by the public phone boxes on Windmill Street in Soho W1; just along from the famous Paul Raymond review bar, waiting for a 'homer', a delivery back to South London.

It was around 5:45 pm when a call came over the radio, "Motorcycle parcel delivery", "W1 to Croydon for cash." I responded to the call with, *"One One I will take that."* The job was to pick up a parcel from a solicitor's office in the West End, London W1 area and deliver it to Daniel Morgan, Southern Investigations, 53 High Street, Thornton Heath, Surrey.

I attended the pick-up address, collected the parcel and proceeded to the offices of Southern Investigations arriving just gone 6:30 pm. By now the sky was completely black and the ambient light was so dim, almost all motorists had turned on their lights.

The offices of Southern Investigations were situated above a High Street shop. Walking into the hallway and up a dimly lit stairwell onto a poorly lit landing, I called out, *"Hello, hello anyone about?"* A short curly haired unshaven fellow with a moustache came out of the back office; he greeted me and said, *"I'm Daniel Morgan".*

My waterproof clothing had dripped a puddle on the floor from the rain but the parcel was dry and clean. I handed him the packet and said, *"That will be £7 cash"*. He said, *"You were very quick getting the job done"*. He then pulled a chequebook from his pocket and began to write out a cheque however, I informed him this was a cash job and *cash meant cash*. He stated he did not wish to give me cash and a cheque would be all right. I picked up the parcel and told Mr Morgan that when he gave me the cash he could have his parcel.

Mr Morgan took some umbrage to this and informed me he was ringing the controller at the courier office to complain. I said be my guest but you will appreciate that waiting time is charged at £6 per hour. I stood firm on my position.

Peter was the courier controller on duty that evening (we had encountered situations of this nature before) and I knew he would tell Mr Morgan a cash job means cash and if the courier did not wish to take a cheque, especially late on a Friday night then perhaps he might like to come and collect his parcel from the courier office on Monday morning and make payment of all the associated charges.

After Mr Morgan spoke to the courier controller he came back to me and he pulled out a large wad of cash and began counting out £7. (In those days we had paper pound notes.) I thought to myself, cheeky bugger, as he had the cash all along.

Then I thought wait until I tell him about the half an hour waiting time that I am about to add to the bill. I informed Mr. Morgan as I had been in his office for 30 minutes the bill was now £9.50 of which he exclaimed, *"What!"* I explained to him time is money. Mr Morgan found this somewhat amusing and from his reactions so did I; I just couldn't help but laugh. We both found each other having an immediate mutual respect in standing firm to our beliefs. He asked me my rider number and name I told him my call sign is One One and my name is David Bray.

Mr Morgan nodded his head in recognition and with a smile on his face he counted out £11 - my fee plus a tip and gave this to me. To my surprise he said, *"David Bray, I like you, you don't take any bullshit off anyone"* and I replied, *"I try not to."*

He told me that in the future when he contacted the courier office and booked a delivery or collection he only wanted me to undertake this service; even if it meant he had to wait longer due to my schedule of work on any one day. I replied, *"Okay"* and that I was happy to oblige. I had not forgotten that he was the proprietor of an Investigation business; that gave me pause for thought and tweaked my interest. As I left his office I knew straight away I like this fellow Daniel Morgan.

So, this is how our friendship began. Daniel would contact the courier office to request me or he would call me at home and this went on for a number of weeks. Each time we got to know more about each other. I became inquisitive about the work he undertook in the investigation business. He shared his experiences with me and I found we had many common interests. It was from this point on we became very good friends.

It was around mid-1984 that I formed a small business venture – an independent courier service from Crystal Palace. I visited Danny and told him of my plans and he said he would assist me as much as he could. He showed great interest and offered me guidance.

We regularly went out drinking and socialising together; I also visited his home and had meals with him and his family. It was at this time I began accompanying Dan on investigative assignments and my role as his apprentice began. Danny could see that I took to investigation work like a duck to water; he took tremendous satisfaction in the fact that he never had to tell me twice how to undertake any task. The more I learned the more my interest in the work flourished.

I later moved my courier operation to Tanfield House, 22 to 24 Tanfield Road, Croydon. This was the offices of Madagan's Bailiff and Auction House; Daniel's ex-employer and friend Bryan Madagan.

Initially Daniel and I arranged that I would share the offices at 53 High Street, Thornton Heath however this did not transpire as I had a number of self-employed staff and the office space required to accommodate this type of business did not prove feasible from this location.

Daniel was a man of his word and he did not want to let me down, he immediately said, *"David leave this with me I have an idea"*. He made a phone call and said we are going to see Bryan Madagan. Daniel and I arranged with Bryan for my business to utilise the spare office space at Madagan's which proved to be an excellent solution.

Bryan Madagan was very kind and gave me the use of a self-contained office, the rental of which was almost nothing. I was based here with my workforce undertaking Southern Investigation's and Madagan's courier work, process serving, vehicle repossession and all mobile operations involving most aspects of private investigative field work. I attended the offices of Southern Investigations and Daniel's home almost on a daily basis.

This work was on the job training and continued until around the early part of 1985 whereby Daniel asked me to work directly with him at the offices of Southern Investigations where I became a permanent staff member. I was now only 20 years of age. Daniel told me that although he was in a partnership, I did not answer to anyone but him.

William Jonathan Rees was Daniel's partner at Southern Investigations. He made it clear to me when I first met him that he wished to be referred to in name as John. He originated from Yorkshire and was a certificated Bailiff working with Daniel whilst both were employed by Bryan Madagan.

Daniel and John established Southern Investigations becoming partners in the enterprise. My first impression of John Rees was a tidy well-dressed individual. He was a married man and his wife's name was Sharon (nee: Vian). The Rees' had three young children. John and Sharon lived in South Norwood less than a mile from Daniel. John was in his early 30's. He was intelligent and at times subtly quick witted - a man considerably different in character to Daniel. John could be most charming, depending on whom he was talking to and I don't think this will come as any surprise to those who knew him.

In all walks of life, as in any profession, people experience differences of opinion with work colleagues and John's northern roots and upbringing could explain this as much as the North and South divide; as I am predominantly south London born and bred. John and I did not see eye to eye however that did not mean we could not exist in the same space. I had my work to do and John had his. John was Daniel's partner and was afforded a level of respect.

Kevin Lennon was the business bookkeeper. I would see him when he visited the office undertaking accounting; he was the father of a large family and over time experienced personal issues. Kevin drank in the local pubs. (See Chapter Something Doesn't Add Up)

Laurie Bucknole was a retired police officer whom Daniel gave work to as a process server. He was one of a number of casual workers. Laurie was a keen white wine drinker and on most days, could be found in the local pubs. He started up his own business, Metropolitan Investigations, initially in Thornton Heath, then moving to offices in Brixton. Laurie was known for sharing business assignments and had extensive contacts and friends within the police. I found him to be a larger-than-life character; Daniel told me that he had his reservations about Laurie and over time he found him to be somewhat unreliable. Daniel said he was pleased when Laurie told him he had started his own enterprise and wished him good fortune.

Daniel employed Peter Newby as the office manager. I recall the hiring of Peter. He was working for Robert West & Co who shared the offices at 53 High Street, Thornton Heath. In getting to know Peter and talking with him mostly passing on the stairs it was established that he was being laid off by the insurance business. I remember Daniel discussing the hiring of Peter with John over a period of about a month. The discussions surrounded the cost in manpower to the partnership and Daniel asked John to offer Peter the position of office manager, initially on a part time basis.

This is an excerpt of Day 3, page 21-22 of the Daniel Morgan Inquest. Mr Peter Newby is examined by the Coroner. Peter Newby's police evidence statement of the 23rd of March 1987 is read to the Court.

"It was whilst working for Robert West that I came to know Daniel Morgan and John Rees of Southern Investigations."

"When I left the employment of Robert West, John Rees approached me asking me if I would like to work for them part-time. I started with them part-time in April 1985 but as the work increased I began working full-time in about July/August 1985. Daniel Morgan dealt with the bailiff side of the work and John Rees did the investigation work. Daniel Morgan

occasionally did some investigation work. During the time that I have worked at Southern Investigations I have known a number of people who have worked for the company. Mr Laurie Bucknel worked on the investigation side of the business and was also engaged in process serving for about 18 months. I think he left us in October 1986. He mainly worked with John Rees. David Bray was engaged in process serving and used to work quite a lot with Daniel Morgan. David Bray was already working for the company when I joined them".

"Malcolm Webb is mainly employed with the bailiff work but if busy, he would assist in process serving. Malcolm would get his work from Daniel and occasionally accompany him on specific jobs. John Peacock works for the company as a process server. He did occasionally go with Danny on jobs. There were a number of people who did security work for the company on a casual basis, i.e. Kevin Quiwckendon, Brian Lawrence. Both these did static security work when our company had a contract with the Co-op. They were used for security at Belmont Auctions". - --- "John Rees' brother-in-law, Glen Vian, and his brother-in-law, Gary were also used on security work. -----, Kevin Lennon was the accountant".

Peter told me he had a long career in business and was involved in the Police Special Constabulary. Peter was responsible for the day-to-day running of the business, affidavit and exhibit preparation and report of findings to clients. We had many discussions over long periods of time. I am aware that Peter was someone that Daniel would confide in and I was privy on a number of occasions when Daniel shared his views and opinions in confidence with Peter.

Patricia Thorne was the office secretary and was an exceptionally nice lady who worked on a part-time basis. She was a working mum and would usually come into the office between 10:00 am and 3:00 pm. She had a good sense of humour and got on with her job, not getting involved in office politics.

Four or five months before he was killed, Daniel recruited Tony Pearce who was an extended member of his family once being married to his mum. Tony was a solicitor however was no longer practising. Tony had an extensive knowledge of the law in commercial distraint and forfeiture. Tony was a gifted academic and an expert in this field but it will come as no surprise to anybody who knew him, he had an unhealthy association with adult beverages.

He suffered from the terrible skin condition of psoriasis which was so bad he would appear to be decomposing whist sitting at his desk shedding flakes of dead skin; he was often in great pain the poor fellow. There were occasions he would not show up for work, he was also found on a number of occasions inebriated in the office he shared with Daniel and I. Daniel always saw the best in people and would give anyone an opportunity to prove themselves even if they thought they couldn't do it themselves. When Tony Pearce did his stuff, he was brilliant and saved the day on more than one occasion.

I shared an office with Tony and I watched him trying to tackle an exceptionally difficult illness, he tried so very hard and wanted to be an asset to Daniel. Daniel knew of the problem that came with Tony however he believed in Tony and tried desperately to help him. I will always remember Tony Pearce as a gentleman with an unfortunate condition.

Malcolm Webb was a Certificated Bailiff. I remember Malcolm fondly as we worked closely together for some time, prior to and after Daniel's murder. Malcolm was a larger-than-life figure. He must have stood six feet two inches tall, a heavy-set man. He was a big lad and was the ideal candidate for a bailiff. As far as being a bailiff is concerned I don't believe there was one field operation he did not conclude successfully.

He got on well with everyone and never failed to put a smile on our face. Malcolm was a great communicator and was quick witted, I was with Malcolm on a number of occasions when he was called upon in difficult circumstances to defuse potentially dangerous situations. He never had to call upon his size and stature; his intelligence, quick thinking and charisma always saw him through.

There are many other associates and individuals that were connected to Southern Investigations and I will refer to some of them as we progress through this story.

Chapter 3
Danny

O ne of the reasons I wanted to write this book was because I have never felt that Danny has been portrayed correctly (in the media) for the man he really was and the work and business that he undertook. The media have reported on the murder since the beginning undertaking sensationalised stories or the submission of inaccurate statements by people who weren't there or who thought they might know him.

Danny was a living, breathing, human being and not a myth or so much newspaper print. I want those who did not know him to have a much better picture and to come away from this book having some idea of who he was.

I would like you to have a clearer understanding of Danny, from my perspective, of what Danny's last few years of life was like. I have a unique understanding of Danny from living this time with him, by working and socialising with him and our shared experiences. It is not my intention to show any prejudice either good or bad.

Daniel enjoyed the time he spent with me because he appreciated our friendship. I have always missed Danny and would have loved to have spent more time with him had he been given the chance. There is no doubt in my mind we were lifelong friends. To me, Daniel was one of the best people that I have ever known in my entire life.

Daniel John Morgan was born on 3 November 1949 in Singapore, his family roots are in Pontardawe, Wales.

Daniel's education was undertaken at Croesyceiliog grammar school, Llanfrechfa, Cwmbran in Wales; continuing his education in agricultural college. Daniel spent time working in agriculture on a farm in Denmark whereby he learnt the Danish language. In the late 1970s Daniel returned to the UK in the London area.

At the time of his death Danny had been married to Iris for about 10 years and they had two children a boy and a girl.

Over the years many people have asked me what Daniel was like as I was one of the very few people who actually knew him. You know when you first meet someone and you just hit it off – well that was Danny and me. We had regular heated discussions but not once did we ever fall out.

It is readily reported that Daniel suffered from a club foot. Yes, Daniel had a club foot however you would never have known this unless someone told you.

This is an excerpt from Day 1, page 39 of the Daniel Morgan Inquest. Iris Morgan is examined by the Coroner.

Q. How would you describe the general health of your late husband? – A. He did suffer from a lot of stress and had been to hospital on two or three occasions.

Q. When you say "stress", do you mean that he became depressed or anxious because of stress? – A. Anxious. He had chest pains constantly. He always had like indigestion and suffered from heartburn.

Q. Did he have any investigation in the hospital? – A. Yes.

Q. What was found? – A. They told him he would have to change his lifestyle.

Daniel was a workaholic and together we regularly worked seven days a week often from early morning until late into the night. We shared each other's company from almost the moment I started working with him up until and including the day he was killed.

Danny had a wicked sense of humour. On many occasions as we were driving along he would tell a story that was so funny you had to stop the car before you crashed. I feel his best comic act was his most silent but deadly flatulence. Picture this; it is 7:00 am and two, three or four of us sitting in a car in traffic on the South Circular Road when all of a sudden, the foulest stench of gas known to man permeates the atmosphere. Now you know there is only one man that can actually create such a demonic pong; he's looking at you with a dead pan, absolute straight face and says, *"Can you smell that?"*

Looking at him you are thinking to yourself, *are you kidding me?* Windows are opened, the fan is turned on and Daniel is looking at you sniffing the air. After windows are closed it happens again. This process repeated until finally Daniel could no longer keep a straight face and in the most proper terms; in the voice of an aristocrat he says, *"You had better pull over as I am in great fear of suffering an unfortunate accident in my underpants"*. Everyone in the car is now in absolute stitches. Danny was amazingly funny.

Danny was well spoken with excellent communication skills with focused facial expression and attentive body language. He was very polite and had superb manners. On speaking with my mother, she reminded me of the first time she met Danny. It was my 21st birthday party and he went up to her and introduced himself saying, *"Hello, I am*

Dave's friend Danny." Her comment to me was, *"What a charming man."* The impression that Daniel gave was that of a gentleman.

Daniel was never led he always took the lead in any situation he was involved in; however, this did not make him a control freak. He was a unique problem solver, he was tenacious and someone who enjoyed a challenge. You needed a high IQ to keep up with him. Daniel was quick minded in any situation. He had many acquaintances but very few friends. He absolutely enjoyed the fact he was able to teach me his craft and called me his protégé. He took great pride in knowing I was an avid student but more so a close friend.

One of Danny's greatest passions was Indian food. He loved a curry and given the chance he would eat it seven days a week. Often after a long day, well past 10:00 or 11:00 pm, we would find a curry house and have a late supper. He seldom got home before midnight and often much later.

Daniel was a massive rugby fan. He would absolutely make time to watch the Welsh national team. He was extremely patriotic and one of the most passionate armchair supporters of the game I have ever known. He would regularly invite me to watch live and recorded games with a few beers and snacks; you know the drill. Danny being Welsh and Iris being Scottish made for some interesting and playful banter between husband and wife when the internationals came around. This was complemented by the most exceptionally amusing and colourful language of banter interaction – all just a bit of fun.

Daniel possessed great empathy and showed kindness to most everyone he knew. Some might think they could take advantage of his good nature but Danny was no mug, he identified these people immediately often allowing them plenty of rope before they hung themselves. He knew his own mind, what he wanted to do and there was no changing him. Daniel was far from naïve.

When undertaking an important business meeting or more formal events, Daniel wore a suit. He was always clean and tidy and almost always dressed casually and was happy in a pair of jeans and shirt with shoes. He was not a great fan of trainers, I tried to get him to kick the habit of shoes (for trainers) but he wouldn't have it. Daniel never allotted a great deal of time for shopping for himself although he very much enjoyed visiting the market at Surrey Street in Croydon.

I recall a visit that I made to the market when I bought myself a blue padded winter jacket. As I walked away from the market stall I thought to myself Daniel might like one so I went back and bought another one. When I got to the office wearing my new jacket, Daniel commented, *"That's a nice jacket."* I said, *"I thought you might like it so I got you one as well."* Daniel was over the moon and he wore that jacket the entire winter.

I know Daniel's home life was very important to him and when he wasn't working for the business he was building his life and family at home. Over time I met most members of Daniel and Iris' family when they would come to visit or undertake an extended stay.

Daniel was always very generous in sharing his social time with me which included time with his family. Due to our hectic work schedule family life became a premium for both of us.

It was a Saturday morning when I first met Daniel's family; his wife, Iris and his children Sarah and Daniel.

Daniel had invited me to call at his home over the weekend. He recently built a ground floor kitchen extension which he was panelling the interior (with pinewood). He wanted to take this opportunity to introduce me to his family. I was very much looking forward to meeting Daniel's family. I was a young man and looked even younger and I wanted to make a good impression. Daniel lived in a three-bedroom, two receptions, semi-detached house with garage and front and rear garden on one of the most prestigious roads in South Norwood. On arrival at Danny's home I found the front door open, I looked through the hallway and saw Danny sawing some wood in his kitchen.

I called out, *"Hey Dan"* and he said, *"Come on in, Dave"*. As I entered the hallway, I was greeted by Iris who had a big smile on her face and a little fella, around three or four years old, who came running along; this was little Daniel. I immediately thought to myself that he looked just like his mum. Sarah was in the doorway to the lounge; she was a little shy and had a beautiful smile. She was the oldest by two years; and was the spitting image of her father.

I found the children to be inquisitive and intelligent and they seemed to be much more advanced in learning than their ages would suggest. I warmed to them immediately. What was abundantly clear was the great love they had for their parents and they adored their father. What was immediately apparent was that Daniel and Iris had two very smart little bairns. I saw a very happy and loving home life; Daniel and Iris were raising the children in a lovely comfortable home environment. Daniel and Iris' hard work was clearly reaping rewards for their entire family. Daniel had created a good life for himself and his family.

I spent the entire day helping Daniel panel his kitchen and getting better acquainted with his family. We shared food and snacks and by the end of the day you would have thought I had known the Morgans for years.

Iris is a Scottish lady from Perth and from the moment I met her, she has always been kind to me. Iris told me she was very pleased to finally meet me as Daniel had been speaking of me for some time. At the end of the evening when I was leaving Iris told me she was happy that her family had established a new friendship.

I was welcomed into Daniel and Iris' home and from that moment on I was treated like one of their family. I have always been very fond of the time that I spent with Daniel, Iris and the children and I retain special memories from the past.

Over time almost on a daily basis, I would be in and out of Daniel's home both visiting and socialising or when undertaking assignments, picking Danny up as we would go out to work at all hours of the day and night. I was always willing and able to lend a hand if the children needed to be picked up or taken to school. I would even get the shopping in from Gateway at South Norwood for Iris when called upon. Even though we worked together the relationship I had with Danny was that of close friends.

As the saying goes, 'Find a job that you love and you will never work a day in your life'.

Daniel was a loving parent and he hated being away from his children. He would talk to his family on his car phone as this was some of the most precious time available for him. Due to our close working proximity (two men in a car at times up to 16 hours a day) it's understandable we both shared each other's special family moments.

The distance we travelled and mileage undertaken on a daily basis caused us to stop regularly at petrol stations. This is where Daniel would find many toys and gifts for his children and wife. Often this was the only opportunity he had to compensate his family for his working commitments and not being there. Almost all of Daniel's time was spent running the business and generating wealth to pay the bills, he almost always put everyone's needs before his own.

We would regularly return to Danny's home late at night and be greeted by Iris with a welcoming cup of tea and snacks. Iris would have put the children to bed hours before and as we did our best not to wake them, they would tip toe down the stairs half asleep for a loving cuddle from their father whom they missed so much. Daniel would go to his bag or his pocket and give them the gifts he had purchased. The children loved this. Iris, in her soft Scottish accent, would often say, *"No Daniel it's late the children have been in bed asleep, give them toys in the morning"*. But when you saw those little tired eyes and innocent smiles it melted your heart. Sarah and little Daniel would always say hello to me and often climb on to my lap for a cuddle too.

I was often invited to dine with Daniel and his family and Iris' fare did not disappoint as she was a most excellent cook.

Weekends, when the workload permitted, were for spending some time with Iris, the children and grocery shopping. These were the days before online home delivery, and as Iris did not drive she would have to rely on Dan for the trip to the supermarket. Her only other alternative was to walk to the stores at South Norwood or get a cab which she was not best keen on. This could cause friction between Dan and Iris if he was delayed or absent with the use of the car in getting the weekly shop. I think most hard-working housewives would sympathise in these circumstances.

I was often in Daniel's company when he took his wife and children to the local toy shop in South Norwood. This was actually quite wicked because you knew he was going to go mental and who wouldn't like going on a mad spending spree in a toy shop. Daniel was well known by the proprietor and it was clear he was his biggest customer.

Daniel would not just pick up any old toy and be out in five minutes; on the contrary he would be in there sometimes for hours. This was better than Christmas. He wanted to know what the toys did and how they worked, with his children studying intently before making their choices. I used to laugh and say, *"Dan can I have that train set?"* He would look at me with a stern look on his face and say, *"No, wait for your birthday"* as if to say don't take the mick; but with a smile on his face you could see he was clearly enjoying himself. It made me wonder was it Dan or the kids who were having the most fun.

Iris was a hard-working mother and housewife and like any young mother there were never enough hours in the day. She took great pride in her home and had excellent taste in choosing the decoration and furnishings.

She and the children were always very well presented. Iris took time in after school education always making sure that homework tasks of the children were achieved. For a large part of Sarah and Daniel's life, Iris had to be both Mum and Dad; the children were so young when Daniel was taken.

Daniel and the children were Iris' whole life. Her family lived in Scotland and Danny's family were scattered across the UK and Europe, so geography did not play a kind hand in her immediately seeing loved ones. She was in London and fortunately had some good friends locally; after Daniel died I did what I could to be there for Iris and the children.

Daniel had a tremendous spirit and character. He was always thinking, calculating and equating. He was a showman and entertainer someone who could 'work a room' like I had never seen before.

Danny enjoyed a game of pool or snooker; although not greatly proficient in this area he had a healthy competitive nature. I had played regularly since I was six years old being taught by my father who was an amateur northeast England snooker champion. I was more than a match when it came to competition which Daniel was well aware. This could be cause for some rivalry between two friends and I recall on more than one occasion Daniel telling me, in a most proper English gentleman's accent, *"If you don't let me win you're fucking sacked"*. This I found hilarious and typical of Danny's sense of humour. However, I did not let him win and this kept his interest and intensity in our games even more.

There were times Daniel could be absolutely bloody minded. I saw this as a method he would use as a 'wind-up' – a ruse for entertainment or a prelude to a passionate discussion. These were times that I thought to myself you're bored Dan and this would lead to some interesting discussions between us often culminating in my resignation.

I must have told Daniel, *"I resign"* at least 20 times in the time that I knew him. It was almost a game we played. I would tell Dan, *"I've had enough, I am on my way and you can stick this job 'where the sun doesn't shine'"*. We both found great amusement with this and with colourful expletives I would make my way down the office stairs with Daniel following me a few steps behind.

He would say to me, *"Don't forget to wipe your feet on the way out"*. I would return a barrage of blue language. Danny would laugh and say, *"Don't let the door hit you in the arse on your way out"*.

As I neared the exit door on the ground floor, Daniel would change his tact and say to me, in his most proper aristocratic voice, *"Now David are you sure you don't want to change your mind and apologise"*. I would then return the volley and tell him in no uncertain terms that he should definitely go and fuck himself. *"Wait a minute, let me get the door for you"*, he would say.

As he was laughing I would turn around and say to him, *"You might be laughing now, but you won't be laughing in the morning when all the work comes in and you don't have any bastard with a brain to go out and do it"*.

This would establish a more sobering thought for Daniel as he followed close behind me while I was walking along the high street and around the corner to Gillette Road. On realizing I was actually going to my car, he would call to me and say, *"David, David now calm down, let's talk about it"*. I would turn around and laugh and tell him, *"I am going to go and find a proper job"* which he clearly knew was not a problem for me.

The nearer I got to my car the more he began to realize that he might have actually gone too far, but I knew he hadn't. I had just turned the table on his 'wind-up'. I would get to my car which most of the time was parked near the Victory pub and on opening the door, Danny would say to me, *"Look don't fuck about, come on see sense"*. The amount of pay rises I negotiated standing by the door of my car, outside that pub, was unbelievable. *"Come on let's go and have a pint"*, he would say. I would say, *"Dan you're buying the next four rounds"*. He would tell me to fuck-off in a most stern manner, and then negotiate it down to two.

Not once did I have any real intentions of quitting my job, because I had no intentions of quitting my friendship with Danny.

Other work colleagues would witness this strange communication between us and our behaviour towards each other would be commented on. On the odd occasion Peter Newby would call us both into his office and give us a dressing down for being a pair of twits. In the tone of a Sergeant Major, Peter would explain to both of us that our roles were supposed to be that of two seasoned professionals and law enforcement agents and not a couple of big kids throwing their toys out of the pram. Both Danny and I were trying not to laugh as Peter was not keen if we started taking the piss. I can remember on more than one occasion when Peter slung us both out of his office.

The work of a private investigator can be dangerous therefore Danny and I developed a close affinity. On certain field operation assignments, we may be in a delicate situation whereby normal conversation was not possible. We developed a language between us using our eyes and body so fine-tuned that a particular look or movement would immediately indicate to the other a significant communication and understanding.

There are some people you meet in your life that you would absolutely go out of your way to help and for me Danny was one of those people. We never had to ask each other twice for a favour. We were always there for each other and experienced a mutual respect.

△ △ △

There was, however, another side to Daniel. He could be terribly reckless and often thought himself invincible. He took unjustified risks in working situations throwing caution to the wind by not taking into account (in its entirety) what might actually go wrong. He could rub people up the wrong way often by arguing to the point of being assaulted. He didn't quite get it that just being right wouldn't necessarily stop you getting a punch in the face. He had his rule book which not everybody played by. He enjoyed the buzz and excitement of confrontation and at times his actions put himself and those working with him at undue risk. He seemed to cultivate excitement and danger and at times, I must admit, it was contagious.

On many occasions I stood shoulder to shoulder with Daniel during field operations we knew were getting hectic. We looked out for each other and depended on the other to keep safe. I am so sorry I wasn't there for Danny on the night of March 10th 1987.

I don't want Daniel to just be remembered as the man who ended up with an axe in his face in a car park or the man who became the most expensive unsolved murder victim in the history of the United Kingdom. He deserves better than that.

On what would have been Daniel's 68th birthday I decided to visit his grave. It had been 30 years since I was last there as I couldn't bring myself to return until now. I wanted to be close to Danny, talk to him and tell him about this book and to say a prayer.

When I found the site of Danny's final resting place, I was completely and totally shocked. There was no memorial, headstone or marker of any kind. Initially I thought I was in the wrong place however from the map (given by the cemetery office) and by matching the neighbouring headstones, I was absolutely in the right place. My jaw dropped and my heart sank; all that was visual was a patch of grass. As I stood in the weak sunshine my mind was awash with my thoughts. I felt so dejected.

I can only imagine, given the notoriety of his death, there were concerns that someone might deface or vandalize his grave. However, after 30 years there is still nothing at his grave to identify Daniel's final resting place.

In 2012, twenty-five years after his passing, a memorial stone was placed at St Peter's, Glasbury churchyard, Glasbury-on-Wye in Powys. A memorial now exists - a black granite stone with gold lettering inscribed with the words 'In Loving Memory of Daniel John Morgan 3.11.1949 – 10.3.1987.

Chapter 4
Misconceptions

Thirty plus years is a long time and it is important to remember what technology was like back in the day and around the time that Daniel was murdered.

Electric typewriters with a golf ball type head were still being used, computers were slowly emerging mainly for business use with word processing and data storage; car phones (non-mobile), mobile phones (if you could afford one) were the size of a brick, photo copiers the size of a small storage shed, pocket pagers, and fax machines that most people had to access at a post office via telecommunications (GPO now BT) to send and receive documents using dial up modems. The youth of today can be forgiven in thinking we were living in the dark ages with the communication technology that is available today.

It was during the early 1980s to the early 1990s that saw the invention and the implementation of the worldwide web and not until the mid-1980s that the internet established itself as an area of electronic communications between people.

What is established as the Web today is different from the mid-1980s; it's forward planning and growth was undertaken slowly. This new technology was not cheap and took time to be integrated across the world, buying it and learning how to use it. It was not until the mid-1990s that the internet really took a foothold in society.

This is an excerpt from Day 1, page 8 of the Daniel Morgan Inquest. Detective Superintendent Campbell is examined by the Coroner.

"At the outset of this investigation a computer was used. This is being fully utilised to date".

This is a prime example of the technological advances at the time in policing and collation of evidence. I find it interesting that the information was deemed of such importance it is actually mentioned and reported to the Coroner what equipment was being used. Today computers are taken for granted and being utilized by billions worldwide.

Daniel Morgan was a County Court Certificated Bailiff with bona fide application criteria extensive in background checks and qualification.

Daniel did not undertake any domestic bailiff work, enforcement of court orders for unpaid debts; by way of removing goods from people's homes to be sold at general sale auctions; the proceeds of which are to pay a creditor. This is work that Daniel and I had no interest in undertaking. Daniel only undertook commercial instructions at business premises, shops, offices, and warehouses etc.

Daniel almost single handily established a portfolio of business clients and acted on behalf for some of the largest landowners and landlords in the nation. They included high street bookmakers, a particularly large high street supermarket chain, and financial commissions to name just a few. Daniel specialised in commercial distraint and forfeiture, acting for his clients permitted in law in the collection of unpaid commercial rents and/or the possession of buildings, land or property.

Daniel's hard work and business acumen was beginning to accumulate Southern Investigations great wealth. The bailiff operations were not limited to the south east; they were being undertaken on a national scale. In 1986 Southern Investigations client bank account prior to dispersal held a comfortably healthy consecutive daily balance of hundreds of thousands of pounds. These client funds were held in a generous interest account rewarding the business an annual dividend for good housekeeping.

Daniel was extremely proud of this and almost daily he would inform Southern Investigations staff how successful the business was and how well we were doing as a team on behalf of our clients.

Southern Investigations had a fantastic client base of solicitors, law executives and credit managers of in-house legal teams from some of the largest finance houses, banks, leasing and credit card companies of the time - all of them household names.

Some of the daily duties and responsibilities undertaken by Daniel Morgan, Private Investigator and the field operation staff at Southern Investigations was, legal process, vehicle repossession, security guards, undercover operations and surveillance, credit status report, certificated bailiff service, tracing agent, debtor location service and civil and criminal investigation service.

The work that Daniel Morgan undertook falls in to the category of civil and criminal law enforcement. Daniel was a court certificated official authorised to act within the due process of law.

Chapter 5
The Offices of Southern Investigations

The offices of Southern Investigations were located at 53 High Street, Thornton Heath, Surrey.

The entrance to 53 was situated to the right-hand side of the front of the building next to the retail shop. Access to the upper levels was shared by way of a poorly decorated, dimly lit hallway leading to a staircase to the first and second floors.

Immediately at the top of the stairs to the left was a small office that was used exclusively by the secretary Patricia or the bookkeeper.

Directly ahead was the manager's office (Peter Newby). This large double office was the day-to-day nerve centre for operations, general meetings, photocopying, etc. This office had a doorway which led to an external wooden staircase down to the garden and to the rear alley which led out onto Gillette Road.

From the middle landing turning directly left up on the right was access to John Rees' office. Directly ahead overlooking the high street was Daniel's large double office.

The second floor was initially occupied by separate business tenants however, about a year before Daniel's murder Southern Investigations also utilised this floor.

The relevance in the early tenancy by Southern Investigations of 53 was the shared access. During business hours the main street door was always open and never locked; something that would be unthinkable today in a business of this type. I cannot remember any working security or alarm system. Basically, people could come and go as they pleased and this will become more important later in the book. (See Chapter Was Danny Afraid)

When Danny first introduced me to John Rees, I noticed that they were friendly to each other and got on well; they had clearly known each other for some time. But what was immediately obvious to me was that they were two completely different personalities.

This is an excerpt from the Guardian online dated Friday 11 March 2011 by Nick Davies and Vikram Dodd: *In a statement read on his behalf, Rees' solicitor said: "When Daniel Morgan was killed it was an awful shock to me and to our business. Whatever anyone may say on 10th March 1987 I lost a friend and business partner.*

The overall atmosphere in the offices between colleagues, in the years which I was associated, was that of focused participation in functioning operations where we all had to be on our game. However, loudness was commonplace due to excitable situations. Someone was always cracking a joke or telling a story of a work incident however tensions could run high and heated discussions and arguments were commonplace.

This is an excerpt from Day 3, page 24 of the Daniel Morgan Inquest. Mr Peter Newby is examined by the Coroner.

Peter Newby responds to the Coroner, *"They argued a lot. Danny used to argue that John was not getting out and doing the work. John used to argue that he could not because Danny was not attending to certain things and therefore he was having to do it. There were many arguments.*

It is my opinion that it was difficult to communicate with John. He had a way about him that might be interpreted as rubbing people up the wrong way. He could be very demanding and verbally intense and this was accompanied in body language. There were also times when John could be amusing.

The daily working routine within the office began between 8:30 to 9:00 am; however, if you arrived later, it was no big deal unless a big operation or meeting was scheduled. On most days it was normal for Daniel to be first into the office and other staff would arrive shortly thereafter.

Most client instructions arrived by way of post which arrived between 9:30 to 10:00 am. If the street door was already unlocked it was often found wide open and the postman would just throw the mail on the entry floor and it would be strewn everywhere. At times, the post was left unattended in full view of the public, totally unsecure; this could contain sensitive and highly confidential documents. We asked the postman to walk the mail up the stairs and place it in the manager's office, however depending on the mailman this did not prove to be a totally fool proof system.

Once the mail was in the office, it was transferred to Peter's desk as every job had to be manually booked in, given a number and placed in a file jacket and this included facsimile instructions received over night and in the early morning. (This was a time-consuming practice as Peter hand wrote and stored the information in the file book.) The legal process for example, all had to be photocopied, and could take some time. The work was then allocated to process servers. Other work such as tracing, observation, and security and bailiff assignments was allocated to each member of staff accordingly. Peter had a large white marker board in his office where he would list who had been allocated what files and so by looking at the board he would know instantly where any files were; Peter was an absolute stickler for this.

There were two main incoming telephone lines and as the business grew trip lines were added. There was direct line access by way of extension to all offices however, in most cases calls would be directed to the appropriate person by either Peter or Patricia. I recall that the main phone line was connected to an answer phone which further had the capability of continued manual recording.

The telephone landline numbers listed at the time were 01-683-3351 and 01-683-3460 the partners mobile telephone numbers were also advertised on the 1986 business pocket diaries as Car, WJR 0860-334712 (John Rees) and DJM 0860 334711 (Daniel Morgan).

Peter's role included liaising with any 'one off' clients discussing with them the terms and the services that we offered; and at times dealing with pre-instruction consultations. Anything he wasn't comfortable with, he passed on to one of the partners.

Peter would deal with the day to day running of the office together with undertaking affidavit and exhibit preparation along with drafting the reports of investigative research findings to clients.

Patricia worked part time from 10:00 am to 3:00 pm and her duties included copy typing, invoicing and general secretarial work. She was great; someone who was a lady and very kind. It was Daniel's rule that no one was allowed to swear around Pat. If you were caught 'effing and blinding' within Pat's hearing you did yourself a favour and you immediately apologized which she found very amusing.

Danny, me, Peter, Pat, and later Tony Pearce and Malcolm Webb, all worked together as a team in field operations with other casual staff that worked on an as needed basis. John's role was very different; on the phone in his office somewhat isolated from what the rest of us were doing. It's important to understand the relationship of all members of staff, their roles and particular skill sets.

Danny was kind and polite with his management skills to everybody in the office however John's approach was very different. In my opinion I found John's management skills to be less desirable.

The actual work undertaken at Southern Investigations was split into two main categories, field operations and intelligence gathering. Field operation staff worked on the street interacting with the public and part of this work included making door to door calls where certain intelligence could be found. More extensive methods in intelligence gathering were by other means, at a desk over the phone or being obtained from confidential sources.

I can say at that time I had limited knowledge of how the information was obtained or who supplied it other than what I have stated. The partners and senior staff members did not share with me the intricacies of this part of the business, but this much I can be sure; it was good intelligence where a subject debtor or asset could be located which made my job in field operations a damn site easier.

Southern Investigations field operations staff would come and go all day depending on the assignments and the areas of operation around the country.

Over time as the business grew so did the amount of work and all the pressures that brought. Both partners had their own ideas as to how the business should evolve; from the kind of work and operations that would be undertaken to the personnel that should undertake it.

John would entertain a lot of different visitors, some you might know and some you did not. Often during the day John's door remained firmly closed and he let you know that was the way he liked it. If an unknown visitor walked into the building, which happened almost on a daily basis and Daniel met them in the hallway or on the stairs, he would ask them who they were and what they wanted. On establishing they wished to see Mr Rees, Daniel would direct them to John's office. Daniel would look at me as if to say, do you know who that was and I would shrug my shoulders as if to say, haven't got a clue. (See Chapter The Best Thing about the Police was Sting)

Clearly Daniel did not know the visitor and the visitor was unaware of John's office location. This could be explained as simply a private client but what it did demonstrate was a lack of communication between the partners. Over time the impression I got was that two separate entities were at work under one roof.

John Rees was a County Court Certificated Bailiff and had vast experience in this capacity however the bailiff work was largely coordinated and undertaken by Daniel. As the bailiff work increased Daniel became inundated and to assist the situation, a decision was made to employ Malcolm Webb as a bailiff for field operations. Tony Pearce was employed for the legal administration dealing with processing of warrants.

John Rees was a perfectly suitable candidate to assist Daniel in bailiff work and he did from time to time; however, his business dealings had him remain almost entirely in his office on the phone or receiving personal callers. Members of staff that shared the most time with John in the office were Peter Newby, Patricia Thorne and Tony Pearce.

Both partners had car phones and it was almost a crime against humanity on leaving the office and once in the vehicle if you failed to switch the phone on. I recall on a number of occasion when office manager, Peter Newby gave John and Daniel a severe talking to along the lines of: *"How do you expect me to run the business when I can't get a hold of you"* - this happened to all of us at some point. It took a lot for Peter to get agitated.

Working in a business of this type and undertaking the work we did could make the daily atmosphere within the office very intense. You felt the stress, the excitement and the emotion. This was not a place for those of a nervous disposition. At times things got so exaggerated within the office; the shared neighbours would complain that we should keep the noise down from the heated exchanges of discussions. Daniel was always very apologetic and visibly ashamed on behalf of everyone. I don't recall any physicality but the air was blue on many occasions.

I recall when John Rees came strutting into the office looking very happy and remarkably pleased with himself. He proceeded to share with Daniel that he was to join a Masonic lodge, and become a Freemason; which he took most seriously. Danny's initial response was playful banter that John was joining the 'funny handshake mob'. Daniel asked John, *"What do you want to do that for?"* John went on to tell us that it would be good for the business and also, he had to undergo some sort of Masonic initiation ceremony of brotherhood. I believe Danny said something to the effect of, *"I hope that doesn't include sheep as that would be classed as cruelty to animals"*. John failed to see the humour in Danny's remark and he proceeded into his office and shut the door. This is how I became aware of John Rees' association with the Freemasons.

Over the following weeks Daniel told me that John was actively encouraging and trying to persuade him to apply for membership and become a Freemason and that in doing so might prove advantageous to the business. Danny told me John went onto say that a large number of the Freemasons were police officers and wealthy businessmen from the local areas. What I do know is, over a period of time, Danny gave some consideration to this.

Daniel eventually told me that he did not like the idea and had no intention of becoming a Freemason. I am convinced that Daniel never did have anything to do with the Freemasons other than knowing acquaintances who were members.

The duties of the permanent office staff were staggered so at least one person remained in the office to answer the phones, during the lunch break, from 12:00 to 2:00 pm. The end of the office working day would be around 5:30 to 6:00 pm. However, Danny and I would often stay much later; left in the office alone or in the pub where I was privy to him having meetings and liaisons both business and private.

For a while the overall atmosphere in the office certainly changed after John Rees was robbed of the takings from the Belmont Car Auctions a year before Daniel was killed. (See Chapter Belmont Car Auctions Robberies)

Southern Investigations working environment changed significantly after Daniel's murder and general staff members had a lot to cope with regarding the entire situation. For me it was never the same without Danny; he was the lifeblood of the entire business and with him gone I felt that Southern Investigations had no soul.

Chapter 6
The Hostelries

Public houses played a major role in Daniel's life and ultimately in his death. I feel it is important to share the experiences I had with Daniel and to tell the story of pub life and how Daniel interacted with work colleagues, male and female acquaintances, family and friends. How he would conduct meetings in public houses and utilise their facilities to the fullest potential. What his behaviour was like around alcohol and the main venues that he used.

The public houses Daniel visited were The Victory, The Wilton Arms, The Harp, The South Norwood Sports and Social Club, Gossips, Uno Plus and Reagan's Wine Bars and the Golden Lion. In this chapter I will discuss each in turn. Opening times were different in those days. Weekdays most pubs opened at 11:00 am and closed at 3:00 pm reopening at 5:00 pm until 11:00 pm. Weekends were different with Sunday opening at 12 noon until 3:00 pm and 7:00 pm until 10.30 pm, alcoholic beverages were not permitted to be sold after these times; an extra twenty minutes was added to closing times for drinking up.

The hostelry which Daniel and the office staff of Southern Investigations visited the most was the Victory or as Daniel and the rest of us called it 'the office'. The Victory was situated at 45 Gillett Road, Thornton Heath, Surrey. The building still stands today however it is no longer serving alcoholic spirit but serving a much higher purpose as that of the Thornton Heath Islamic Centre. The demographics of Thornton Heath have changed significantly over the decades and I think that Daniel would find the change of use of the building (*the office*) to be an inspiration that would put a smile upon his face.

The Victory sat at the junction of Gillette and Garnet Road, some seventy yards or so away from the main high street, an area where most of the staff of Southern Investigations parked their vehicles. At the time limited parking restrictions were present around the busy high street. It only seems like yesterday but I know it has been well over 30 years.

The Victory was a traditional English workingman's pub; it had a public and a saloon bar where prices differed for the same beverage depending on which bar you used. Daniel utilised the public bar 90 percent of the time for no other reason than it was more cost effective.

The Victory was tucked away just far enough from the main high street to be obscured. The house served cask ales, good lager and an excellent top shelf as well as offering home cooked food and handmade sandwiches on a china plate which you could serve yourself from a glass display cabinet on the bar. The landlord of a type of days gone by; serving mostly regular patrons from white-collar workers of the high street, to the locals of the residential area.

The Victory's most prominent patron was Daniel Morgan, Private Detective and his entourage. Danny knew all the patrons and if anyone visited he didn't know, it didn't take him long to find out who they were and introduce himself, especially the ladies. Daniel appreciated camaraderie and attention - in fact Danny loved it - and felt very much at home and comfortable in the Victory, a place he could relax.

I often watched Daniel as he would share stories of his casework exploits with the entire public bar, everyone listening intently. He was fantastic and it was like a drug to him; and the crowd couldn't get enough. This was a regular routine for Danny. My personal opinion was that Daniel's behaviour was unprofessional and indiscreet. I would say to him, *"Daniel, are you sure you should be sharing these details in public?"* However, Daniel was Daniel and he did what he wanted.

Daniel was a sought-after customer so much so the landlord allowed him a *slate* (a credit account) behind the bar that he used every day ordering food and drinks. I remember Daniel would settle his slate usually on a Friday evening or when the landlord felt the balance amount was getting rather large. Some weeks the bill could be in excess of £200 which would probably equate to around £550 in today's money. At times it pained Daniel parting with the cash saying he was going to cut back but he seldom did. He saw it as a business expense and he could afford the cost.

Daniel was known to be very generous in treating others to a drink. For example, if he had a particularly good day and earned well, on arriving at the bar and ordering a drink he would call out, *"drinks all round"* and bought everybody in the bar a beverage, sometimes this could add up to 30 or 40 drinks. This made him popular with many patrons but occasionally unpopular with one or two thinking he was a bit flash and showing off, however Daniel's immediate response would be another round for everyone. This would normally put pay to any patron's opinion of his actions.

Daniel would enjoy a variety of alcoholic beverages. He could make a pint last a couple of hours yet other times he could drink quite quickly, slowing down when he felt the effects of intoxication. Daniel could become most jovial or intense but never violent or rude to the point of deliberately causing offence. Daniel liked to stay in control of his persona. He was a regular consumer drinking on an almost daily basis however I cannot recall ever knowing him to actually be drunk. He would enjoy one or two pints of lager with a curry. Daniel did not use drink as Dutch courage or for any purpose other than social enjoyment. Apart from lager Danny didn't have a regular daily usual. I found myself constantly asking Dan what his drink of choice was on any given day as this could change dramatically from Guinness to Dubonet depending on his preference.

The opening time for the Victory was 11:00 am and lunch was available from 12:00 noon till around 2:00 pm. At least one member of the Southern Investigations staff had to stay in the office to answer the phones and this was alternated between Patricia and Peter. Other staff could be found in the pub most weekdays enjoying a hot lunch and depending on your individual workload return to the office around 2:00 pm. All sorts of meetings would take place from social interaction with wives and girlfriends to more formal business meetings with other colleagues from within the bailiff and investigation industry; solicitors, media contacts and persons known to the senior members of staff as police officers, serving and retired.

When Daniel or any staff member was required back in the office, Patricia or Peter would telephone the landline for the Victory and speak on the house phone. This was the mid-1980s and there were no pocket mobiles, tablets or public Wi-Fi hotspots. On many occasions I recall Peter actually having to walk into the bar from the office to speak with the partners when his telephone calls to the pub went unanswered.

The business day within the offices at Southern Investigations would come to a close around 5:30 pm however; most weekday evenings Daniel, I and other members of staff would spend a couple of hours in the Victory. Field work operations were a 24-hour a day task and for some of us the time was spent waiting for the rush-hour traffic to die down and then proceed on the road with the evening casework.

The Wilton Arms public house was situated at 61 High Street, Thornton Heath. This was the nearest hostelry to the offices of Southern Investigations positioned on the corner of Gillette Road. The building still stands and continued business in the name of the Thomas Farley Public House until closing in 2018. The venue in the mid to late 1980s was a large multi-level high street saloon type establishment which was very well kept with nice furnishing, plush carpeting, providing a fine level of comfort and one of the nicest pubs in the area at that time.

Many of those who patronised the Victory would also use the Wilton Arms. Daniel only used this pub when other people he knew were present. Due to the size of the Wilton Arms and the transient clientele Daniel always seemed somewhat wary about these surroundings; he never seemed totally comfortable there. Daniel would meet with local lawyers and businessmen, private clients and girlfriends at the Wilton. Daniel told me he once had a slight altercation with some builders who were regulars at the pub and I believe this put him off the venue for a period of time.

The Harp public house was situated at 97 to 99 Parson's Mead, West Croydon, Surrey. The Harp was a traditional English workingman's pub and served the general community including local residents and light industry workers. The pub was positioned just off the main London Road. The partners of Southern Investigations were well known at the Harp by the locals. The pub was in close proximity to the homes of other Southern Investigations casual staff and family members. The Harp was used less and less by Daniel in the last 12 or so months of his life. It was not a place that Daniel and I frequented on a regular basis, almost to the contrary. The Harp ended its trading days as a Rock Venue Bar. The building no longer stands and has been replaced by a block of flats. The Harp played a major role as a support venue while Southern Investigations was undertaking the on-site security of squatters and the eviction of travellers and the possession of the land at the site of the old Co-op London Road, West Croydon, Surrey. (See Chapter The Irony of an Axe)

The South Norwood Sports and Social Club was situated at 26 Avenue Road, South Norwood, London. The building still stands and is now the Waterside Centre. Back in the 1980s the venue was a member only club with a licensed bar. This was Daniel's local bar close to his home. A place he could walk to with his family where they spent time together. I recall many hours here socialising with Daniel. This was not a venue he shared with everyone. The fact that you had to be a member and guests had to be signed in, gave Daniel the opportunity to be selective and I believe this was the place he felt ultimately at peace whilst socialising. I recall on more than one occasion watching Danny as he would stare out of the windows onto the lake, daydreaming for a number of minutes. I would not break his meditation however I wondered to myself what was he thinking, and what fascination had taken his thoughts out of the room. This was a side of Daniel that few people ever saw other than his closest family. Daniel was a member of the Thornton Heath Luncheon Club which would meet once a month. This was set up by a group of local business people. Here he would meet acquaintances and business men and women. The venue could change on a month to month basis attending different restaurants and bars in the local area. This was a very popular event which Daniel always looked forward to. I personally never attended any of these functions other than to drop him off or pick him up.

Depending on the talent (females) present, lunch could go on into the early evening, with club members moving on to pubs and clubs; and Daniel, on occasions, partying well into the late night.

The Ship at 55 High Street, South Norwood, London is now closed. Daniel frequented the South Norwood Conservative Club (where he attempted to play snooker), The Cherry Tree on Station Road, South Norwood, and the Albion 26 High Street, South Norwood, were all pubs that Daniel and I used within walking distance of his home.

Gossips Wine Bar, Gypsy Road, West Norwood, London is no longer in operation. The concept of the wine bar in the UK was relatively new being introduced in or around the mid-1980s. Daniel was known to entertain lady friends at wine bars. Gossip's was situated in a small parade of shops around the Paxton Green area, in a small village type setting, well away from the main high streets of West Norwood and Crystal Palace. At that time after around 7:30 pm the area became very quiet almost tranquil with hardly any traffic flow. Gossip's was operated by friends of Daniel. He would spend time here entertaining, drinking and dining. This was a place Daniel would use when he wanted something a little more upmarket than the average pub or restaurant. Daniel and I spent some quality time at this wine bar.

Uno Plus Wine Bar London Road, between Norbury and Thornton Heath, London was a place that Daniel frequented and where he entertained girlfriends. I never accompanied Daniel to this venue however he would share with me his exploits of the women he would meet there.

This is an excerpt of Day 2, page 8 of the Daniel Morgan Inquest. Margaret Harrison is examined by the Coroner.

Q. *"Our meetings were mainly for lunch time drinks, occasionally in company with other people. The meetings were not normally pre-arranged. He would normally ring up in the morning. We would normally go to the Uno Plus Wine Bar but sometimes we went to other pubs. – A. As I say, it was not that often.*

Reagan's Wine Bar was new, it was situated on Brigstock Road just along from Thornton Heath railway station a short distance from the high street. This business is no longer in operation. This was a venue that Daniel visited and where he told me he met girlfriends. Also, this is where, on the last night of his life, Daniel shared a bottle of wine with Margaret Harrison in the early evening on the 10th of March 1987 before travelling to the Golden Lion Public House in Sydenham. (See Chapter Ladies Man)

The Golden Lion is located at 116 Sydenham Road, Sydenham, London. This building stands to this day and continues the business of a public house. Daniel was not a regular and did not drink at the Golden Lion. He is only known to have visited the Golden Lion on two separate occasions, the 9th and the 10th of March 1987.

Daniel utilised public houses throughout the entire country as they were convenient and were found to be a place of rest for the tired motorist which Danny was almost on a daily basis. Daniel never gave a second thought in undertaking a business or private meeting in a public house or a wine bar as frankly they became a second home to him.

Daniel would be totally unsuspecting and it never would have occurred to him that his life might be in jeopardy walking to his car at a public house; a place he would have seen as a public sanctuary.

Chapter 7
The Motor Vehicles

Daniel was an avid collector and restorer of classic motorcars. Daniel's collections consisted of a restoration project MGA, a Daimler Sovereign and his pride and joy a 1957 Austin Healey 3000. When Daniel had free time, you would find him happily welding away in his garage. I would often call at his home and spend time sipping a few beers watching him turn a rusting relic into a beautiful classic serviceable motor car.

He spent a fortune in restoration parts; a passion only fully appreciated by a true connoisseur. Daniel would spend time driving around the country picking up panels and other parts for his beloved collection. We would regularly drive over, on a Saturday afternoon, to a specialist classic parts supplier in Hounslow, Middlesex and pick up the next pieces of his project.

I recall Danny had purchased an old beat up white 1969 Volkswagen panel van which he initially had plans to convert into a camper. He would always laugh every time he got in that van. He left it parked on his drive outside his house and it was temperamental to start. He used it a lot for taking waste down to the dump; we would bomb around in it. I think out of all the vehicles Danny had this old white van gave him the most fun; bringing out the teenager in him. He never did restore that van but he got it mechanically sound and moved it on to a young enthusiast who was able to give it more restoration time.

Danny enjoyed attending specialist car shows. An Austin Healey event was held in north London on the Sunday two days before he was killed. Danny asked me if I wanted to accompany him that day however I declined his invitation. I now wish I had accepted as it would have given me another special memory with him.

At home, Daniel only had space for one car in his garage and shared a two-car drive with his neighbour. Even though there was plenty of space on the street outside his house to park a number of cars he was sensitive to any concerns to his neighbours so he looked for storage for his Austin Healey 3000. The Healey was almost complete as Daniel used the services of car restorer Brian Crush who originally had a restoration repair garage on Albion Place, South Norwood, London. Brian moved his business to Norfolk sometime prior to Danny's death and I recall this was where Daniel's Daimler Sovereign was having restoration work done.

Daniel rented an underground garage at the Council flats where Jonathan Rees' mother-in-law, was resident. This was on Handcroft Road in West Croydon, Surrey. Daniel made a deal through John Rees' family and subsequently rented the garage for an indefinite period.

On one occasion I accompanied Daniel to the garage which, he visited regularly to make sure the car was safe and nothing had been interfered with. The area was not the ideal place to store an expensive classic car and Daniel was concerned about the neighbourhood. As he opened the garage door immediately a smile was met on his face. There she was the most beautiful example of an Austin Healey 3000 you are ever likely to see. This was an almost completely restored classic motor of some value. I believe Daniel mentioned to me at the time a figure in the region of £20,000 to £25,000 which in the 1980s was nothing to sneeze at. I remember Daniel did not want to leave his pride and joy motor; he had already spent about 40 minutes just admiring his handy work caressing the body and looking her over like a fine sculpture, Danny was in his element. I said, *"You do know the pubs are open"*. This promptly gained his attention and obtained the desired effect. He placed some blankets over the vehicle like he was putting one of his children to bed and closed away his precious. We popped upstairs to one of the flats where Daniel met a middle-aged lady, he dropped off a pint of milk along with some money which, I believe was for rental of the garage and then we left. That was the last time I ever saw the Austin Healey.

Daniel's day to day ride was a 1984 metallic green BMW 320i registration number A155 DFG and John Rees drove a dark blue BMW 518i, sensible robust vehicles for business users.

I absolutely remember the day when Daniel picked up his BMW. I was in the office dealing with some paperwork and we all new that Danny was getting his new wheels on that day as he hadn't shut up about it for a fortnight. Daniel rushed up the stairs and came into the office he said, *"David you must come downstairs I need to show you my new wheels"*. I laughed and said, *"I do know what a BMW 320i looks like."* He replied, *"I know but you haven't seen mine"*. This remark was typical Daniel. I accompanied him from the office and we spent the next hour and a half cruising around Croydon. You could not take the smile off Danny's face. Little did we know, at that time, the roll and significance that car would have in being the vehicle Daniel drove to the venue of his murder.

Shortly after Danny was murdered, Iris was contacted by John Rees who told her that arrangements needed to be made to move the Austin Healey from the garage at Handcroft Road. I felt the timing of the request and the pressing for the removal of the vehicle seemed somewhat insensitive.

I recall that Iris was not immediately able to do this as she was obviously grieving and trying to come to terms with the murder of Daniel. She also had to deal with a number of other more important issues including dealing with unfinished financial issues involving Southern Investigations. (See Chapter Belmont Car Auctions Robberies)

After a period of time Iris was finally in a position and made arrangements to remove and store the Austin Healey from the garage at Handcroft Road. She arranged for a vehicle remover to attend at the underground garage and on arrival it was established that the car was missing, Daniel's prized Austin Healey had been stolen.

I cannot ignore the fact that Danny told me he was always concerned about the security of the garage and the area in which the car was stored. However the situation is seen, it cannot be said that notice to remove the Austin Healey from the garage had not been given.

I believe Danny had the car insured for theft however it is possible this may have lapsed in the time after his murder. As if Iris didn't have enough on her plate she now had to suffer yet another loss and any associated thoughts, was the theft of the Austin Healey in anyway connected to Daniels murder?

After extensive police investigation and some 19 years after it was stolen Daniel's Austin Healey 3000 was finally located by police in a London lock-up garage in September 2006.

In June of 2007 the police contacted me and asked me to assist as a witness in their inquiries regarding Daniel's Austin Healey. The police told me the person who sold the car to the current keeper in 1998/1999 had nothing to do with the murder and that the person who purchased the car was completely unaware of the vehicles history and was in no way involved in any wrong doing in obtaining the vehicle; and it is pure coincidence and somewhat ironic that that person just so happened to be a police officer.

Two men have since been convicted in connection with this matter.

Daniel was a skilled gifted individual in the restoration of classic motor vehicles and instead of looking at the obvious negatives surrounding this situation I would like to think that even after all is said and done something positive does exist from this.

Daniel was very proud in his skill, craftsmanship and hard work in restoring that Austin Healey 3000. It stood the test of time and 19 years after his murder his cherished motorcar was still sought after and a desirable classic example; having continued its life being appreciated and loved as much then as when Daniel was custodian, showing love and care for that vehicle whilst he was alive.

Chapter 8
The Irony of an Axe

t was around the early part of 1986 when Danny received instructions from lawyers to remove travellers from the site of the old Cooperative Wholesale Society, London Road, West Croydon, Surrey. The travellers that were in occupation of the land were seasoned habitual offenders who knew exactly what they and we were doing.

This was a very large site with a car park, loading bays and warehouses, derelict commercial buildings and extensive grounds. This job included the use of on-site security guards undertaking hourly patrols round the clock; the security aspect involved perimeter containment including fencing and boarding. Also undertaken was the service of legal process and eventual eviction of person's unknown together with site clearance of fly tipped waste.

The travellers had entered and taken over the site and were illegally squatting. Numerous caravans, pickups and tipper lorries were present however the biggest problem was the fly tipping which was already prevalent. A site of this size could become a tip for hundreds of tons of industrial waste from hard core rubble to garden waste and general rubbish and if this was left unabated could cost the landowner tens of thousands of pounds just to clear.

Danny had the task to secure the site and limit access to vehicles that had the potential to fly tip.

Danny and I arrived at the site around 8:00 am on a Saturday morning. After undertaking a walk of the site, we had a good idea what was required to secure the perimeter. We had a quick breakfast at a café on the main London Road, where we noticed a good quality hardware store a few doors down.

We needed to buy some tools to assist in securing the site, the cost of which would be passed onto the client. With no expense spared we proceeded to fill the basket with hammers, nails, screws etc. Then Daniel came across a hand axe that was about 16 inches long with a chrome head and shaft with a black perforated handle. He started to wield this around in a way that you might imagine from a Chinese martial arts film and in amusement said, *"Hey Dave what do you think of this?"* I replied, *"It's an axe Dan"*, he said, *"Yes but it's a nice axe"*, I replied, *"What do you want with an axe. I don't think we need an axe on this job"*. He said, *"I know but I haven't got a decent axe"*. I replied, *"Oh I see buying ourselves a little present, are we?"* He said, *"Yes, you could put it like that, I think I will treat myself"* – which he proceeded to do.

We returned to the site and began the process of fencing, boarding and securing the perimeter. During the day Danny went out of his way to use the axe and with a smile on his face said, *"See Dave we did need to use the axe"*. I just smiled and shook my head.

Some of the tools that we used that day remained in the boot of Danny's BMW for no other reason than he thought they may be needed on the next job and were stored for ease of access. I asked Daniel if he thought it was a good idea to leave these tools – possible weapons in the boot of his car and what his response might be if the police stopped him. Daniel's logical answer was that he was a certificated bailiff and could explain that he used the tools in his day to day routines connected to his business.

During the police investigation into Danny's murder, I was asked if he had ever threatened anyone with an axe and to my knowledge he never did nor do I believe he ever would.

I find it ironic that Danny and I would have a laugh over buying an axe for the sheer fun of having one and then he is brutally killed by such an implement.

This is an excerpt of Day 1, page 7 of the Daniel Morgan Inquest. Detective Superintendent Douglas Campbell is examined by the Coroner.

Q. May we look at the axe that was actually used at the murder? It is not to be taken out of the container. May I see that? – A. Yes. (Same handed)

Q. I do not think the members of the jury wish to look at the axe in detail. It is bloodstained and so forth. I have asked Mr. Campbell to purchase a similar axe so that we can see the axe in greater detail. That is the one that was actually used. – A. Yes, and that is a copy.

Q. Before we go any further this is the axe. It was a new axe that was used in the killing. – A. Yes.

Q. This is referred to as the diamond brand. This axe, I understand was made in China. – A. Inquiries revealed that this type of axe is imported into the United Kingdom by various wholesalers from China. One wholesaler interviewed caused 30,000 to be imported between April 1986 and April 1987, and numerous other companies import similar quantities. A great many come into this country. They are sold at various hardware shops throughout the British Isles. They retail at about £4.50.

Q. I would also like you to note that the handle of this axe is bound with some adhesive tape. The usual method of putting tape on here is to take it in your grasp, where you would hold the axe handle. This is for two reasons. One is to get a greater grip on the axe itself, especially if your palm is sweaty. It tends to move. The second, and this is probably more important, is that it is virtually impossible – it is well-nigh impossible – to take fingerprints from that material. Would you agree, unless there is some solid medium embedded into that that would take a print? – A. We did look at the axe and more so the underside of the adhesive tape for fingerprints on the original axe, but no marks were found.

Q. Putting tape on here serves two purposes, does it not? – A. It would be very difficult to try and find fingerprints on the face side, if you like, of the tape because of its material.

Q. Its material. Lay people are not au fait with forensic details and have the impression that you can take fingerprints from any type of medium. Obviously, if the surface is very absorbent or if there is a break in the continuity of the surface it makes it very difficult. We cannot get any lead, as I understand it, by the adhesive tape because this is common adhesive tape which is purchased at any chemist shop. – A. That is correct. It is made by the Elastoplast Company. They make thousands of yards of it.

This is an excerpt of Day 4, pages 28-32, of the Daniel Morgan Inquest. Dr Michael John Heath is examined by the Coroner.

Q. You are Dr Michael John Heath. You are a forensic pathologist, and you a lecturer in forensic medicine in the London Hospital Medical College which is part of the University of London. – A. That is correct, Sir.

Q. You performed an autopsy on Daniel John Morgan....... – A. My examination took place in the presence of a number of senior CID officers. .....

Q. The axe was found in situ in the temple region having penetrated to a depth of four inches and would be in the anterior cranial fossae. – A. Yes, Sir. ....

Q. Would I be right in saying that that blow would have caused death instantaneously in any event? – A. It would certainly have caused brain stem death, but there was obviously evidence of respiratory movements after this unconscious phase. He would have been rendered unconscious virtually instantaneously.

Q. Again I think the family should know, but as far as pain is concerned, and as far as his sensibility is concerned, he would have been absolutely senseless from these blows that had been rendered on his brain. – A. That is correct.

Q. Can you tell me which was most likely the first blow? – A. No, it is difficult to say which was the first blow. Obviously the last one was the one that the axe was embedded in. The other four are more difficult to determine. One of the other four appeared to be consistent with actually having been inflicted as he hit the ground. So, three of the other wounds could have been caused by an axe blow, but which order they were given in I do not know.........

Q. With regard to blood splashes, lay people tend to think that because you have such an horrific attack on somebody's skull and from the amount of bleeding around the head, that the *assailant or the would-be assailant must by virtue of that amount of bleeding be covered with some splash marks. – A. No, that is not necessarily so.*

Q. Would you be able to explain to the jury and the court that this is not necessarily so? – A. Yes, it is not as though the skull has been pounded in the same place. If you start pounding the same place then the initial damage causes bleeding, and then on the next injury that splatters blood about, but as these are essentially separate injuries they are relatively clean injuries and they will not actually cause much, if any, spraying of blood.......

Q. I would like to draw your attention to the first photograph. Members of the jury, those of you who are somewhat squeamish do not need to look at the photographs. This is a close up of the axe embedded into his head through his face. – A. Yes. If you actually look at this photograph it shows – we are looking at the face and upper part of the trunk of the deceased – some splash marks over the handle of the axe. Over the handle of the axe you can see a number of, what appear to be, splash marks. It is my opinion that those were actually caused not during the infliction of the wounds, but during the terminal episode. Blood has tracked over the face and over the front of the mouth area, and during the terminal respiratory episodes blood has then been aerosoled and sprayed out over the direction of the axe's handle and the upper part of the clothing. I do not think there is any evidence from the post mortem, sir that blood would have sprayed separately from the other larger vessels.

Q. I was especially mindful of the shirt. If there had been a lot of splashing from the pulsating artery of a larger calibre artery on the surface one would have expected the right-hand side of his shoulder of his jacket and the shirt to be splattered too, and they are not. – A. There was a bit of splattering there, but it would all go with the actual breath movement, that is the actual spraying of blood and the frothing of the blood.

This is an excerpt of Day 8, pages 123-124 of the Daniel Morgan Inquest. The Coroner, Sir Montague Levine is summing up.

It might seem somewhat strange to you, ladies and gentlemen that those horrific gashes in the skull, and an axe blade placed in four inches through the side of the head, could not cause splashing. I can assure you that in this court, with many pathologists who have given evidence before me time and time again, that undoubtedly it is possible. The amount of blood you are seeing oozing out is most likely the body moving when the brain is almost dead. It is frothing, caused by its exhaling of oxygen or air through the windpipe and pushing the frothing blood down across the front of the chest.

Looking at it you would say "Surely this must have made some splashing?" Not necessarily so. I would certainly accept the view of Dr. Michael Heath who did the post mortem.

The gashes themselves, horrific as they are, there is every reason to believe that all those gashes could have been struck in a very short passage of time. I think Dr Michael Heath talked about five and six seconds, but if you increased it to seven or eight seconds or nine or ten seconds, it is a very short passage of time when that axe would be applied against the skull. The important point is this: each and every one of those wounds could easily have rendered Daniel

Morgan unconscious, oblivious, no control of his limbs and he could easily sink to the ground. I mention that when you think of the possible scenario of Daniel Morgan putting up a fight.

What we are led to believe from the expert forensic evidence is that the assailant would not necessarily have any blood transfer or any *visible* blood transfer from the assault. I do not believe Danny would have had any chance to defend himself and I have always prayed that he didn't suffer or feel any pain.

Conspiracists can confer all they like but what is absolutely sure and without any shadow of doubt are the preparation of the murder weapon and the premeditation of the murderer.

Experts all concur that the axe was purchased and prepared for one purpose and one purpose only, to kill Daniel Morgan.

Chapter 9
Repo Man

The 1980s was a prominent period in United Kingdom history when consumer credit established a mainstream presence in our society together with the advent of the computer. Almost like an explosion on the high street people were putting pen to paper for HP (hire purchase). Finance was being used to purchase televisions, hi-fi, videos, early PCs and larger more expensive items, motor vehicles. Consumer credit had arrived and was available everywhere.

In the mid-1980s credit managers informed the Investigation industry as their agents that UK household borrowing was increasing dramatically; on average around 20 to 50 percent of a debtor's entire household income. These figures were projected to rise even further over the coming decade to 75 percent of an entire household's actual income liabilities - borrowings which may not be sustainable if wages and incomes did not keep up with inflation.

This was the business of money lenders – financial institutions charging huge interest rates and Joe Public couldn't get enough. HP credit terms were available over three to five years on average; a time when the credit reference agencies were in their infancy; the 1980s establishing their commercialization.

Initially everything seemed just dandy until problems arose; paying the money back. Expensive purchases like motor vehicles were particularly susceptible to debtor default. Debtors either *could* not or *would* not honour their agreements and fell into default by not making the repayments to creditors and that is when they would get to meet the repo man.

This chapter contains excerpts taken from the Hire Purchase Act 1965 and the Consumer Credit Act 1974 and is public sector information licensed under the Open Government Licence v3.0.

A significant amount of the field operation work undertaken by Daniel and I was that of vehicle repossession. Daniel's clients included some of the largest finance houses, credit organizations and vehicle leasing managers in the country. We were managing client default accounts running into the millions of pounds. Regulation pertaining to credit services was facilitated by the Hire Purchase Act 1965 and the Consumer Credit Act 1974. Procedures in debt management and vehicle repossession were significantly different in the 1980s than the strict rules and regulations that are in place today.

There were two main ways a person could obtain credit/lease for a vehicle and it is important to explain the details of how these agreements were entered into with the credit company and what the repercussions were for the debtor if they fell into default.

Hire purchase allows a customer with limited money to make an expensive purchase which otherwise would not be possible. A customer would enter into an agreement with a finance house or credit organisation (creditor) borrowing money to facilitate credit in obtaining a motor vehicle at a car sales showroom. The creditor would undertake credit worthiness checks of the customer (debtor) including employment status, home and work addresses, means to pay, etc., however credit checking of the 1980s was nothing like it is today. In many cases all you had to do was make an application and by merely applying you would qualify for credit. This was mostly undertaken over the phone in just a few minutes.

In the 1980s to establish a valid HP agreement a contract would be drawn up and signed by the Creditor and the Debtor. Our clients contracts would include a number of standard provisions: 1) a full description of the goods, 2) the full cash price of the goods, 3) the HP price, the total sum that must be paid including the cost of interest, 4) the cost of the monthly repayments and the applicable interest rate, 5) a deposit (usually 10 percent of the vehicle value) by way of a down payment, 6) a comprehensive statement of the parties rights, including the right to cancel an agreement and a cooling off period for a borrower to change his mind, 7) the right of the consumer to terminate the agreement, 8) a motor insurance policy in force for the vehicle and; 9) at least two forms of identification from a prescribed list. Our client's contracts also included debtor and creditor rights and obligations.

Once an agreement was entered into by both parties the purchase price of a motor vehicle minus any deposit is paid to the car sales showroom by the creditor to release the vehicle to the debtor.

Interest is included as part of the monthly repayment. Part of any agreement informs the debtor that payments must be made on a regular monthly basis until the entire amount has been repaid to the creditor.

Debtors Rights: The debtor has a right to buy the motor vehicle outright at any time by giving notice to the creditor and by paying back the balance of the HP less any rebate. The debtor has the right to return the motor vehicle to the creditor subject to the payment of a penalty to reflect the creditor's loss of profits. This was usually undertaken by selling the motor vehicle at public auction by the creditor, and any difference in monies of the contract losses to be made up by the debtor and any gains paid back to the debtor by the creditor. The debtor would also have a right of recourse where the creditor wrongfully repossesses the goods.

Debtors Obligations: The debtor must pay all the agreed repayment instalments on the dates specified. The debtor must take all reasonable care of the motor vehicle and keep it in a safe and roadworthy condition. The debtor must inform the creditor where the motor vehicle will be kept and inform the creditor of any change of address or residence. The debtor is permitted to sell the motor vehicle if and only if he has fully purchased the motor vehicle outright or in some circumstances under the strict permission and with the agreement of the creditor.

Creditors Rights: If the debtor does not make the repayments or violates any of the terms of the agreement he would fall into default. In law the creditor has the right to end the agreement at any time and is entitled to keep any deposit paid, to keep any repayment instalments already received and undertake the recovery of any balance due, the creditor retains the ability to instruct his agents servants or otherwise to repossess the motor vehicle, (which in certain cases may have to be dealt with by way of a court order and be dependent on the percentage of the total balance already paid) and finally the creditor retains the right to sell the motor vehicle by way of public auction to recover its monies however, if the value at auction did not meet the outstanding debt further action would normally be taken against a debtor to recover the balance of the creditors money. This would also include any associated costs over and above the original debt and interest that was incurred by the creditor in the repossession of the vehicle and in the recovery of their monies.

Vehicle Leasing and Personal Contract Hire: These are contracts entered into by an individual or business by way of a lease; long term rental, in the 1980s this was usually 36-months. A fixed fee is agreed to cover the use of the vehicle and accumulated mileage over a period of time. The payment terms are monthly. With a vehicle leasing company, the vehicle is never actually owned by the lessee; at the end of the lease term the vehicle must be returned to the owner. At their discretion the vehicle leasing company may include as part of the agreement at the end of lease term the opportunity for the lessee to purchase the vehicle outright by way of a (balloon payment) final payment.

When a vehicle is repossessed it is only the vehicle that is the property of the creditor. Any contents or goods found in the vehicle at the time of repossession are deemed to be the property of the debtor who is contacted and given ample opportunity to collect these belongings.

Phew! Okay now you have some idea about the law and the provision of an agreement between creditors and debtors and the standard operating procedures in the action of vehicle repossession. However, just because there was an agreement, freely entered into by both parties, didn't stop defaulters getting pissed off when the vehicles were repossessed.

Daniel would receive client instructions (default notice, termination of agreement notice) for vehicle repossessions (known as snatch backs in the trade) by fax, post, courier or personal collection. These instructions would consist of a copy of the original agreement and a letter of authorisation to repossess from the creditor together with a default termination notice addressed to the debtor.

Daniel and I undertook the repossession of some of the most prestigious cars manufactured: Mercedes, Jaguar, Porsche, Ferrari to name a few. Repossession wasn't just limited to motor cars, we would repossess anything where instructed, coaches, lorries, commercial plant including JCB's, cranes, marine equipment, boats, aeroplanes, medical equipment, you name it Daniel and I would have a go at snatching it back. When instructed Daniel and I would undertake repossessions all over the world. (See Chapter The Malta Repossession)

Over a period of years Daniel and I made some excellent contacts within the motor trade and working with many of the top vehicle manufacturers and car companies we established a system (and it was brilliant) to obtain automobile keys for almost every vehicle built from the early 1980s. By merely obtaining a vehicle's registration and identification number, we were able to attend an auto key cutter in south London and within a couple of minutes have a key that would open and start the vehicle.

This was an invaluable service to Daniel's clients and word travelled fast to finance managers across the nation as it meant potential savings in the use of tow trucks and other associated costs. In addition, it limited any damage that may be caused by forced entry of a vehicle during repossession. Our ingenuity in obtaining keys established a cost saving exercise that revolutionised the vehicle repossession industry at that time.

Not all vehicle repossessions were as simple as merely entering the vehicle and driving it away. A lot of the vehicles were not 100 percent road worthy and sometimes you found this out the hard way; whilst driving it. Some debtors absolutely knew the vehicle was in a dangerous condition yet would fail to make that clear to Daniel or me. Tow trucks and flat beds were utilised to remove vehicles that were not driveable. At times it was necessary to immobilise vehicles using wheel clamps to prevent a debtor driving the vehicle away. This method was used on the odd occasion when we were unable to obtain a key.

Private property was an area where difficulties were found in repossession and consideration had to be taken with the law of trespass. Vehicle condition reports had to be completed often supported by photographs as debtors were not always truthful or accurate when dealing with discrepancies such as mechanical or bodywork damage.

This had valuation and/or cost implications, which would inevitably lead to a greater debt for the defaulter as a vehicle would be sold, as seen, by the creditor at auction to the highest bidder, sometimes for next to nothing.

Due to the nature of the business, the work involved in debt recovery and vehicle repossession; together with the time period (1980s) and the evolution of society, the attitudes and opinion of some defaulters expressed an unhealthy disregard toward the repo man.

Vehicle repossession was seen by some defaulters as theft. Repo men were disliked; hated by some. Daniel and I met an array of debtors and these we would gauge by the good, the bad and the ugly.

The GOOD: Debtors who were at the addresses listed and contacted creditors to explain circumstances why they were unable to make their repayments. They were willing and would agree to hand back the vehicle and honour the terms of the agreement entered into; debtors who realised and understood their responsibility.

Daniel would do everything he could to assist genuine cases of hardship and unfortunate circumstance. I watched Daniel on numerous occasions act as middleman for debtors and creditors. In the majority of cases he was able to barter a deal so that family cars remained at the homes of the people who truly needed them. Daniel knew genuine cases when he encountered them and he would find solutions acceptable to all parties. In some cases, Daniel would spend hours when it was clear that these folks just needed help and assistance. He wouldn't even bill for his time which, was unusual for Danny. He knew that this would cause more hardship and more costs and he genuinely did not want to make a difficult situation worse.

The BAD: Debtors who just did not make their repayments, who would move away from the addresses they gave in their agreement with the creditor and who failed to inform the creditor of any change of circumstance. Debtors who would have to be traced to establish current work and/or home addresses; that had no interest in paying their debts or fulfilling their obligations and responsibilities. Debtors who would refuse to hand over keys. Debtors who would hide the vehicle or change its identify; who would do anything to retain a vehicle as long as possible and use it without paying for it. Debtors who did not care if they got a County Court Judgement against them or that their credit rating was being trashed, because in those days no one was overly bothered about credit ratings or County Court Judgements.

The UGLY: These ranged from professional debtors to career criminals obtaining credit by way of fraud and deception often working with shady car sales operations for the purpose of defrauding creditors.

The credit industry was fully aware that holes in the system existed but in the early days it took a number of years before this area of default and losses (running into millions of pounds a year) was fully identified and dealt with. Even today the system isn't fool proof. The finance houses were making so much money from those that did pay; creditors could merely adjust their interest rates to cater for the losses by way of bad debt provision. It was investigators like Daniel that were able to identify, from investigation and intelligence, how criminals were accessing, infiltrating, undertaking and laundering cash in this area of consumer finance, also establishing some of the first innocent purchaser defences seen in this area of investigation.

Daniel would study the files and undertake some background inquiries to establish an address where a debtor or the subject vehicle may be located. He would then mark the files on a scale of one to ten (one being the worst and ten being highly likely) as to the likelihood of establishing a vehicle being located at any given address.

Certain files would end up on John's desk with an understanding of what trace and location was required. A day or so later the files would be returned to either Daniel or me with the new intelligence provided inside the file. The information could include some or all of the following: the debtor's new address, telephone number, employment address details, etc. This was invaluable information for the field operations team. The result of this new intelligence in tracing these debtors increased asset location dramatically. The vehicle repossession success rate went from one in two to nine out of ten; and the clients loved it.

I recall a particular occasion, from intelligence obtained, in the tracing of a debtor and the subsequent repossession of the vehicle, the debtor said to me, *"How have you found me? The only time I have used this address was when I changed my vehicle registration documentation with the DVLA"*.

My response was that of surprise and I told the debtor to hold fast. I returned to my car where Daniel was sitting and I told him what the debtor had said, Daniel replied, *"really"*. I said to Daniel, *"This bloke is not pleased and he is talking about calling the police"*. This caused Daniel to be concerned. Danny told me to go back and tell him that we spotted the car by chance out on the highway and followed him back to the address where we found the vehicle. I said to Daniel, *"No we didn't"*. Daniel replied, *"Yeah, well he doesn't know that, does he and that will take care of any concerns he might have"*. I returned to the debtor and told him, and the debtor replied, *"That's a long story if ever I heard one"*.

The debtor absolutely did not believe the circumstances surrounding the locating of the vehicle (even though he was well in default of his repayments). I got back to our car and Danny said, *"I am going to have a word with John about this"*.

Danny and John were partners in a private detective business and offered the services of tracing agents and debtor location. I cannot believe that Daniel would not have had some awareness in the methods used in the tracing and locating of debtors or vehicles that field operations alone could not locate.

Daniel and I would sometimes collect up to 30 different car keys from the auto key cutter for the vehicles we were looking for. With instructions and keys at hand we would saddle up and be on our way.

Here are some examples of vehicle repossession work Daniel and I undertook on an almost daily basis.

Good Debtor Repossession: Daniel would contact the debtor by telephone and make appointments and arrangements to either collect the vehicle for the purpose of disposal at a public auction, collect full payment of the outstanding balance or a payment to bring the account up to date and out of default. When necessary Daniel would liaise with both parties undertaking financial status reports of a debtor and reach an amicable agreement due to economic hardship. These activities were most civil and the majority of those debtors were thankful for his help.

Bad Debtor Repossession: These were debtors who fell into default for a number of reasons, often never making any repayment whatsoever. The necessity to trace debtor companies or individuals was unfortunately increasing. Background searches and intelligence would establish new home and business addresses of defaulters. Experience informed us that in most cases it was futile in attempting to contact these debtors prior to establishing the whereabouts of the motor vehicle asset. If the debtor had any intention of being present and cooperative, the debtor would not have absconded in the first place and we were under no obligation other than to secure the asset on behalf of the creditor.

Vehicle repossessions were mostly conducted between the hours of 11:00 pm and 6:00 am which was the best time to find the subject vehicle outside of an established address. Night time meant we could travel far greater distances whilst most everyone was tucked up in bed and the roads were clear. Repossessions would be undertaken by area, for example Monday night in Kent and Sussex East and West. Daniel and I may have up to 40 repossessions at any one time in and around these areas. Daniel would not knock at the address; he would merely take the key from the file open the vehicle and it was repossessed and then he would start the car and drive it away. Daniel would place in the debtor's letterbox notification from the credit company that the vehicle had been repossessed and how and when to collect any personal belongings that might be in the vehicle. We would immediately contact the police to inform them that the vehicle had been repossessed and was not stolen.

We would alternate who drove our vehicle and either Daniel or I would undertake the repossession. Repossessed vehicles were then driven to the next address of another defaulter, where we would park the first repossessed vehicle. We would go to the file take the key open the second vehicle and undertake another repossession; driving the second vehicle away leaving the first repossessed vehicle in the vicinity of the house of debtor number two.

Using this method, we would repossess cars all night if necessary until around 5:00 am. Daniel and I may have repossessed anywhere between 10 or 15 cars in one night, just the two of us. A different debtor car outside a different debtor address none of them any the wiser to our actions. We were safe and secure in the knowledge that all we had to do was contact the police and inform them that the vehicles had been repossessed, that they were not stolen and were no longer in the debtor's possession.

At around 6:00 am telephone calls would be made to contact the debtors we had removed vehicles from to further inform them of the actions taken in the repossession. We would then return at a later time to remove the vehicles to auction or to return them to debtors who had made arrangements and paid the creditor in full. Debtors were always given the opportunity to collect their personal belongs from the vehicles prior to them being removed to auction.

There was the odd occasion when things didn't exactly go to plan. I remember one especially cold night in particular. Daniel and I were undertaking our normal nocturnal routines and arrived at the address of a debtor. Daniel proceeded to open and enter the vehicle to be repossessed. He was turning the engine over again and again and the bugger just wouldn't start. I was watching the address of the debtor for any sign of activity, lights coming on, dogs barking, etc. This did not faze Daniel that the car would not start, he popped the bonnet got out of the car, got a torch from his pocket and proceeded to adjust the engine in an attempt to get it started. Then all of a sudden, a bedroom light at the debtor's address came on.

Now to be fair the debtor may be forgiven in thinking that someone is nicking his jam jar and you can imagine that he is probably not best pleased to what he's seeing especially at 3 o'clock in the morning.

Daniel is not blind and notices what is happening. Now you might think he would turn tail and be on his toes and get back in the nice warm motor that I am sitting in, oh no, not Daniel. He gets back in the motor, starts turning the engine over and it fires up; he then gives me a thumb up through the windscreen. I notice the downstairs lights are on and the front door of the debtor's house opens and outcomes this colossus of a man dressed in nothing but Y fronts, screaming and shouting. This fellow must have been 6'5" and 18 stone. Daniel is pulling away in the motor but seems to be struggling, and this barefooted, Y fronted almost naked man is running after his car, and gaining on it. Finally, Daniel is able to pick up enough speed to drive away. I followed in our car and passed the Y fronted beast who attempted to hail me down saying, *"someone's just nicked my motor."* I pulled up a few feet past him and told him, *"no mate it's been repossessed."*

I carried on my way catching up with Daniel about a mile or two down the road. As we pulled over by the side of the road. I got out of our car and went to see if Daniel was okay. I found Daniel laughing his head off, which was quite contagious. I asked him what was the matter with the motor and why couldn't he pull away. He tells me that his feet were slipping off the pedals and he had not adjusted the rear-view mirror so couldn't see what was going on behind him. Daniel only stood about 5'8" and that's when he told me he realised that the driver of this car must be huge. That was the last time Daniel ever got into a repossessed vehicle without first adjusting the driver's seat and rear-view mirror before driving away.

The Ugly Repossessions: This was an area of fraud and deception that took time to establish and was not immediately apparent. It could take up to three or four months sometimes longer before finance houses or credit managers would place any individual account into default and start pressing for an asset to be located and repossessed.

Daniel would study the initial credit application. Inconsistencies would be established by good old-fashioned detective work and knocking on doors to prove that the details submitted to obtain the credit were either false or misleading. The home address and/or the employment status given for the debtor were incorrect or false; together with other information submitted at the time of the application which again was either incorrect or false. In many of these cases no payment had ever been made and the asset vehicle had been sold for cash sometimes within 48 hours from the credit agreement actually being signed and authorised. These vehicles were often located sometime later in the hands of innocent purchasers who had absolutely no knowledge as to the background and the history of the vehicle. Common practice today is undertaking HPI checks however the 1980s was a different time. Daniel was a great proponent of fair play assisting many innocent purchaser defences in this area of investigation.

Investigations into these cases established intelligence and evidence, and it was quite apparent that shady car dealers selling used cars were heavily suspected of involvement in fraudulent activities. These so-called businesses had tremendous incentives by way of car sales profit and were seen to be aware and willing participants in fraud collusion; however, prosecutions were difficult to prove. To police the situation themselves the finance houses started to withdraw credit services from any suspect car dealers, no longer giving them the status to submit applications to the finance house for credit on behalf of their car buying customers.

I have tried to make it as clear as possible that the work Daniel undertook was not as straight forward as it may appear. Vehicle or asset repossession was huge business for Daniel, and due to the nature of this work and just by kicking over the wrong stone, he could sometimes find himself inadvertently being involved with major fraud investigations involving organised crime and the police.

There was one side of Daniel's behaviour regarding repossession that was rather unprofessional. We might be looking for a particular defaulter or vehicle for a number of weeks and the defaulter would be aware that Daniel was looking for the asset. Like a game of cat and mouse both would do all they could to outwit the other. Inevitably we would locate and repossess the vehicle; often outside a premise's where a defaulter felt the vehicle would never be found. This is where Daniel could be a little bit naughty. He would contact the defaulter by telephone and he would identify himself and ask the debtor to look out of their window and tell him what was missing; obviously he is referring to the car that we had just repossessed. This was a complete wind up by Danny, and he would say to the defaulter, *"You are not so clever now are you and have you got a bus pass to come and collect your personal possessions as all your stuff is in bin bags"*. *"Oh look"* he would say *"your motor has just been loaded on the flatbed truck to be taken off to the auction, don't think it's going to fetch much"*. Believe me, I did not promote this behaviour but you just couldn't help but laugh, Daniel was wicked.

Sometimes the defaulter actually found the funny side of it, but in most cases Daniel was called every name under the sun and oh my god the threats! On the odd occasion we actually had irate defaulters turning up at the office wanting to kick off. We all had a word with Danny about this unprofessional behaviour as this affected our safety. He said he would stop and mostly he did but every now and again he would be up to his old tricks. I told Daniel if I caught him doing it again I would no longer accompany him on repossessions and I meant it.

Repossession work always had the potential to become messy, but it was just one of the many services that Daniel and Southern Investigations offered to its clients.

Is it possible from Daniel's work and reckless behaviour in this area that a motive might exist for his murder?

Chapter 10
Process Server

The definition of a Process Server is, 'A person authorized by the court to deliver legal process papers to a defendant or respondent'. The service of legal process (in the main part) must be done in person by the process server upon a defendant or respondent.

Daniel Morgan was a process server and this was one of a number of services that Southern Investigations offered to clients. This type of work involves dealing with complete strangers from a diverse demographic. We dealt with civil and criminal law which includes matrimonial, domestic violence, financial matters including bankruptcy petitions, witness subpoena, high court writs and county court orders, etc.

As a process server you deal with discrimination, race and religion; people who are in financial difficulty, who are violent, who have mental illness, sex offenders, drug users, child abusers, any example you can think of we dealt with them all.

A large proportion of legal process issues are fraught with a high level of emotion and situations that are potentially dangerous. As the process server you are meeting individuals and placing in their hand Orders of the Court, instructions from the court telling these people what to do and in many cases how to conduct themselves and behave. Some of these people didn't appreciate the situation they found themselves in or you because they saw that you represent the enforcement of the law.

There was a time in the United Kingdom if a man or a woman was assaulted by their spouse, the police in the majority of cases would say the matter was a domestic dispute and they would not get involved. Can you imagine that? The police would actually walk away from volatile, violent and dangerous situations leaving almost no protection for the injured party; arrests in these cases were almost non-existent. Thank goodness, the 1980s saw a change in the domestic violence law. Judge granted power of arrest could now be attached to non-molestation court orders, providing the police the power to intervene and to arrest these defendants. Process servers with these court orders were now able to assist with some protection for battered spouses.

Such court orders were not straight forward to obtain. Plaintiff and defendant lawyers battled it out before a judge or by way of a plaintiff ex partie application to the court where the defendant was not represented in person or at all. Evidence would have to be submitted to the court by the plaintiff or their solicitor to show cause as to why a court order with power of arrest attached should be granted.

Once granted by the judge these non-molestation orders in document form were usually served by hand (unless instructed by the judge otherwise) by the process server to defendants. Until personally handed to a defendant the court order content is not enforceable. Defendants became aware of this and some did everything in their power to elude the process server and the will of the court.

The process server would have to track down defendants, day or night. For identification purposes we would obtain photographs of the defendants from the plaintiffs as many defendants would deny they were the person stated in the court order. Once located and identified they would be served/handed with the papers.

Immediately after the defendant was served you would have to file a duplicate copy of the court order with the desk Sergeant at the plaintiff's local police station; occasionally some distance away which could take time. This could leave the plaintiff vulnerable to assault by the defendant, his agents and servants or otherwise. Attacks on plaintiffs by these defendants were commonplace; often literally moments after the process server had successfully served the defendant with the non-molestation court order.

The process server would have to act fast to assure that if a further instance of domestic violence occurred by the defendant upon the plaintiff the police had a hard copy of the court order on hand, giving them the power to arrest the defendant named in the court order.

The matter for the process server doesn't end there, once you had successfully served the defendant you would draft an affidavit/report of service and attach, by way of exhibit, a further copy of the court order then attend the offices of a commissioner for oaths (a solicitor) and swear on the bible the content of the affidavit/report was true. This document would then be filed at the issuing court for their records.

If you are thinking that all sounded a bit long winded imagine having to do this sometimes up to 40 times a day, six days a week and that could be just one process servers' workload. This gives you some idea of how many people at the time required protection from domestic violence. Service of any type of legal process back in the day was not permitted on Sundays, Good Friday and Christmas Day.

The majority of cases involving domestic violence and family matters sometimes took years to be resolved with further court hearings and legal process being served pertaining to the same case. Daniel and I might meet a particular defendant 10 or 11 times. As you were able to identify the individual you would likely stay on the case. Some of these defendants would make it very clear, in no uncertain terms, that you were not on their Christmas card list.

Think of an area of a town or city that has a poor reputation, a place you personally would not want to visit. An area filled with anti-social behaviour. Separately and alone Daniel and I would go into these areas 99 percent of the time without police backup. Half the time the old bill didn't want to enter these areas themselves because they knew of the potential dangers and on a number of occasions we were informed that due to police staffing they were unable to assist us anytime soon. The process server worked in some of the most volatile and dangerous areas of our society. We entered these areas on a daily basis carrying out court ordered business.

You see on television today civil law enforcement officers; they wear anti stab vests; body armour and they record everything on body cameras. They do this because the work they carry out is dangerous, they put their lives at risk for a paycheque - it is their chosen profession.

Way back in the day, when we undertook these tasks we did so with only a piece of paper in hand and our wits. This was not work for the faint hearted; we had to be tough, resilient, quick minded and brave. We had to be able to react in any situation, be able to communicate at any level, with exact thought of mind as things could go terribly wrong at any moment and on occasion they did.

In my capacity as a legal process server I have been threatened with a meat cleaver, a three-foot samurai sword, and the strangest weapon of all a nine-foot wooden boating oar. You did not make many friends in this business.

Southern Investigations was a tremendous resource for plaintiffs, lawyers and the courts in the service of non-molestation orders. Process servers were hated by many of the defendants in this particular area of legal process as you were seen by some to be interfering and being invasive in private matters. Often the defendant would forget the purpose of your visit, which was to enforce a court order to protect a spouse. A spouse who in some cases had been beaten and abused mentally and physically so badly the scars never healed. We would meet the plaintiffs (mostly women but also some men) and we would see for ourselves in person or study the photographic evidence of the terrible injuries of domestic violence by their so called loved ones. You couldn't believe that a human being could inflict such pain and suffering on another person; the controlling and mental torture their victims had endured all in the name of "I love you". So many times, plaintiffs would take the defendants back and then the phone would ring - it's happened again.

One court order that can be obtained and has the most emotional impact is that of custody care and control. A mother or father attends court with their lawyer for the purpose of obtaining a court order for child custody. Once this has been granted it gives the plaintiff rights of custody care and control of a minor or minors.

Danny and I were often called upon to undertake what is known in the trade as, *'child snatch backs'.* This was part of the legal process system not every investigation business got involved with however, at the time Southern Investigations undertook operations in this area of work.

This work involves a team effort, in most cases, tracing, locating, and tracking of fathers who had fled the family unit taking a child or children. Mothers were often left in absolute despair, pulling their hair out over whether they would ever see their child and/or children again either dead or alive. We would do all we could to reassure these mothers.

We were well versed in these procedures and we promised the plaintiff parent their child and/or children would be returned as soon as possible. We would travel day and night where ever necessary in the jurisdiction of the court, sometimes this could go on for days. We would not stop until the child/children were located and returned safely home. Danny and I always felt a great sigh of relief once the child and/or children were found unharmed and placed into the custody care and control as per the instructions of the court.

The last child snatch back Daniel and I undertook together was around the 14th of February 1987; we were acting for a law firm in South East London. The case was to remove a girl from her father and place the child into custody of the mother. We obtained the court order and picked up the mother from the lawyer's office to accompany us.

We proceeded to an address in the Southwark area which the mother had a key; we entered the flat and found that the father and the child were not present. The mother was very upset but we were able to calm her and it was decided to undertake observation from the kitchen in the flat to wait and see if the father and the child would make a visit. After a period of time we observed the father and the child drive into the car park. They proceeded to the flat and entered the property. A few words were said and the father was visibly upset; we assisted in calming him down. After a period of time, both parents felt comfortable, reasonable and calm and on that basis, we felt that the child was in no immediate danger. Mother and father went into an adjoining room and chatted calmly for around half an hour. The mother re-joined us and collected some clothing for the girl.

We escorted the mother and her child to a place of safety at a hotel in Southwark. The events concluded peacefully in what we would class as a textbook operation. All the operations we undertook ended with all the children being found safe and well.

You feel for the children and the family and it is not the process server but the judicial system, a judge in a court of law that decides from legal argument what the outcome will be. Process servers are merely the instrument that executes the judgement of the court. Yet when emotions run high and adults are in a battle, especially over children, it can be the officer of the court, the process server who becomes the object of collateral damage by way of verbal and physical abuse.

This was an area of Daniel's work together with the risks involved that was clearly taken into consideration in the summing up of the Coroner in the Daniel Morgan Inquest prior to the verdict of unlawful killing.

Chapter 11
Quarter Days the Bailiff is Coming

During the time I worked at Southern Investigations Daniel Morgan and John Rees were both Certificated Bailiffs. Their certificates were issued from Croydon County Court. The main part of the bailiff work undertaken by Southern Investigations was commercial distraint and forfeiture.

Tenants and leaseholders would meet the bailiff when they were in breach of their contract with the landlord for non-payment of rent and/or service charges.

To fully understand Daniel Morgan, it is helpful to appreciate the entire nature of his work. The work of a bailiff consists of domestic and commercial. Daniel Morgan only undertook commercial bailiff work (businesses) he did not deal with domestic bailiff work (private homes). It was very early in our relationship that Daniel told me he did not undertake domestic bailiff work. Daniel was very clinical regarding this and said the money and profit was in the commercial bailiff market.

In the 1980s commercial distraint and forfeiture provided landlords and landowners (who rent or lease property or land) certain rights in common law; and depending on the agreement with their leaseholders and tenants (the covenant) they could instruct a bailiff to collect unpaid debts for rent and/or charges.

In the last few years of his life Danny was extremely focused on commercial bailiff work. His final business meeting (on the day of his murder) was with a huge landowner client for the purpose of securing more bailiff work.

This area of work is so complex he hired an in house legal executive. Danny could see that a lot of money could be made quickly and the legal system seemed advantageous toward landlord and landowners almost preferential in procedures of debt management; an area he felt he could fully exploit to the maximum.

Laws were in place and had to be followed. Bailiff fees were controlled by a percentage scale for the actual rent debt; and it was mostly the associated fees where extra costs would arise. The removal of goods, van fees, disbursements, etc., were costs that were tremendously profitable to the bailiff. These extra fees were left to the imagination and conduct of the individual bailiff and if not undertaken responsibly could leave the leaseholders and tenants open to abuse.

This chapter includes excerpts taken from the Control of Goods Regulations 2013 which contains public sector information licensed under the Open Government Licence v3.0.

Bailiff work involves complicated legal issues regarding what can and can't be done under regulation of law. Due to a vast array of performance issues (specially to do with bailiff conduct in the charging of fees and disbursements to leaseholders and tenants) on the 26th of July 2013 The Lord Chancellor made the Taking Control of Goods Regulations; the law was changed and came into force on the 6th of April 2014.

The new regulations saw the rights of landlords in common law relating to distress against his tenants to recover rent arrears for commercial premises using certificated bailiffs changed.

Even with the changes in the regulations landlords are still strongly supported and continue to have the ability to recover rent without the use of the court system.

The new regulations that replaced the landlord's common law right of distress are called Commercial Rent Areas Recovery (CRAR). There are significant changes in how a landlord is now permitted to recover unpaid monies. A landlord is now only permitted to recover rent arrears. Any service charge arrears must now be recovered separately via the county court; then by way of CCJ (county court judgement); this can then be dealt with through the high court for enforcement.

Daniel Morgan, in his duties as a bailiff, would attend a commercial premise and if the tenant or leaseholder were unable to pay the rent or the service charges in default he could remove the business stock or other goods in lieu of the value of the outstanding rent or charges. These goods he could then sell at public auction to pay the landlord. However, in a lot of the cases Daniel handled, he would enter into a walking possession agreement with the leaseholder or tenant giving a further period of time to pay the outstanding monies.

Under this walking possession agreement Daniel would enter the premises and undertake an inventory and valuation of the goods on site owned by the tenant or leaseholder. The goods would stay at the premises and were not permitted to be removed by the leaseholder or the tenant. An agreement of time to pay was entered into with Danny and the tenant or leaseholder; usually from a few days to a couple of weeks.

Danny would return on the date as per the agreement to collect the outstanding debt or to remove the goods if the debt remained unpaid.

Regulations stipulated that certain items could not be removed by a bailiff and sold at public auction. Items that were not permitted to be removed would include any motor vehicle or other goods that were on hire purchase or that were rented; items such as tools or other equipment in connection with a person's employment or vocation. Daniel was always very careful not to violate this regulation.

A landlord's tenancy or lease agreement would include clauses or covenants that tenants or leaseholders must pay the rent and charges every 13th week (one quarter) and if not paid a bailiff could remove goods to the value of the rent and/or charges. Covenants would usually include a clause for the possession of the entire building or land by way of forfeiture.

There were four specific quarter days in a year and it is was from these dates that leaseholders or tenants who had not paid their rent or charges on time may face enforcement proceedings at any time thereafter.

In the time leading up to quarter days Daniel would become very excited knowing that big pay days were on the way. Bailiff instructions were eagerly awaited by Daniel and they would arrive by fax, post or courier.

Daniel's clients were some of the biggest commercial landlords and landowners in the country. These companies had portfolios worth hundreds of millions of pounds. These business landlords did not become successful by allowing their leaseholders or tenants to default on paying their rent or charges. These clients did not delay in sending Danny in to collect their money.

The bailiffs associated with Southern Investigations worked on a national scale. Landlords could instruct local bailiff firms but chose to use Daniel because they trusted him to manage their entire portfolio in rent collection.

The morning of quarter days Danny would arrive early at the office and like a ritual take a position around the fax machine which took pride of place on his desk. Daniel eagerly waited for this goose to lay the golden eggs. The first fax of the day was always the most exciting for Daniel and he would say, *"at least we know the fax is working"* and believe me it worked. That fax machine was looked after better than a royal baby. The machine would start to spit out warrants (rent collection instructions) from clients. Danny would say, *"Oh, oh look at this big one a 500-quid fee!"* or, *"Oh my God a two-grand fee!"* or, *"A building possession jackpot!"*

Danny was like a kid at Christmas opening his presents. He would read one, throw it down and grab another one to see if it was of greater value. I would watch Danny during this time as he was the consummate showman; he was very entertaining with his running commentary of the value of the fees from the warrants. Then the first post of the day would arrive with more warrants. Couriers would arrive with even more.

Danny's enthusiasm was contagious and quite outrageous, you just had to laugh, we all did and this went on all day.

Daniel would be on the phone in regular contact with clients asking what other instructions might be coming through. He would contact established clients who had not started sending warrants to make sure there was no problem or that he hadn't lost any clients from the previous quarters work.

The warrants had to be enforced immediately and everyone had to be on the road either that night or no later than the next morning before dawn; to start work that could take up to a month to complete depending on the amount of warrants that were received. Any delays might mean a tenant paying the rent, the warrant being cancelled which Southern Investigations would lose out on fees and commission. Daniel could be on the road for days at a time before returning to the southeast and home.

In the mid-1980s there were only a handful of big commercial bailiff companies around the country – some might say a monopoly. Daniel's work in this field made him unpopular although there were many regular default tenants that Danny had a respected rapport. Often tenants had to fall into default and meet the bailiff to be able to negotiate time to pay. The majority of cases with regular defaulters were merely a cash flow situation why payment had not been made. Many leaseholders and tenants incorporated the extra bailiff costs as a quarterly billing expense within their turnover and actually utilised the bailiff service for their business benefit. This was easy money for Daniel and on that basis relationships lasted for long periods of time.

However, just the word 'bailiff' would send many debtors into ranting tirades of hate. Many businesses failed and closed at the hand of the bailiff; at times destroying livelihoods. You seldom make friends in this line of work.

Basic economics tells you if a business is not making a profit then it is not a good business. In turn setting off a chain of events with creditors that has a knock-on effect destabilising other support businesses or suppliers; so, it was important for the economy that powers were in place to deal with defaulters efficiently to protect industry at large.

Depending on the amount of work or the location of the jobs Daniel would call in associate independent bailiffs, people that he knew and trusted who were able to follow his instructions to the letter.

Daniel Morgan was a sought-after member of the bailiff community. He had vast experience in this field of operation. Daniel would often undertake some of the biggest bailiff assignments, large multiple occupancy premises possessions, conducting a team of bailiffs dealing with all the legal process, and any subsequent evictions, security and site clearance. (See Chapter The Elnathan Mews Possession)

Daniel received this type of instruction when a client was either selling an entire site, a large land area was under redevelopment or where leases or tenancies were being terminated by the landlord.

Since the 1980s a great deal has changed in the bailiff civil law enforcement agency business. There are now set practice guidelines to be followed when enforcement is being carried out, how enforcement agents are expected to behave, and the conduct of their agents.

Enforcement agents must act within the law, respect confidentiality, be dressed appropriately and act in a calm, dignified and professional manner, not to discriminate but to be fair in their actions, to fully identify themselves when requested to do so; and to abide by, the Taking of Control of Goods national standards April 2014.

Bailiff and enforcement officers are not to be overly assertive in their duties nor should they be aggressive or violent undertaking their daily responsibilities. They should not expect to have placed upon them the threat of physical or verbal assault or be subjected in any way to aggression or violence from tenants, leaseholders or the general public.

Penalties of imprisonment or fine exist if any enforcement officer is threatened or assaulted in their duties; those responsible will be punished. The reason that these penalties are in place is because the work undertaken is known to be dangerous.

Is it possible from Daniels's work as a bailiff that a motive might exist for his murder?

Chapter 12

The Best Thing about the Police was Sting

You might have an idea about what a private investigator could be involved in regarding the police. You may have watched television shows or crime drama movies depicting the actions of fictional P.I. characters; ultimately saving the day when the bad guys come calling with the police taking all the credit.

Well this is real life non-fiction. A real man was horrifically murdered and these events actually took place.

You may find it surprising or hard to believe that a private detective would not have numerous contacts or sources across the plethora of law enforcement and you would not be wrong in thinking that. However, over the last 31 years, not one serving police officer (that I am aware of) has ever come forward or made any admission that Daniel Morgan offered or colluded with them for any financial incentive for the exchange of intelligence.

A lot of the staff employed or associated with Southern Investigations was retired or ex-police officers and from this fact you might expect they would have established friends or acquaintances in the police service. However, the difference between friends and sources is something completely different. I believe Danny only had one police source contact.

Daniel and I spent many hours together on a daily basis; *we were mates.* We worked together and socialized together, we liked each other's company and what comes from that is a sound knowledge of what makes a person tick. From early on, in our friendship, it was clear to me Danny did not have a great love for the old bill and other colleagues within Southern Investigations knew this. Now don't get me wrong, as a business of certificated bailiffs and process servers we would come in contact with the police on an almost daily basis from our involvement with case work. This was a purely professional association with police and to be fair the old bill would assist us as best they could and mostly that was where the relationship began and ended for Daniel Morgan and myself.

This is an excerpt of Day 3, page 26 of the Daniel Morgan Inquest. Peter Newby is examined by the Coroner.

Q. Did Danny get on with the police or did he have anything to do with the police? – A. As far as I know, speaking in general, he got on reasonably well with them.

Q. Who Danny? – A. Yes.

Q. But did Danny have much to do with the police? – A. Not a terrible lot, no.

Q. Who had dealings with the police more? – A. John.

Q. Did the police come and visit the office? – A. On occasions.

Q. Did they visit the office for social reasons or did they visit the office on business? – A. I assume it was for social reasons. When they came, they met John in his office. He was upstairs and I was on another floor.

Q. You were never present at the meetings. – A. No.

From his testimony Peter Newby alludes he had some level of awareness of Daniel's activities surrounding his association with the police and what went on in the office. Danny did not go out of his way to ruffle the feathers of any police officer. He would say to me, *"David, the best thing about the police is Sting"*. Danny clearly had a particular attitude towards the police; I do not believe he ever really trusted them. This mistrust would probably have come from knowledge and experience from the behaviour of certain police officers of an unlawful nature. Daniel was no fool and he had been around police and ex-police as a private detective for a long time.

Daniel had a great camaraderie with Solicitor Michael Goodridge who was a partner at Coffey Whittey & Co. Their offices were just along the high street from Southern Investigations. On interacting with both men, I could see that Daniel had a healthy appreciation of Mike and they got on well. Mike had become friends with both Danny and John from the time Southern Investigations began operating in Thornton Heath. Mike dealt with criminal law which brought him into contact with the police and the crown prosecution service. Mike was a down to earth fellow someone who enjoyed his work and also enjoyed the social benefits that came with it. Mike was always inviting Daniel to join him and extended numerous invitations to his friends for social events, many of which were police functions. Danny was always keen to join his friend at this type of gathering.

This is an excerpt of Day 3, pages 75 and 76 of the Daniel Morgan Inquest. Michael Goodridge is examined by the Coroner then is cross examined by Miss June Tweedie.

Q. Did you ever think that Morgan was a little aggressive towards police whereas Rees was not? – A. No. I used to go with Danny Morgan to police CID parties whereas I did not go with John Rees. We used to go to parties where hundreds of police attended.

Q. With Morgan? – A. Yes. I mix, obviously, with police every day of the week.

Most of the time, I was probably more with Danny Morgan than with John Rees. Certainly, for social activities, I was invariably always with Danny Morgan.

Cross-examined by MISS TWEEDIE

Q. You say that you were aware that they went to Catford to see the police. Was that both of them or just Mr Rees? – A. I thought it was both of them.

Q. How did you come to get that impression? – A. That was the impression that I was given, that they both went, or both were friendly with Catford police. It is only now that I realise that it was not that.

Q. Who told you that? Did anyone actually say to you: "I am going off to meet some police at Catford?" – A. John Rees, on occasions, said that he would meet police, yes.

Q. But Daniel would not or was it just an assumption you made? – A. It was just an assumption I made.

In that last couple of years of his life, Daniel began to socialise more with police in pubs and restaurants; most likely at venues where he would be accompanied by others, this is where he would find police officers present. I only ever knew Daniel to seek out one particular serving police officer.

I had been present with Daniel and John on numerous occasions in the company of serving members of the police and in my opinion Daniel's involvement was purely social. On many occasions in a large group that were all old bill Daniel may have acquaintance with maybe one or two at most. From the expression on his face I could see he often felt out of place around these individuals only remaining in their company for a few minutes before taking his leave.

John Rees was quite different as he had established friendships with these officers. Daniel told me on more than one occasion that even he was surprised, *"very surprised"* at the amount of old bill John had become acquainted with.

This is an excerpt of Day 8, page 91 of the Daniel Morgan Inquest. John Rees is cross examined by Miss June Tweedie.

Q. Do you have friends in the Kent police? – A. There are officers I know in the Kent police, yes.

Q. Do you meet them socially? – A. Occasionally, yes.

Working at Southern Investigations meeting people in the office you did not know, but who were established to be police almost became an occupational hazard. These people did not wear a uniform but other members of staff knew who these individuals were and could identify them. Over time you would develop an instinct in identifying them however, *there were so many* and even Daniel did not know who the large majority of them were and I feel the evidence demonstrates this from the entire inquest transcript. I would wonder to myself what are all these, old bill doing coming in and out of here, Daniel certainly raised his eyebrows on many occasions, it was like they were using the office as a transport café yet there was no tea.

Danny would say: *"There is more, old bill in the pubs and clubs of Thornton Heath than all the custody suites in southeast London combined; if you ever need a copper don't bother going down to the local nick you won't find any there just nip into one of the local pubs"* and that's just the way it was.

The 1980s was a different time and a lot of the private detective bureaus were set up by retired or ex-police officers; instructing clients almost expected this. I have known clients withdraw their consideration in using a detective service that did not include ex-police officers. Some of these detective businesses were highly likely to have established and continued relationships with serving members of the police and exchange of intelligence, for reward, may well have been taking place and would not have been seen as a big deal by those involved.

This was the genesis of the 'dark arts' and what would morph into one of the biggest scandals (News of the World, Phone Hacking, and Hackgate) this country has ever known. However, it is important to be mindful that no one should be cast as guilty by mere association alone. (See Chapter The Daniel Morgan Independent Panel)

Daniel Morgan was a private detective however that did not automatically qualify him as a person lining the pockets of any unscrupulous individuals. And if he did I certainly didn't know about it and I am sure I would have had some idea; I am not being naïve in saying this.

If Daniel had any association with police officers for intelligence it would have been a relationship of a whistle blower. He would only have had involvement to bring light on law breakers or corruption exposing this through media contacts. In my opinion Daniel was very aware in this aspect of what was going on around him yet that didn't mean he was a lemming. Certainly, in the latter months of his life, there is evidence to show Daniel had a healthy disrespect (in some aspects) of the police. That itself should ponder the question why?

On one occasion when Danny and I returned to his home he told his neighbour Doris, *"You know Doris all coppers are bastards!"* (See Chapter Detective Constable Alan 'Taffy' Holmes)

Just because Daniel was a scoundrel in certain areas of his life doesn't mean he was totally devoid in his moral judgement. Daniel would say, *"There is no success in failure"*. He was a seasoned professional in investigative research, a fantastic asset in field operations and in my opinion a champion in civil and criminal law enforcement.

Chapter 13
Where is Danny's Rolex?

t was a midweek day in the late summer of 1986. I was undertaking my normal duties in the offices of Southern Investigations when Danny came in and said, *"Hey Dave, take a look at what I just bought"*. He showed me a Silver Rolex Oyster watch on his left wrist. The timepiece had a twist dial on the face. It was a beautiful and prestigious example of watch making excellence. He said to me, *"You are not going to believe how much I paid for this. Guess how much it cost?"* I answered, *"2 Grand"*. He laughed and said, *"A mere £700"*.

To purchase a brand-new Rolex Oyster, at that time, was around £1800. Danny was such a perfectionist he actually pointed out one or two very minor scratches on the glass face almost unnoticeable to the naked eye. I said, *"Are you sure, for what you gave for it"*. He showed me his receipt and mentioned this because he had it specially insured. Danny had talked about wanting a Rolex almost from the time I met him; he was exceptionally proud of this status symbol.

This is an excerpt of Day 3, page 20, of the Daniel Morgan Inquest. Peter Newby is examined by the Coroner.

Q. What sort of wristwatch did Danny Morgan wear? – A. Rolex.

Q. Did he always wear a Rolex? – A. No. The first time I saw it was about three or four months beforehand. He was writing on my desk and the watch, the strap was very loose, and it slid over his hand. I remarked at the time "You will lose that" and he just laughed and pushed it back.

Q. Are you sure it was a Rolex? Rolex have very distinctive faces and very distinctive bezels around the face. There are certain types of Rolex, are there not? What sort of Rolex was it? You describe it to me. I do not want you to tell me the type. What sort of Rolex was it? – A. It was chrome with a chrome band. I think the face was a light-coloured face. It was the size of a crown.

Q. Metal strap or leather? – A. Metal.

Q. Metal strap hanging loose. Can you tell me what the bezel was like round the face? Do you know what the bezel is? A. Yes. No, I do not think I can.

Q. You cannot. But you noticed the inside face. If you look at my watch, what would mostly strike you about it? – A. The black face.

Q. Did you notice the bezel? – A. I think it had numbers around it.

Q. Was it coloured? – A. I cannot recall.

Q. As far as you were concerned, he had only had it three months previously. – A. Sorry?

Q. As far as you were concerned, you had only seen it ------ -- A. Three, or four months earlier.

Daniel had purchased the Rolex as nearly new and as such the watch was not tailor fitted.

Daniel had become friendly with an old-time watch repairer and jeweller in Croydon. This was a shop he would go into from time to time and had asked the proprietor to keep an eye out for this specific item and when one came along for sale to give him a call. I recall the proprietor had telephoned Daniel on at least two previous occasions over a period of months to visit the shop and view potential watches that Daniel had subsequently declined.

Peter Newby said that the Rolex watch strap was loose when Daniel first purchased it and indeed it would slide on Daniel's wrist. Daniel initially wanted the strap adjusted however this was not immediately possible. The metal strap was original Rolex and he had concerns that this might become scratched or damaged if any attempt in adjustment was undertaken by a non-experienced person. Danny did take steps and had the strap adjusted to size. I recall this because after it was adjusted Danny mentioned that the watch was very comfortable and no longer moved up and down his wrist. The relevance being that it could no longer just slide off his wrist or be lost.

Danny always liked to share his good fortune with me; he had worked hard for himself and his family over many years. I never saw Danny as a flash Harry in this regard; going out every week buying new clothes or wasting money in the bookies. Danny saw a purchase like this as a sound investment, an item that would appreciate in value over time or something that he could bequeath to his son. A Rolex Oyster was what Danny wanted for himself and he could now tick this off his wish list.

Over the years, a great deal has been written in the media and online about the Rolex and its significance on the night of the murder.

(Author's note: Some of the following excerpt is repeated from chapter 1 to ease the flow in reading)

This is an excerpt from Day 3, pages 13-14 and 17 of the Daniel Morgan Inquest. Thomas Terry is examined by the Coroner.

Q. This is a statement you made on 10th March 1987. ----- "On Tuesday 10th March 1987, at about 9:40 p.m. I had just finished work at the BBC. At 9:05 p.m. I drove into the car park at the Golden Lion public house, Sydenham Road, SE26. I stopped my car, a Vauxhall Cavalier, index A334 RGW in the car park and in the headlights, I saw what I took to be a dummy lying on the ground. I pulled my car up to the body and went to have a look. I saw that he had an axe in the right of his neck. I also saw two packets of crisps by his left hand and that his trousers were ripped on the right side. He was wearing a grey striped suit. He was dressed quite smartly. I then went into the saloon bar and told the barman, Mr. Joe O'Brien. We both went into the car park where I showed Mr. O'Brien the body. I touched the body with my right hand on the back of his left hand just to make sure it was real. We both then returned to the pub and Mr. O'Brien called the police." That is signed "T.D. Terry." It is witnessed by Noel Cosgrave.

Q. How long was it before the police arrived? – A. Within minutes.

Q. Can you remember how many minutes? – A. Certainly five or less.

Q. During those five minutes, there was nobody out in the car park. – A. Not that I know of, no.

Thomas Terry makes statement that he touched the back of Daniel's left hand. However, his testimony does not actually disclose if he saw or knew Daniel's Rolex was on his person. I am not suggesting in the slightest that his account is not accurate. He goes on to say the police arrived within minutes and that he was not aware during those minutes if anyone was out in the car park. The police officer who witnessed Thomas Terry's statement was DC Noel Cosgrave.

A few months after the murder I was informed by an officer who was present at the crime scene on the night of the murder that Danny's watch had been seen on his body as he lay in the car park. However, later that night Daniel's watch was reported missing. The officer made it clear to me, in no uncertain terms; the murderer had not taken the watch. I was advised not to mention our conversation.

On the night of the murder crime scene witness statements were taken in abundance. The police and later the Coroner must have had a level of awareness that the murderer was not suspected in taking the watch. However, the way that the watch came to be missing was not examined in any great depth at the inquest, that itself I found most surprising.

Perhaps I am being a little sarcastic but I am of the opinion that when police officers attend a murder scene they establish immediate responsibility and a care of duty to undertake trained procedures to protect the integrity and control of that crime scene. You may believe, like me, to expect this to include the personal belongings of the murder victim.

It would seem that the police certainly have some explaining to do in satisfying this aspect of the investigation. It beggars belief what else may have actually transpired that we are still yet to learn about the crime scene evidence on that night.

For over 31 years the information available in the media and online regarding this aspect of the murder may leave some readers feeling they may have been misled or confused into believing the missing watch was linked to Daniel's killer, when from the outset, this seems not to be the case.

The missing Rolex clearly demonstrates that at least one piece of evidence or property was allowed to be mishandled, contaminated or lost and may have been stolen by anyone present at the scene of the crime after the police took control.

Those present and involved in handling Daniel's corpse would include police, civilian workers, ambulance staff, mortuary workers, etc. We, the general public, are left questioning the integrity of the police investigation and we should never be placed in that position - ever.

Daniel's Rolex has never been found. No civilian or anyone associated with the police service has ever been disciplined for it being lost or charged and prosecuted for it being stolen. I am unaware if any internal investigation by the police even took place. Questions remain and clearly need to be answered.

In the early summer of 1987, I joined the Territorial Army the 8th Battalion Queens Fusiliers (City of London Regiment). Whilst training as a soldier, and by chance and pure coincidence, I met, served and became friends with non-regular permanent staff, Private Niall Cosgrave who told me he was the son of DC Noel Cosgrave. During this time, I met Niall's family. DC Noel Cosgrave was one of the first detectives on the scene the night of March 10th 1987 at the Golden Lion where Daniel was found murdered.

What are the chances that my new friend's Dad had been involved in investigating my best friend's murder?

Chapter 14
The Algarve Trip

Daniel Morgan and John Rees had both worked for Bryan Madagan before Daniel decided to establish Southern Investigations. Daniel had a good working relationship with a number of Madagan's largest clients and when Daniel began Southern Investigations some of these clients accompanied him in this new venture.

In the 1980s B.E. Madagan and Co. was probably one of the largest bailiff companies in the southeast. Over time part of their organisation saw them operate a general sale auction when the business moved to their new light industrial premises at Tanfield House, 22-24 Tanfield Road, South Croydon, Surrey. I became well acquainted with Bryan Madagan being introduced through Daniel. I came to know Bryan to be a gentleman and someone whom Daniel admired. Daniel always spoke very highly of Bryan and someone he would go to for advice.

Bryan was kind, a helpful and knowledgeable man. I worked for Bryan undertaking process serving and investigative research in the mid to late 1980s. Madagan's business was a serious operation and Bryan Madagan remains well thought of throughout the industry. I always liked Bryan; I knew him to treat people properly and I can see why Daniel would confide in him.

Around September 1986 Daniel told me that he and his friend Bryan Madagan were going on a business trip to the Algarve in Portugal. The trip was to last seven days and was part business part pleasure. It was Daniel's intention to discuss a business merger on behalf of Southern Investigations with Bryan and my immediate thought was wow, if this merger happens it has the potential to become one of the biggest business operations of its kind in the country. John Rees remained in the UK as agreed to by the two partners.

Bryan and Daniel flew to Portugal from Gatwick. Daniel telephoned the office daily keeping up with the events back home. On returning to the UK Daniel stated that discussions with Bryan were sociable and constructive yet no firm decision hand been made to progress with a merger; immediately or at all. Daniel's demeanour was quite normal; calm not overly excited but not disappointed either. He actually looked like he had time to rest, charge his batteries and by all accounts had enjoyed this time with his friend.

A week or so after returning from the trip, Daniel contacted a Southern Investigations client, speaking with the accounts manager on the telephone. Daniel told me that whilst he and Bryan had been away (discussing a possible business merger) a colleague of Madagan had contacted the client of Southern Investigations to offer the business services of Madagan's.

When Daniel learned of this he was furious - almost spitting teeth, he immediately contacted Bryan regarding the situation. Daniel took a little time to calm down. On speaking with Daniel, I got the impression not everyone within Madagan's organisation was in total support of the proposed merger. The response he received from Bryan must have satisfied Daniel as Southern Investigations continued to undertake subcontract work from Madagan's unabated. However, Daniel's relationship with Bryan's colleague, who had been involved in the misunderstanding, remained civil but had certainly cooled when I observed their interaction when we all met in a pub in Croydon.

This is an excerpt of Day 1, page 26-27 of the Daniel Morgan Inquest. Kevin Lennon's police statement is read to the court.

I have been asked by police if I was involved in any proposed merger between Southern Investigations and B D Madigans, in November 1986. "There was a proposed merger between the two companies arising from Wendy Madigan leaving Madigans. She managed the part of the company which could be filled by John and Daniel. I knew at this time that both John and Daniel had been employed previously by Madigans before setting up their own business. I became involved in the financial side of the merger and advised John and Daniel not to go ahead with it. This was because Madigans could not give me any details of any liabilities involved which would affect Southern Investigations. I asked Madigans for certain details which were straight forward and this was ignored and about ten days after this negotiations were broken off by Madigans. From addressing the records of Southern Investigations over the period that I have been employed by them I can say that they have no serious liability and I cannot recall any financial difficulty involving the company".

I recall the matter that Kevin Lennon's statement refers to. This was a situation of partner separation, between Bryan and Wendy Madagan, with Madagan's business assets being divided. That may well have been why Kevin Lennon was ignored as he says in his statement. At the time Daniel told me of Kevin Lennon's role regarding the proposed merger. I have no doubt that Daniel, John and Bryan would have resolved this matter and not necessarily informed Kevin Lennon of the finer details.

This is an excerpt of Day 8, page 39 of the Daniel Morgan Inquest. John Rees is cross examined by Miss June Tweedie.

Q. *Were you aware during your business relationship with Daniel that he was considering setting up another partnership which would not involve yourself? – A. With whom?*

Q. *I am asking you whether you knew of any such arrangement that Daniel Morgan was thinking about? – A. Only apart from what myself and Daniel discussed between ourselves.*

Q. *What had you discussed between yourselves? – A. One was joining Madigans and setting up a business relationship with Madigans. Another alternative was taking Tony Pearce into the relationship.*

Q. *Did you know that part of that plan might have been that you would be an employee and not a partner? – A. I would not have accepted that and it certainly was not put to me.*

Q. *You did not know that? – A. I did not know anything and I do not believe that was discussed.*

This is an excerpt of Day 3, page 22 of the Daniel Morgan Inquest. Peter Newby is examined by the Coroner.

Peter Newby says *".... Tony Pearce was brought into the company towards the end of November 1986 by Danny to oversee the work on the bailiff side and also to boost the amount of work coming into the company. As a direct result of this, the company styled 'Morgan, Rees' was set up to deal solely with this work.*

Subsequently Southern Investigations and Madagan's never merged and in November 1986 Daniel and John established a second specialist business called Morgan Rees and Co. Daniel told me this was to specifically operate the commercial bailiff business. Tony Pearce (who was once a practising solicitor and who originally introduced Daniel Morgan to Bryan Madagan) was appointed as a consultant with a caveat of becoming a potential shareholder to deal with the credit managers of clients pertaining to executive legal matters. Daniel said that part of Tony Pearce's role also included a remit in establishing an even larger client portfolio for Daniel and John; many of which were believed to be existing clients of B.E. Madagan and Co. (See Chapter Morgan Rees & Co)

In the winter of 1986 (through inter agency exchange of instructions) it was Madagan's who referred the finance house client to Daniel for the Range Rover repossession in Malta. (See Chapter The Malta Repossession)

Daniel's relationship remained strong with his friend and business associate Bryan Madagan. Daniel continued to confide in Bryan on a number of occasions during the winter of 1986 until his murder in March 1987. (See Chapter Detective Constable Alan 'Taffy' Holmes)

Bryan Madagan has made a number of significant witness statements since Daniel's murder. Surprisingly he too was not included on the witness list by the Coroner to give evidence at the Daniel Morgan Inquest in April of 1988.

Bryan Madagan has maintained a social relationship with John Rees since they met in the early 1980s.

Chapter 15

The Elnathan Mews Possession

aniel received instructions from a large corporate landowner to act as bailiff for the purpose of serving legal process and undertaking the possession of approximately 32 mews garages situated at the site of Elnathan Mews, London, W9. The tenancies and lessees had been ended by the landowner and were not being renewed. The landowner was seeking vacant possession of the mews garages which were being used as day to day car repair businesses, storage and car parking.

This job was one of the largest multiple occupation premises possessions that Daniel had ever undertaken. A job of this size did not come without challenges and the significant use of extensive resources. These are the circumstances and events which took place and almost ended in a full-scale riot.

Elnathan Mews is located in one of the most prestigious areas of London – Maida vale and is in close proximity to Warwick Avenue tube station.

I recall Elnathan Mews to have a cobblestoned access entered by way of Formosa Street to the south and Shirland Road to the north.

On initial reconnaissance of the site Danny and I found the majority of the garages being used by mechanics and auto body and taxi repairers. Other units were used for business storage and private car parking. Clearly people were running businesses and livelihoods were at stake once the site was repossessed.

There are clear procedures in law that must be undertaken by landowners and bailiffs in the possession of land and property. Legal process had been served on all the units. Plenty of notice was given to known tenants, occupiers and lessees informing them of the notice of possession of the garages and the date which they must vacate the premises; however, a large number of the garage occupiers ignored the notice of possession and remained in situ.

Daniel and I attended Elnathan Mews prior to the date of possession and held a meeting with all those present. He had spoken to everyone and informed them when they must leave. Daniel met with some resistance and was struggling to get an amicable resolution from the occupiers. Daniel said to me, *"These folks are just not getting it; they just don't want to leave"*.

Daniel contacted the landowners informing them of the situation. He told me the response from the landowner was, *"You have carte-blanche for resources for the removal of the occupants and the possession of the site"*. Daniel was well versed in dealing with the possession of land and buildings and would often think up innovative and creative ways of obtaining his objective.

Knowing that most, if not all, of the garages would be unattended after 6:00 pm on a Saturday night, Daniel decided that the best time to take possession would be between 8:00 pm Saturday night and 6:00 am Monday morning.

The day of possession arrived and Daniel, as bailiff, had lawful right of entry and possession of the garages. With bolt croppers at the ready Daniel proceeded to forcibly enter all the garages under order of possession. This was a major undertaking. The majority of the garages were full of cars, tools, business equipment, you name it and it was in there. He quickly realized the removal of these goods and personal possessions would be a nightmare. The logistics and storage alone would be insurmountable.

Daniel quickly put staff and resources in place for the task ahead. He arranged flood lighting to light the mews for night operations, ordered two lorry loads of ready mixed concrete, instructed scaffolders and spoke with a colleague who was able to lay his hands on a large number of six feet lengths of industrial RSJs (rigid steel joists). Now you might think to yourself what Daniel could possibly want with lorry loads of concrete and a load of RSJs and you would be right to think that.

It was around 4:00 am on day two of the possession that I arrived at the site of Elnathan Mews and my jaw dropped at what I witnessed and I couldn't help but laugh. I said, *"Hello Danny, someone's been a busy boy, have you been here all night?"* Danny replied, a little tired and somewhat flustered, *"Yes, we finally have control of the site."*

Daniel had instructed cement mixer lorries to deposit, outside the front of a number of the garages, a mound of concrete in which he had placed a number of six feet length RSJs. The concrete had dried and set leaving an immovable barrier of concrete RSJs. The majority of these garages had motor vehicles in situ. I said, *"Dan, how are we going to get the cars and stuff out of the garages?"* Danny's response was, *"Well, Dave, that's the whole idea. We can't get it out and neither can they. We will access the garages one by one when we are ready by breaking up the barriers"*.

My first thoughts were and I said to Dan, *"You do know this is going to piss them right off?"* Danny looked at me and replied, *"Fuck 'em, those that were still in occupation had plenty of opportunity to get out and now we are in possession of the garages"*.

I looked to the south end of the site near the Formosa street entrance where I saw a large roofed scaffold-built structure which had not been present before. This building was no little shed, far from it. Daniel had instructed scaffolders who had in turn erected a two-storey high storage compound that was probably 70 feet long by 25 feet wide, the temporary structure was quite secure. It was wall clad and roofed with 6 feet by 3 feet corrugated iron panels topped off with barb wire and was floodlit using petrol generators; and entry was by way of two large gates.

The compound was to be manned 24 hours by static security guards. I asked Dan why he built the structure and he told me it was a temporary warehouse storage facility so he could control the movement and storage of the possessions in the garages, keeping them safe so the occupier's possessions could be collected by their owners thereby clearing the garages.

A tremendous amount of work and effort had gone into securing the site. Cars and vans had been placed at each of the entrances of the site to form barricades stopping access to the mews. Daniel asked me to man the Shirland Road entrance barricade, limiting vehicle and pedestrian access to the site. Daniel told me that no one was allowed entry to the mews without his strict permission and all persons would have to sign in using the site visitor's book and then be escorted throughout the entire duration of their visit. Daniel also told me that he had made arrangements with the local police that mobile patrols would drive by every hour or so and that police remained on standby if any breach of the peace transpired.

I recall most of the staff of Southern Investigations was present on site together with numerous independent bailiff colleagues of Daniel some of whom were unknown to me. On weekday mornings Peter Newby was in place at the office taking telephone inquiries pertaining to this job.

Staff started emptying goods and possessions from some of the garages and placing them in the temporary warehouse. Daniel had instructed me and other staff that when removing the goods and possessions an inventory should be taken to include the garage number and the items removed. Daniel told us to use whatever vehicles we could get our hands on, including our own personal cars to undertake the transfer of goods and possessions along the mews to the storage compound.

As night turned into day and the sun came up occupiers of garages started to arrive. Initially, Daniel told those guarding the barricades that no access was permitted whatsoever. This did not go down well with those wanting access to the units and groups began to gather at each end of the mews.

As the morning progressed tensions began to brew and the situation was becoming verbally hostile. Daniel was called upon to calm the situation and explain the circumstances of the possession. Again, this did not go down well with the tenants and occupiers.

Daniel realised he had to do something to ease the stress so he started to allow one or two of the garage occupiers access to the site however, when they saw the concrete and the RSJs blocking access to the garages they became infuriated. They saw that goods and possessions had been removed from some of the units and there were a number of allegations of damaged goods and theft.

Daniel's attitude was confrontational as he had limited sympathy for the tenants and occupiers who had plenty of time to amicably remove their goods and possessions but chose not to.

I was guarding the Shirland Road entrance; myself and others were doing all we could to calm the situation as attempts were made by some of the crowd to charge the barricades and forcibly enter the site. Daniel called up even more support from other bailiff colleagues to attend the site as things were beginning to get out of control. Police were called as large crowds were beginning to gather at each end of the mews and a mob mentality was brewing.

Daniel returned to confront the crowd at the Shirland Road entrance as we were all receiving abuse and threats to our safety and well-being. Daniel just seemed to escalate the rage in the crowd until finally one of the bailiff's said to me, *"Dave get him outta here and off this site! This is gonna go off in a minute"*. I literally grabbed Daniel by the scruff of the neck and I said, *"Sorry, Dan, but we are leaving!"*

I kind of frog marched Danny to my car and assisted him inside then we sped away. Daniel looked at me and did not utter a word. We had driven as far as Park Lane before he said anything to me. His next words were, *"Well, fuck me, that didn't exactly go to plan, did it?"* I almost laughed and I said, *"Dan you do know I had to get you out of there, don't you? If we hadn't left when we did we all would have been lynched".*

Daniel knew leaving the site was the right thing to do and putting his pride aside, he thanked me for putting his safety first. I am pretty sure the events at the mews surrounding the possession of the garages actually made the national newspapers and London radio at the time.

Daniel had done nothing unlawful and was well within the boundaries of his remit as bailiff. Although his actions in dealing with the job were initially ingenious he must have realised his actions were going to raise tension. I have no doubt Daniel knew exactly what he was doing.

Over the next couple of weeks, the Elnathan Mews situation was resolved and the site handed to the landowner successfully as instructed.

This situation was yet another example of the risks posed to bailiffs and court officials undertaking their lawful duties. Circumstances often present themselves to be challenging - especially where livelihoods are at stake. Tensions ran high and the mentality of rage and hate was prevalent and directed at Daniel so much he had to flee the site for his own safety.

This is an excerpt from the Guardian newspaper written by Duncan Campbell on 13 September 1994,

Private Eyes make many enemies. It is the nature of their business that they encounter people at the sharpest points in their lives. Morgan was, according to Malcolm Webb, not the most tactful of men and did not back down from a confrontation. So, one obvious line of inquiry was his work and anyone whose cage he might have rattled.

Is it possible that the events surrounding the Elnathan Mews possession (which occurred literally a few weeks before he was killed) or any other possession or bailiff work undertaken by Daniel or Southern Investigations could have generated a motive that may have led to Daniel's murder?

Chapter 16
The Malta Repossession

There has been a great deal reported and tremendous speculation online and in the press over many years regarding Daniel's trip to Malta and the Range Rover repossession. Much has been said about threats to Daniel's well-being surrounding this assignment or links with drugs or organised crime. It was I who accompanied Daniel throughout the entire duration of the trip. This is the account of what took place.

It was mid November 1986 and I was in the office undertaking my usual duties. Danny received a call from a staff member of B.E. Madagan & Co asking if Southern Investigations were interested in undertaking the repossession of a vehicle in Malta. Danny told me the offer of the job was because B.E. Madagan staff were unable to undertake the repossession due to staffing commitments. Daniel said that he would be willing to go to Malta for the repossession. The client was a finance company based in the West Midlands. It was agreed, by Madagan's, that Southern Investigations would deal with them directly.

Daniel contacted the finance company and liaised with the account management and they agreed a deal that Daniel should travel to Malta for the purpose of vehicle repossession. Instructions for the job arrived around the middle to end of January 1987.

The instructions were to repossess a 1984 fully loaded Range Rover; the vehicle was no more than 2 ½ years old and at the time had a potential resale value of approximately £13,000. The finance company was keen to recover this vehicle and reduce their loss deficit. The vehicle had been supplied new and leased and the payments were in default. Even with the associated costs of repossession from Malta to the United Kingdom it was still financially viable for the finance company to take this action and not to write the vehicle off as lost.

The finance company had established good intelligence where the Range Rover might be located and had prior communication with those involved with the vehicle in the UK and in Malta.

I have not included the actual names of all the parties involved and refer to the actual events as seen. This matter was connected to an active police investigation into serious fraud which was eventually dealt with by way of a criminal court case.

The accounts manager of the finance company told Daniel the vehicle was being stored by a gentleman who I will refer to as the **vehicle custodian,** and that he was represented by a lawyer, who I will refer to as the **custodian's lawyer.** The original contract assignee, I will refer to as the **vehicle lessee** and it was he who was responsible for the vehicle being taken to Malta.

The **vehicle lessee** had known connections to a residential address; a large detached house just outside the main town Victoria on the island of Gozo. Daniel's instructions were to visit the address and to make contact with a Maltese lawyer of Valletta who I will refer to as the **client's lawyer** who was acting on behalf of the finance company as their agent in Malta.

Malta is made up of three islands, Malta, Camino and Gozo situated in the Mediterranean Sea. In 1987 Camino was almost uninhabited; occupied by the odd shepherd and flocks of sheep. Malta, its capital Valletta, was a bustling vibrant multicultural city and Gozo a less urbanised and much slower developed yet beautiful island, built at a walking pace which its capital is Victoria.

Daniel spent little time preparing the operation; only arranging accommodation and flights at the last minute. It was decided that I would accompany Daniel and we would leave for Malta on Sunday the 1st of February 1987. We booked British Airways flying out of Gatwick one way.

On the morning of Sunday 1st of February 1987 I drove to Daniel's home where I left my car. I walked around the side of the house into the kitchen; Daniel and Iris were sitting at the table. I sat down, had a cup of tea and we all discussed the pending trip. Daniel's bags were already packed and Iris was offering her husband the normal, don't get into any trouble routine as I know what you two are like or something to that effect.

Daniel had ordered a taxi that arrived shortly after me. Daniel grabbed his bag from the hallway and I got mine from the boot of my car. Daniel kissed his family; we said our goodbyes and went on our way.

The drive to Gatwick was uneventful and we arrived at the terminal, checked in, sat in the lounge and had some hot drinks, then proceeded to the departure gate and boarded the flight to Malta.

We arrived in Malta sometime after lunch. We dealt with baggage reclaim, immigration, passport control, and found our way out to the arrivals concourse by the taxi rank. The weather was nice, sunny and warm and a damn site better than the cold winter February weather we had just left behind in the UK.

We hailed a taxi and told the driver to make his way to St Paul's Bay. On driving through the capital of Valletta the first thing we noticed was immaculate examples of vehicles from the 1940s 1950s, 1960s and 1970s. Fords to Bedfords, Commas, Austins, Morris, Hillman the list just went on. These cars were everywhere; it was like we had entered a time warp. The buses and lorries all pristine examples of vehicles from a time gone by; we had never seen anything like it on this scale. We tried to establish an explanation to this phenomenon however the taxi driver did not speak English. Daniel was extremely excited with what he was seeing. It was about an hour drive from the airport to St Paul's Bay and I don't think he shut up once talking about these classic motor vehicles.

We arrived at St Paul's Bay, paid the driver grabbed our bags and found ourselves in a very quiet sleepy seaside fishing village. We were looking around and probably thinking the same thing, okay where is the hotel and isn't it always the way; no bugger about to talk to or who speaks English to tell you where to go. St Paul's Bay was situated in a horse shoe like configuration. In the distance I saw some form of life so we walked along the shoreline to the other side of the bay. We had been in the bay for around 15 minutes and not one car had passed in either direction. Luckily and quite by chance we found our accommodation.

We checked in and had separate rooms with en suite both of which had a balcony overlooking the bay. Now this was wintertime in Malta and well outside the tourist season and as it turned out we were the only hotel guests in residence for the entire duration of our stay. Daniel commented this felt a bit odd and perhaps we were a little vulnerable due to the nature of our visit. I did my best to alleviate these concerns and said, *"It could be worse but we do have the bar all to ourselves"* this almost immediately put pay to any doubts in his mind. But joking aside he was right and immediately we established that a diligent approach to this job was the order of the day.

We went to our rooms, unpacked and had a rest; we arranged to meet downstairs in the bar in a couple of hours then proceed to supper. When I woke from my rest it was dark outside, the bay was poorly lit and it was a little cold. I proceeded downstairs where I found Daniel sitting at the bar talking to the barman who I learned was the manager of the hotel. Daniel ordered two steak dinners; we had supper at the bar and continued talking with the hotel manager who was an excellent host.

As it was out of season the hotel manager asked the purpose of our visit and was it to visit family or friends. Daniel felt confident enough to tell him that we were here on business and said that we had come to visit a gentleman who drove a 1984 Range Rover on British number plate. To our complete surprise the hotel manager told Daniel that he knows of a man who drives such a Range Rover and he has seen him with the vehicle and that he lives on the island of Gozo, he went on to say that he had a nickname. We had a few more drinks and Daniel and I discussed our plans for the next day; we then retired to our rooms.

Monday 2nd of February we awoke about 6:30 am and went to breakfast. We left the hotel for the car rental office in St Paul's Bay and hired a car. We travelled north to Cirkewwa harbour and boarded the 10:00 am car ferry crossing to Gozo. The ferry crossing took around 35 minutes arriving at Mgarr Harbour Gozo. We drove to the capital Victoria. On calling at an address for the vehicle **custodian's lawyer** we received no reply. Daniel decided to attend the main police station in Victoria. On speaking with the desk sergeant on duty, whose English was reasonably good; Daniel established, surprisingly, that police were aware of who was in possession of the vehicle and where it could be located however they said Daniel must contact the vehicle **custodian's lawyer**. We then left the police station.

Daniel commented to me that everybody seemed to know the vehicle and the **vehicle custodian** and what a popular figure he must be.

Daniel made some local inquiries and it was confirmed that the Range Rover was known to locals and had been driven by the **vehicle lessee** however he had not been seen for some time but the vehicle was seen recently being driven by the **vehicle custodian**.

Daniel made further inquiries whereby on a hill just outside of Victoria we found the detached property, the address given on Gozo for the **vehicle lessee**. The house was boarded up with no one in residence. The property was in good repair however the surrounding foliage was overgrown and we were of the opinion that the property may have been empty a number of months more than empty for years. We then proceeded to the other side of the island where Daniel established a further address connected with the **vehicle lessee**, in that of a female, of well-known origin to locals as a gentleman's escort. We headed back to the main town of Victoria.

We visited the office of the vehicle **custodian's lawyer** again and on calling we received no reply. A short distance away by the side of the road we saw a motorcycle police officer passing the time of day. We approached the officer and Daniel asked him if he had any information regarding any persons associated with a 1984 Range Rover, on British plate. Remarkably the officer replied, *"Yes I do."*

The officer spoke excellent English and told Daniel in no uncertain terms not to mention the conversation they had regarding this situation. Daniel replied *"Whatever you tell me I will treat in the strictest confidence"*. The police officer quite out of the blue said, *"Okay get in your car and follow me"*; okay we said and did as instructed. We followed the officer out of Victoria, driving south along the road toward the coast. Approximately two miles later the officer slowed down and stopped alongside a newly built warehouse type garage by a derelict farmhouse; this was a large detached building that could house two, 70 seat coaches.

The police officer told us the vehicle we were looking for was likely to be found in that garage. There was a four-foot-high steel cattle gate at the entrance of the driveway that was chained; we proceeded to climb over this. The doors to the garage were about 12-foot-high with small clear windows at the top of which you could see in. Daniel told me he wanted to get on my shoulders so he was able to peer in, and on doing so he identified the Range Rover we had been seeking.

Daniel thanked the police officer and just before he left Danny asked him a question, was the officer aware of any nickname for the **vehicle custodian** of the Range Rover. The officer, who suddenly looked surprised, replied, *"Yes"* and said a nickname and in English replied, *"Head of the family"*. After the officer left, Daniel and I got back in our rental car and took a few moments to ponder our thoughts. The nickname had matched the one that had been given to us by the manager at our hotel residence. I said to Danny, *"Did he just say what I think he did?"* Danny looked at me and said, *"Yeah he did"*. We just looked at each other in a state of contemplation no words were necessary as to what we were both thinking.

Daniel then said that I was to remain at the farmhouse while he would drive back to Victoria in an attempt to locate the **custodian's lawyer**. I remember saying to Danny, *"Oh cheers mate, I'll just sit on the wall in the middle of fucking nowhere and hope it's not duck hunting season"*. Danny found this rather amusing however; me not so much. So, this is what we did. Daniel had been gone for around 45 minutes when he returned telling me the **custodian's lawyer** was still unavailable but that he had left a written message that contact was desired.

Only two main roads serviced the towns between Victoria and that of the coastal village a couple of miles ahead and we were on one of them. Daniel decided that we should position ourselves in the driveway of the farmhouse, sit and wait in the car which would certainly draw attention to any passers-by as no other buildings or access roads or anything else for that matter was visible in the near vicinity.

About 75 minutes or so later a Land Rover on British number plate passed our position and pulled up about a hundred yards down the road, Danny said, *"I bet that's our man"*. The driver of the Land Rover waited for a minute or so and then drove off south towards the coastal village. About 20 minutes later the same Land Rover returned and pulled up alongside us. Danny approached the gentleman driver and introduced himself and asked him if he was the **vehicle custodian** of the Range Rover that we had been sent to repossess, the man replied *"Yes"*. We informed him we were from the finance company and we had come for the Range Rover. The **vehicle custodian** spoke perfect English.

The **vehicle custodian** proceeded to open the gate to the farmhouse and then the gates to the lock up and allowed us to inspect the Range Rover; we found the vehicle to be in excellent condition. Daniel and I checked the vehicle identification chassis number which coincided with the British logbook. The vehicle was still displaying the original British registration number plate. The **vehicle custodian** informed us he was unable to release the vehicle to us as he had been storing the vehicle for in excess of 192 days and that storage charges and other costs had been incurred and compensation was required.

He informed us there were fees for repairs to the vehicle and costs for import/export which we didn't initially understand. The **vehicle custodian** explained to us he had to export the vehicle out of Malta and re-import it back into the country because six months was the maximum legal time limit that a vehicle of this engine capacity was permitted to remain in Malta or the vehicle would have to be modified to turn it into a van (commercial vehicle) or it would be seized by the Maltese authorities.

At the time Maltese law only permitted private motor cars up to a maximum specific engine cc size. The **vehicle custodian** took the action of export and re-import to safeguard the vehicle from being seized by the Maltese government. This information was confirmed at a later date.

Unknown to Daniel, the finance company, the **vehicle custodian** and his lawyer had already begun negotiations into an arrangement regarding a compensation package in exchange for the Range Rover to be handed over to us-the repossession agents. The **vehicle custodian** wanted a compensation package to consist of four Maltese pounds per day (eight English pounds per day at that time) for a total of 192 days for storing the vehicle together with other costs and expenses.

The **vehicle custodian** invited us to a private domestic residence for some refreshment; we accepted his kind invitation and followed him in our rental car for some two to three miles to a coastal village residence. I do not recall ever knowing the address. On arrival he made us comfortable in a lounge area as we drank spirits which made for a pleasant afternoon. Most of the time was spent discussing the **vehicle custodian's** compensation.

Whilst in the company of the **vehicle custodian** and using his phone, we contacted the finance company account manager in the UK and told him the **vehicle custodian** wanted £2000 sterling. Daniel was becoming rather agitated with the **vehicle custodian** that this was a lot of money for looking after the vehicle. I recall that I intervened in the conversation and apologised to the **vehicle custodian** and said to Daniel that it was not our decision to make and that we were merely on site to repossess the vehicle. Danny looked into my eyes where he could see I was telling him to shut up. What I was really thinking was Danny don't wind this bloke up, we are a long way from home with no back up.

The accounts manager of the finance company agreed it was a lot of money and negotiations continued. Danny asked the **vehicle custodian** if he was willing to accept payment by way of a solicitor undertaking, the **vehicle custodian** rang his lawyer, to take advice, however he decided that was not suitable and that he would prefer cash.

Finally, it was agreed by all parties that £2000 sterling would be telex transferred to the finance company lawyer's bank, who was acting as their agent in Malta.

The **vehicle custodian** agreed that when the finance company lawyer received the telex bank transfer, which was to be paid into a Maltese, bank in Sliema, the **vehicle custodian** would be satisfied that he would be paid; and then release the Range Rover into our custody.

Numerous calls were made back and forth from Malta and the UK between the offices of the finance company, Southern Investigations and the **vehicle custodian.** The **vehicle custodian** further requested that he be compensated for the international call charges for the use of the phone; this was agreed and Daniel paid £30 in cash and also gave him the hotel telephone number where we were staying by way of contact.

The entire meeting with the **vehicle custodian** lasted around two hours and all parties were civil without any aggravation apart from Danny's agitation in negotiations. We reached an amicable agreement and were merely awaiting the transfer of funds from the finance company and for the vehicle to be released to us.

Arrangements were made for further contact later in the week. We all shook hands and took our leave. We headed to Mgarr harbour ferry terminal stopping along the way at a bar for a swift half. I asked Danny what was he thinking when he was talking in an argumentative manner to the **vehicle custodian,** he said that he was not impressed to have had to negotiate and pay for the Range Rover and thought the **vehicle custodian** needed a smack in the mouth. I told Danny you cannot take this personally and that he needed to lose his attitude. Danny calmed down and told me he understood my concerns and it wouldn't happen again.

We continued our journey to Mgarr harbour where we boarded the 7:00 pm ferry crossing to Cirkewwa harbour in Malta, returning to our hotel for supper and some refreshment at the bar. We retired to our rooms around midnight.

On Tuesday 3rd of February we had a bit of a lay in and then went to brunch around 10:30 am. We checked with the hotel manager to enquire if there had been any calls, he said there had not but he would take any messages. We decided to take the day off.

The weather was around 68° and sunny so we took the opportunity to explore Malta. We made our way into the capital Valletta and spent time sightseeing but mainly looking at these unbelievable examples of classic vehicles. Around 2:00 pm and after feeling a little leg weary, we found a fantastic old art deco cinema in the heart of Valletta. Screening that day was the 1986 Rob Lowe movie "Youngblood"; we bought two tickets for less than the price of a cheese sandwich. We went up a flight of stairs to a concession area. They were selling a 12-bottle wooden box of cold lager for what worked out to be less than five pounds. The crate of lager you were able to take to your seats; they even gave us a bottle opener which they were happy we returned later. We found the hospitality at this venue tremendous and most accommodating.

There we are - me and Danny sopping a box of cold lagers watching a Rob Lowe matinee; the theatre was almost empty maybe five or six patrons. Danny insisted that I open the beers as he had paid for them and he refused to be moved on the subject. There was an exchange of expletives but I just shook my head and smiled. It's funny what you remember. We left the cinema around 4:00 pm and returned to the hotel for dinner.

On checking in with the hotel manager he informed us that no messages had been left. Daniel telephoned his family and then spoke with either John or Peter at the office whereby we were both shocked to learn that the offices of Southern Investigations had been burgled the night before. Daniel was very concerned to establish if any files were missing, but by all accounts, and with reassurance from Peter Newby these were all in place and intact. We were both very disappointed to learn the news of the burglary but Daniel decided that we shouldn't let bad news interfere with the work at hand and said we will deal with the break-in when we get back home. (See Chapter The Office Burglary)

The hotel manager informed us that the singer Sinnita was performing at a nightclub only 20 minutes away so we booked a cab and decided to go to the show. We arrived at the club and obtained admission and got change from a tenner. The show was about to start however there were only some 40 people in the club, a venue that could hold 400. We enjoyed the show and shared a bottle of vodka then returned to the hotel getting to our rooms around midnight.

It is important to stop for a moment and explain one or two things regarding the Malta assignment. Firstly, communications; this was 1987, we had no mobile phone or car phone and had to rely on public call boxes and the hotel for making calls. There was a time difference, Malta being ahead of the UK by two hours. We received communication by way of utilising the hotel as a message taking service when we were out. The hotel manager was happy to oblige; however, we did limit the content of the knowledge of our communications by informing anyone calling the hotel to merely leave their name and we would call them back. Secondly, in 1987 there were strict rules governing imports and exports of motor vehicles in Malta. Private motorcars were only allowed into Malta up to a maximum engine cc; anything above the limit would be classed as a commercial vehicle and would have to be modified into a van to be permitted to remain in Malta. We saw many examples of vehicles like this as we drove around, the back and side windows would have metal coverings by way of modification. The finance company Range Rover was at least 3500 cc and could only remain in Malta for six months unless modified to meet with government guidelines. Furthermore, only the importer of the vehicle was legally allowed to remove the vehicle from Malta and it was the **vehicle custodian** who had the importation documents so we had to meet with Maltese customs to have the vehicle paperwork transferred into Daniel's name to be able to export the vehicle out of Malta and back into Europe and the UK.

On Wednesday 4ᵗʰ of February we awoke around 9:00 am and proceeded down to breakfast. Daniel contacted the finance company and spoke to the accounts manager to establish if the money transfer had taken place. We were unable to ascertain if the monies had been received in Malta. We left the hotel and enjoyed the day sightseeing and touring. We returned to the hotel around 5:00 pm whereby the hotel manager informed us that the **vehicle custodian** called and had left a message that we were to meet him the next day at a café in Valletta for the purpose of attending the Valletta Customs house. We spent the rest of the evening having supper and drinks at the bar.

On Thursday 5ᵗʰ of February we awoke around 8:00 am and had breakfast at the hotel. Daniel made some calls to the UK again speaking with the accounts manager at the finance company and with the staff at Southern Investigations. Daniel was still unable to establish if the funds had been received by the finance company lawyer in Malta. Around 11:30 am we left the hotel and proceeded to our planned meeting with the **vehicle custodian**. We arrived at the café meeting place around 12:30 pm. The **vehicle custodian** arrived and he was joined by another gentleman who he identified as his lawyer. The **vehicle custodian** said that he would like to take us for a drink at a bar which he highly recommended; away from the café venue. We thought this unexpected, however; not to offend we agreed and accepted his invitation. We left our car parked and went with him and his companion to his car whereby we all travelled together to a bar on the outskirts of Valletta.

On arrival at the bar we were allocated a table outside. This was a civilised lunchtime meeting and quite normal. I recall Daniel and the **vehicle custodian** were initially discussing the bank transfer funds and that Daniel was unable to confirm that the funds had arrived in Malta. The conversation then moved on to cars.

The **vehicle custodian** told Daniel that he was involved in the car trade. He also said he had lived in the East End for some years and knew the London area very well and that Malta was a good place for business in the classic stock of 1950s, 1960s and 1970s cars of which many hundreds had been restored to original showroom condition in Malta.

He said that he imported classic car parts and vehicles; part of his visit to the customs house at Valletta that day was to get other documents stamped for his business. He also informed Daniel that the Range Rover **vehicle lessee** also had a BMW that belonged to a finance company and it was he who had collected it from the UK and imported it to Malta and kept it also on behalf of the **vehicle lessee**. He then informed Daniel that the **vehicle lessee** had been deported from Malta to the UK by a northern constabulary who was investigating a multi-million-pound fraud. During the meeting Danny gave the **vehicle custodian** his Southern Investigations business card and said he drove a BMW 320i in the UK.

Around 1:30 pm the **vehicle custodian** said we should leave and go to the customs house; he dropped off his companion on the way. The three of us continued on to the Valletta docks customs house. We arrived around 2:00 pm and walked up to the first floor and went into the office that was identified as head customs officer. The **vehicle custodian** seemed to be acquainted with the customs officer as they exchanged pleasantries in Maltese. He dealt with his business first getting documents stamped and paying the fees in cash. He then submitted the documentation for the Range Rover which seemed to be all in order; the customs officer stamped the documentation and wrote an export permit in Daniel's name so we could leave Malta with the vehicle. The cost of this was £20 in Maltese money. The **vehicle custodian** said, *"That's it all done"*; the **vehicle custodian** retained the export paperwork.

The Range Rover documentation was now in Daniel's name and he was authorised to export the vehicle from Malta on Saturday 7th of February.

The three of us drove back to the café where we had originally met and had parked our rental car, we agreed to communicate further and to finalise the details to handover the vehicle. We exchanged pleasantries and went our separate ways.

We returned to our hotel and Danny telephoned the Maltese lawyer acting on behalf of the UK finance company who informed him that the money transfer had still not been received. Danny contacted the UK finance company and was told that £2000 sterling had been forwarded to a bank in Sliema in Malta. We spent the rest of the afternoon and evening enjoying supper and spending time drinking at the bar until retiring to our rooms around 11:00 pm.

Friday 6th of February we awoke around 7:00 am and had breakfast at the hotel. Daniel decided to attend a travel agent in Valletta to book ship passage for us and the vehicle from Malta to Reggio di Calabria, mainland Italy on Saturday the 7th of February. Daniel undertook this action because there were only two car ferry crossings per week, one on Saturday and one on Thursday, however the Thursday car ferry had broken down and no bookings were possible for the foreseeable future. If we didn't have the Range Rover in our possession and were not able to board the 9:00 am car ferry on Saturday the 7th then we would have to remain in Malta for another week.

On leaving the travel agent we contacted the UK finance company Maltese lawyer who informed us that the monies had been safely received and communication had been forwarded to the **vehicle custodian** and his lawyer and it had been agreed that the vehicle would be handed over to Daniel and me at our hotel at 7:00 pm that night. We drove back to St Paul's Bay and returned the rental car and walked back to the hotel.

At the hotel we packed and prepared for the imminent arrival of the Range Rover and as agreed the **vehicle custodian** arrived at our hotel with the Range Rover and export documentation just after 7:00 pm; he was accompanied by a companion in a second vehicle. The handover of the Range Rover and the paperwork was undertaken; we said our goodbyes and that was the last we ever saw of that gentleman or his associates.

At that time of the evening it was already dark and the street lighting in the local area was rather poor. Daniel and I decided we should examine the entire vehicle for roadworthiness; to be as sure as we could that the almost 2000-mile journey ahead would be as uneventful as possible.

We drove to a nearby petrol station which had reasonable forecourt lighting whereby we spent the next 45 minutes to an hour meticulously examining the entire vehicle. Now why you may ask would Daniel undertake this task; as stated general roadworthiness and safety of the vehicle and its passengers. Daniel was able to build a car from its chassis up; he could identify any mechanical problem or fault from a visual inspection. Torches in hand we checked the underside, the engine bay, wheel arches, suspension, everything. We undertook a mini service checking the oil lubricants, water, tyre pressure etc., nothing was untoward and there were no visual signs of any crash repair or other interference in any way with the vehicle. We moved on to the interior checking under the seats in and around the boot area, storage compartments, etc.

We checked the vehicle to make sure that no personal belongings of the **vehicle lessee** or the **vehicle custodian** of any kind had been left in the vehicle. This is common practice with vehicle repossession as it is the vehicle that is the property of the finance company and not the individual goods which may be found or left in the vehicle and we didn't want any unforeseen hold ups in getting safely out of Malta.

After undertaking these checks, we returned to the hotel. The vehicle was parked outside on the main road from around 9:00 pm overnight. The vehicle was not parked in a secure compound or any area being monitored by CCTV, merely on the local road outside the hotel; the vehicle was locked and alarmed.

We returned to the bar of the hotel around 9:15 pm and had a late supper. Daniel settled our bill that night so we would have no delays in leaving early the next morning, we returned to our rooms about 10:30 pm arranging an alarm call for 5:00 am.

Saturday 7th of February I woke around 5:00 am and called Daniel from the internal telephone system. Daniel was already awake and told me that he would meet me in the lobby at 5:30 am. I looked out the window and through the darkness I could see the Range Rover parked where we left it. I must say, throughout our entire stay, after about 8:00 pm until approximately 7:00 am almost no cars or foot traffic passed through St Paul's Bay. To say the place was quiet is an understatement. I grabbed my bag, checked my room and headed to the lobby where Daniel was sitting. We shared some chocolate bar snacks and orange juice then grabbed our bags and walked to the Range Rover whereby we began our road trip back to the UK.

We drove from St Paul's Bay to Valletta harbour arriving around 7:00 am. There was already a large queue in the boarding lane. We drove to check in and were issued a boarding card, then moved onto customs and presented the vehicle paperwork and documentation; all of which was in order. Customs did not undertake any search or inspection of us or the vehicle. We were marshalled with the vehicle to the boarding area and allocated a boarding lane. We remained stationary until around 8:15 am when boarding started, eventually boarding the ship around 8:45 am. The Range Rover was parked in its allocated bay and our passage was booked through to Reggio di Calabria mainland Italy. We left the vehicle and proceeded to the ship's canteen where we sat down to enjoy breakfast.

The ship pulled out of Valletta harbour around 9:15 am and we were both pleased to be leaving and heading home. The weather that morning started off rather damp, cold and dull however by the time we set sail and were watching Malta fade away in the distance the weather had become bright, sunny and warm.

Whilst on board we established that the first stop was Siracusa, Sicily and the sailing time was about five hours. We were told with all the stops the ship had to make including the sailing time; it would take at least 12 to 13 hours or more to reach our final destination of Reggio di Calabria. However, if we got off the ship at Siracusa then drove across Sicily and got the ferry from Messina Sicily to Reggio di Calabria we could save anywhere between five and seven hours off the journey time; so, this is what we decided to do.

We spoke to the ship's crew and they agreed that we could disembark at the port of Siracusa, Sicily. We were told that Italian customs officials would board the ship at some point outside Siracusa and that immigration and passport control would be undertaken while still aboard the ship. This was duly undertaken and at the port of Siracusa those permitted were allowed to disembark.

We drove through Sicily from Siracusa to Messina to board the ferry crossing to Reggio di Calabria mainland Italy. I recall the oranges and the limes on the trees; we passed the smoking volcano of Mount Etna. We made no stops as the fuel tank was full from Malta.

The drive through Sicily was uneventful and took around two hours. Daniel drove this leg as he preferred daytime driving. On arrival at Messina ferry terminal we booked the next available crossing to Reggio di Calabria and boarded a ferry around 5:00 pm. The crossing took around 45 minutes on disembarking we were back on the road around 6:00 pm.

We travelled north through Italy via Napoli. We pulled over and got some snacks and fluids which we ate in the vehicle; it was getting late (around midnight) so we decided to rest and slept in the vehicle. We awoke cold and stiff around 5:00 am on Sunday the 8th of February and continued on our way until we found a truck stop where we got some hot tea and pastries.

We continued north bypassing Rome through Firenze to Bardonecchia Italian Alps border at an elevation of 10,000 feet. At around 10:00 pm we entered the Frejus tunnel driving through the mountains to Modane, France. I recall the descent down the mountain into Chambery and how beautiful it was with the snow and the lights and the

SNCF railway - a Christmas card picture. Daniel and I spoke of how we had seen all four seasons all within a few hours during our trip; from the summer weather in Malta and Sicily, the spring conditions around Napoli to the severe winter conditions of northern Italy at the Alps with the sleet and snow.

We pressed on through the night taking turns driving and sleeping bypassing Lyon through Macon, onto Dijon, Troyes, Reims and finally reaching the ferry port of Calais around 9:00 am on Monday, 9th of February.

We booked the next crossing to Dover arriving in the UK around 1:00 pm. The Range Rover was only left unattended whilst on board ships. The vehicle was never unattended at any other time apart from outside the St Paul's Bay hotel overnight. We had passed through some five sets of customs and border control without incident; we met no other persons that gained access to the vehicle during the road trip. The entire journey of 1900 miles was uneventful. We proceeded from Dover to London and arrived at Daniel's home around 3:30 pm that day. The Range Rover was left parked outside Daniel's home until the following morning.

On Tuesday the 10th of February, Daniel drove the Range Rover to the office of Southern Investigations and parked it on Gillette Road, which was the last time I actually saw the vehicle. The vehicle was then driven to the Midlands by a Southern Investigations agent and returned to the custody of the finance company.

Daniel contacted the finance company and undertook a detailed report of the findings from the trip. There was a concern that a threat might have been made to Daniel and this was mentioned by Peter Newby.

This is an excerpt from Day 3, page 32 of the Daniel Morgan Inquest. Peter Newby is being examined by the Coroner:

Q. ...... *"The only other time that-I was aware that Danny may have been threatened was shortly after he returned from his trip to Malta to bring a Range Rover car back. I walked into his office about 10:30 a.m. one morning and I heard him slam the phone down. His face looked white. It often went like that if he was worried or tired. I asked him what was wrong. He said: 'I've just had a phone call about that job in Malta.' I said: 'What sort of phone call?' I think his words were 'a bit heavy.'"* – A. I think that is what he said, yes.

Q. *Did you interpret that in any other way?* – A. I interpreted it as being leaned on.

Q. *Being leaned on. Being threatened?* – A. Yes.

At no time did Daniel tell me that he felt threatened or had received a phone call containing threats about the Malta repossession. If Daniel had received any threats regarding this I have no doubt he would have told me straight away.

As to the conversation which, Peter Newby refers to I know Daniel liaised with a Northern Constabulary and he was asked to submit a report of the events that had taken place in Malta. This would have included any consideration that he might have surrounding any fraud or corruption concerns. This was a normal routine that Daniel would undertake especially in the repossession of property, goods, and vehicles or when establishing police involvement regarding any casework that he may be undertaking.

The original **vehicle lessee** was the subject of a serious crime squad fraud investigation and the exchange of information with the police may have enlightened Daniel as to the possible depth of the police investigation which may have given him reason to express concern to Peter Newby.

This is an excerpt from Day 6; page 2 of the Daniel Morgan Inquest. Detective Sergeant Davidson recalled and further cross-examined by Miss June Tweedie.

MISS TWEEDIE: I have a number of points.

Q. The first point was about Woman Detective Constable Benfield. – A. Yes.

Q. The relevance of that being that she told or asked the sister of Daniel Morgan whether he had made an appointment with the Sydenham CID for a day or two after his death. – A. I have been unable to speak to Miss Benfield. She is on leave. There is no answer from her home telephone number. However, I have searched my records and I can say that there is no information relating to any appointment made by Mr. Morgan with the CID Officers at Sydenham. However, there was a telephone call received in our office the day following the murder, the 11th, from two officers from the West Yorkshire Fraud section, who said this morning that they had contacted Southern Investigations with a view to visiting them in order to obtain a statement from Daniel Morgan. The circumstances of that were that Mr. Morgan had recovered the car from Malta and they wanted to take a statement to that effect. That is the only record I can find of any possible appointment that Mr. Morgan may or may not have had with the police prior to his death.

It's important to point out that at no time during the repossession of the Range Rover and the subsequent financial negotiations was there any bribe payment paid to anyone. The payment made to the **vehicle custodian** of £2000 was agreed through the finance company and lawyers. These fees were for costs of storing the vehicle and actions in safe guarding the vehicle from seizure by the Maltese authorities under acts of law.

The **vehicle custodian** had no involvement in any wrongdoing surrounding the events that took place in Malta in the handling or the repossession of the Range Rover.

At a time after Daniel's murder I was informed by a Northern Constabulary that a Crown Court trial was to take place involving the original **vehicle lessee** and that I had been included on the witness list. However, I was later informed by the police that the prosecution no longer required me to give any evidence and I was released from that witness subpoena.

Chapter 17
The Office Burglary

On the night of the 2nd of February 1987, the offices of Southern Investigations were burgled. Daniel and I were told of the break-in on Tuesday the 3rd of February when we telephoned the office from Malta where we were undertaking a vehicle repossession. This is what I recall of the events.

Peter Newby informed us that the burglar had entered through a window on the first floor to the rear of the building. Daniel was most concerned about what had been stolen but more so the integrity of confidential files. The office manager, Peter, was an absolute stickler about keeping track of the files and making sure he knew where and who had any particular file at any given time. He assured Daniel that the files were intact. Peter said that goods and monies had been stolen and the matter had been reported to the local police.

I am unable to confirm what actions were actually taken at the time of the incident as Danny and I were in Malta. Daniel decided that when we returned to the office he was definitely going to establish what took place, for his own peace of mind, as he too was a stickler for detail and if anyone would know if the files had been touched it was Daniel.

During our time in Malta I could tell Daniel was worried about what exactly had taken place and also the fact that the robbery occurred in our absence whilst out of the country; Daniel said there was nothing he could do about it until our return to London. Daniel was kept updated by Peter and I do not recall, at any time, that any files were ever reported as missing from the burglary.

I watched Daniel over a period of days after our return to London as he was troubled by the break-in. He meticulously examined the filing cabinets and individual files that he believed contained information of a sensitive nature or that might be useful by way of intelligence. He was clearly weighing up in his mind the evidence until finally concluding (and this was his actual opinion) that the break-in was a random goods burglary.

Security at the office was almost non-existent and under the cover of darkness access to the rear of the building would have been easy. Basic security of today is light years ahead of what was classed as secure in 1987 at 53 High Street, Thornton Heath.

No one has ever been charged or prosecuted by the police for this burglary and this crime is yet another that remains unsolved.

Is it possible that this burglary was far more sinister than first thought? Was the real purpose of the break-in to examine Southern Investigations files? Had any been copied or photographed without any actually being removed? The office had a state of the art fully functioning photocopy machine situated in the manager's office. Did the burglar obtain any sensitive intelligence? Did the intruder stage a random goods and monies burglary to cover tracks as to his real intentions? Did the burglar know that Daniel was out of the country undertaking an assignment? Or was this a mere coincidence. There have been far too many coincidences surrounding Daniel's murder for my liking and this is just one of many.

In 1986 Southern Investigations received instructions to obtain witness statements surrounding the activities of a prominent member of the Conservative party on a visit to Germany. In January of 1984 the BBC programme Panorama had broadcast, "Maggie's Militant Tendency" claiming a number of Conservative MPs had links to far right organisations in the UK and Europe. Two MPs were named, one being Neil Hamilton.

The Panorama programme alleged that during a visit to Berlin Neil Hamilton goose stepped and gave a mock Hitler salute; an act which was not permitted at that time in Germany. Tory MPs vigorously denied these allegations and sued the BBC.

The instructions that Southern Investigations received which Daniel and I worked on were to trace and interview witnesses in an attempt to defend a libel case brought by Tory MPs regarding the documentary. As much as this may seem far-fetched, this type of instruction might have brought Daniel and Southern Investigations under the gaze of senior government intelligence agencies.

I remember this was somewhat of a rushed job which my involvement included attending a number of addresses in the central London area in an attempt to interview individuals and obtain witness statements in the defence of the libel claim. I recall this because of the prominence of the case but more so because out of the 10 plus people I was to interview I do not recall obtaining any witness statements which I found most unusual. Either I was told, 'no comment', or people made themselves unavailable to be questioned.

I also formed the opinion that Daniel did not place his normal resource into these instructions; for if I had ever returned to the office without completing my task (obtaining witness statements), Daniel would have said, get your arse back out there and do your job. However, this was not the case, he merely asked me had I attended all the addresses and reported my findings accordingly; which I had.

I don't think Daniel felt entirely comfortable being involved with this particular job. I could tell he felt this assignment was stretching the political boundaries and the effects of any damning evidence we established might have and any potential repercussions on his career or business. Daniel said to me, *"These are powerful people who have powerful allies so be careful in your approach to the task at hand"*.

In 1986 the BBC withdrew from the case and Neil Hamilton MP was awarded substantial damages in compensation.

Is it possible the burglary at the offices of Southern Investigations could have constituted a much more sinister motive such as espionage or was Daniel correct in his conclusion that the break-in was a random goods burglary? I doubt we will ever know.

Chapter 18

Sir Monty and the Inquisition

On the 11th of April 1988 a public inquest began into the death of Daniel John Morgan and was held at Southwark Coroners Court, Tennis Street, London SE1; the presiding Coroner was Sir Montague Levine.

The inquest lasted a full eight days over a period of two weeks between the 11th and 25th of April 1988. In the Coroner's summing up he said, *"This has probably been one of the most unique inquests that I have had to deal with over the years. I am sure people who have been involved with inquests will probably agree with me".*

My story centres on Daniel Morgan when he was alive and the time I knew him. The assignments we undertook, the work we did, the people he knew, how his behaviour affected those around him. However, it is important to spend a little time with my thoughts and opinions regarding the evidence and findings of the witnesses who gave testimony in April 1988 at The Daniel Morgan Inquest.

The significance in time is extremely important regarding witness testimony. Witness statements would or should have been taken by the police immediately after Daniel's murder when the findings or the recollections of those witnesses should still have been relatively fresh in their minds. Over time opinions of witnesses in their testimony can change or could actually be different in some way from what was first said to what they may recall later, sometimes at a much later date. I would put this down in the most part to memory good and bad especially in an unsolved homicide that has been ongoing for over 31 years.

Sir Montague's inquest is a momentous chapter in Daniel's murder and the transcript is a very important document of record. It was the first time that any witness testimony had been heard and explored in any degree in an open court to a conclusion. It is important to remember the Coroner's Court admitted hearsay into evidence.

The inquest was set up by the Coroner and took into account any police evidence and witness statements obtained during the initial police investigation into the murder of Daniel Morgan. It is from this evidence or witness statements that some of the witnesses are called to the court as chosen by the Coroner to give testimony in open court. Notice of attendance to these witnesses would have been given prior to the start of the inquest. Witnesses are in a position to seek legal advice or to obtain legal counsel to be present on their behalf if advised or required.

The Coroner's Court is not a trial, nobody is charged here, and it is a court of record which is inquisitorial in nature not adversarial. It is the purpose of the court to ascertain who the deceased was, how, when and where the deceased came by his death. A jury was convened whose job it was from hearing the evidence to reach a verdict, the Coroner's Court is to determine the facts of all these questions.

The structure and the record of the inquest included:

SIR MONTAGUE B. LEVINE – The Coroner

MISS J. TWEEDIE (instructed by Messrs Gagg & Co., Crickhowell) Appeared for Mrs. Isobel Mary Hulsmann and Mr. Alastair Morgan.

MR. J. NUTTER (instructed by Messrs Coffey Whittey, Thornton Heath) appeared for Mr. John Rees.

MR. I. GOLDSWORTHY (instructed by Messrs Russell Jones & Walker, WC1) appeared for Detective Sergeant Fillery, Detective Constable Foley and Detective Constable Purvis.

MR. J. GOMPERTZ Q.C. AND MR. J. NORRIS (instructed by The Solicitor to the Commissioner of Police) appeared for the Commissioner of Police.

(Transcript of the Shorthand Notes of Marten Walsh Cherer Ltd., Pemberton House, East Harding Street, London EC4A 3AS. Telephone Number: 01-583-0889)

The Coroner and the Legal Counsel in representation all had the ability to examine or cross examine all the witnesses.

The inquest into the death of Daniel Morgan began, the jury was sworn in, the Coroner (with the assistance of DSI Campbell) arranged the order of the witnesses to start with an event that took place prior to the murder, which may or may not be related, but was explored surrounding Daniel Morgan's demise. The witnesses with their relevant evidence occur in sequence. I was called and examined on day four; surprisingly I was not included on the Coroners original witness list.

Detective Superintendent Campbell was the lead police investigator handling the initial investigation into the murder. He informed the court as to what investigations had been undertaken together with the police resources utilised to that date in the process of trying to ascertain the murderer of Daniel Morgan.

DANIEL MORGAN SOUTHERN INVESTIGATION

This is an excerpt from Day 1, pages 8 and 9 of the Daniel Morgan Inquest. Detective Superintendent Campbell is examined by the Coroner and Campbell reports the following:

Apart from the United Kingdom, inquiries through the various police forces have been made in Eire, Malta, West Germany and Denmark. The press interest in this case has been extremely high. There have been some 47 separate reports in newspapers. Additionally, appeals were made on LBC, Radio London, Capital Radio, Police 5 and Crimewatch UK. Crimewatch UK reconstructed events and broadcast the programme nationwide on 23 April 1987. Some one hundred appeals for assistance notices were printed and displayed outside police stations and business premises in South London and Surrey. In view of the nature of Mr. Morgan's business a telex was sent to all stations in the Metropolitan Police District, asking for police officers who had any dealings with him to come forward. Two special police publications were also printed in April and November and circulated to all forces in England and Wales. These notices gave details of Daniel Morgan and information regarding a Rolex watch that was missing from his body on 10th March 1987. On 17th March 1987, exactly a week after Mr. Morgan's death, a mobile police station was in attendance outside the Golden Lion Public House, where in addition to detective officers employed on the investigation, some 20 uniformed officers were engaged interviewing customers in the public house and persons passing through Sydenham. The dedication of all the officers employed on this investigation has been of the highest quality. These officers have worked long and hard in an attempt to find the person responsible for Daniel Morgan's death. Unfortunately, to date their efforts have been unrewarded. The police have not been in a position to charge any person with Mr. Morgan's death. The investigation is on-going.

The Coroner: At this particular stage, I would suggest that I ask you about some matters which occurred some considerable time before the event. They concern the Belmont Auctions. I think that at this particular stage we do not know whether the matters we are going to discuss this morning with regard to the Belmont Auctions, and various people involved, including police officers, may or may not have a direct bearing on the demise of Daniel Morgan. But I think that it is absolutely essential, as you will see as the inquest proceeds, that this matter is investigated here and now. If counsel at the beginning of this wish to make any submissions on this, it will be my duty to ask for the jury to leave.

What I notice is how Campbell refers to, "*The dedication of all the officers employed on this investigation has been of the highest quality*". I am afraid I have never been of the same opinion.

Detective Superintendent Campbell goes on to inform the court of his main lines of inquiry which he established were relevant and important to the demise of Daniel Morgan.

This is an excerpt from Day 1, pages 11-12 of the Daniel Morgan Inquest. Detective Superintendent Douglas Campbell is examined by the Coroner.

The Coroner: At this particular stage all I want you to do is to outline to the court – do not go into this in great detail – the investigation, as far as you were concerned, which has relevance—that is very important—to the case of the demise of Daniel Morgan. – A. That is in relation to Belmont Car Auctions?

Q. Yes. – A. Belmont Car Auctions is in South East London. In February 1986 an armed robbery took place where approximately £20,000 was stolen. Resulting from this, Mr. William John Rees of Southern Investigations was introduced by police officers to the Director of Belmont Car Auctions. He undertook security cover at the auctions. Security was provided on 4th, 5th, 7th, 8th, 11th, 12th, 14th, 16th, and 18th of March 1986. A number of men were employed at the auctions. On 18th March William Jonathan Rees collected a sum of £18,280 in cash from the auctions. He was unable to deposit the money at the Midland Bank night safe because apparently the night safe lock was jammed. He took it to his home address in South Norwood. Outside his home address he was robbed by two men and the money was stolen. He reported the matter to the police. He attended the Mayday Hospital where he was detained for a number of days, having had some corrosive fluid sprayed in his eyes. The matter was fully reported to police and investigated. No person was ever arrested for that robbery.

About three weeks into the murder investigation I became aware that Belmont Car Auctions were pursuing a civil claim against William John Rees for the loss of this money. The solicitors acting for Belmont Car Auctions had written to three police officers who were present at the auctions at various dates whilst Mr. Rees was providing security cover. The three police officers had not notified either me or the Metropolitan Police that they were to be interviewed. On 3rd April 1987 I caused those three police officers and Mr. Rees and two other men to be arrested in connection with the murder of Daniel Morgan. It is fair to say with regard to all the men who were interviewed that there was insufficient evidence to charge any of these persons with the death of Daniel Morgan.

The Coroner: We shall hear in more detail about this later on as it fits into the sequence of events, but I think at this particular stage we should leave this matter as it is at the moment. (To the witness) We shall recall you to see how it fits in to the order of events.

This was obviously intriguing and most compelling and would have had the entire attention of the court. However, it was nothing compared to what the court was about to hear from the next witness; testimony so explosive it started a media frenzy across the tabloids.

This is an excerpt of Day 1, pages 12-18 of the Daniel Morgan Inquest. Kevin Lennon is examined by the Coroner.

Q. You have made various statements to the police. – A Yes.

Q. Three in number. – A. Yes.

Q. I should like to ask you some questions. I understand that you became friendly with a person known as Laurie Bucknall, a friend of yours, who was at one time in the police. – A. That is correct.

Q. Through him, he introduced you to a man by the name of John Rees. – A. Yes.

Q. Do you see John Rees sitting in this court? – A. Yes.

Q. *Subsequently you became very friendly with John Rees. Some six months after being introduced to Rees he in turn introduced you to his partner, a man named Daniel Morgan, the deceased.* – A. *Yes.*

Q. *You learned that John Rees and Daniel Morgan were in business together as private investigators with a firm known as Southern Investigations, with offices at Crown House, Crown Point, Norwood.* – A. *Yes.*

Q. *Shortly after this introduction to Daniel Morgan you had occasion to visit him and John Rees at their offices. You became extremely friendly with them and you accepted their offer to start working for them as an accountant.* – A. *Yes.*

Q. *What was your work actually?* – A. *At that stage I had my own business in Croydon as an accountant. They became one of my clients, collectively.*

Q. *Did you actually go and work in their business completely? Did you give up your own job?* – A. *No. I was working as a professional accountant with my own firm. They became one of my clients.*

Q. *Did you say that you came to the conclusion over the first few weeks that business-wise John Rees and Daniel Morgan were a good partnership.* – A. *That is correct.*

Q. *They were two entirely different individuals but, nevertheless, they worked together as a team. You say here that Daniel Morgan was better educated than John Rees and was more knowledgeable on matters of law than Rees. However, you say that Daniel Morgan never dressed smartly, whereas John Rees did, but that they complemented each other in lots of ways.* – A. *Yes.*

Q. *But, unfortunately the partnership, as far as you were concerned, soured somewhat. You then go on to say that as time went on Daniel Morgan's mannerisms and behaviour began to annoy John Rees intensely. Eventually this became public knowledge.* – A. *That is correct.*

Q. *How long did it take for that to take place? How long did it take before you realised that all was not well between the two partners?* – A. *About eighteen months.*

Q. *Had you left your own firm and were working for them?* – A. *No. I went to attend their offices as and when necessary, to write up the books and prepare the end of year returns and so on.*

Q. *You then make a somewhat damning statement here. You say that one of the main reasons why John Rees came to despise Daniel Morgan was because of his attitude with and towards women. What do you mean by that?* – A. *It became obvious through my conversations with John and Daniel that whenever the opportunity arose, either through client contact or otherwise, Daniel was always very keen to become friendly with any female staff who were present at any meetings. He would make efforts to ingratiate himself with females in those positions in order to invite them out for a drink or for dinner.*

Q. *He felt that this was extremely embarrassing to the business. Was it causing problems for John Rees?* – A. *John considered it to be very unprofessional behaviour.*

Q. *Are you suggesting that this caused problems with the clients, that clients were leaving the business because of this? – A. I would consider that on occasion, if it became known, it would cause problems with the clients, yes.*

Q. *You went on to say that another thing John Rees did not like about Daniel Morgan was the fact that Daniel had a deformed foot. Most people would be sympathetic to somebody with a deformed foot. What had happened that they argued about his deformed foot? – A. I think that John gradually grew to dislike Daniel because of what I have said earlier, regarding his behaviour with female clients and so on. John would pick on this particular aspect of Daniel's physical build to poke fun at him.*

Q. *You say that as time went on you realized that John Rees' dislike for Daniel Morgan had in fact turned to hatred. Hatred is a strong word, to hate someone. Surely it was not because of Morgan's deformed foot and his attitude towards women. Can you explain what you meant by that? "Turned to hatred" is the term you used. Can you explain what you meant by that? – A. John and Daniel were entirely different people. John was far more professional in his approach to his work and far more capable of getting his work done, whereas Daniel, on the other hand, would quite often ignore or forget to attend to current matters, which in turn would lead to client complaints in the office. By the nature of the work John would spend much more time in the office than Daniel would. He would be at the receiving end when clients would ring in to complain.*

Q. *Here you are working for two partners. It is very dangerous sometimes to run with the hare and the hounds. Did Mr. Morgan realise that you were now hearing tales about him from Mr. Rees? This is what you were doing. You were having private conversations with Mr. Rees, were you not? – A. I think that Daniel did realise it. I was present on several occasions in the office when these problems with clients arose. John and Daniel argued fiercely about the causes of all these problems.*

Q. *You cite three individual cases here. You say that John often spoke to you – this is hearsay evidence, obviously – about arranging to get Daniel breathalysed or arrested for drinking and driving. Did he tell you that or is that something you found out for yourself? – A. John told me that.*

Q. *Did this surprise you; that somebody was going to try and get him arrested for drinking and driving? – A. At this stage the relationship had deteriorated from John's point of view, where he would have liked it if Daniel could no longer operate as an effective partner in the business. As Daniel needed his driving licence to perform his particular duties, if he were breathalysed this would have meant that he could no longer perform as a partner.*

Q. *You then go on to say: "I frequently advised John Rees in the strongest possible terms to effect an agreed dissolution of the partnership." I can see your point there. They were not getting on together. There were lots of problems. "But John Rees would not listen." Why did they not break up the partnership if things were so bad? They obviously were bad if one partner is trying to get the other one breathalysed so that he cannot function as a partner in a private detective agency. Why did they not dissolve it? – A. I think the reason why John never* approached Daniel with regard to this proposal is that John would have been loath to pay Daniel any money on the dissolution of the partnership, had it been agreed to.

Q. Was that a fact, or was it your idea that he would not pay any money or did Mr. Rees say that he would not pay any money? – A. John did say this to me that he felt that this was not the right course to take.

Q. The next statement here I want you to think about carefully. You say: "It was during the course of one of these" – this is one of the talks about dissolving the partnership; this is you talking to Rees confidentially and privately, I presume. Was this privately? – A. Yes.

Q. You say that it was during the course of one of these by now regular conversations that you had with John Rees that he revealed to you his idea for having Daniel Morgan killed, because he thought there was no other way of getting rid of Daniel. That is a terribly damning statement. In conversation people say things in jest, "I wish I could have so and so killed." It is part in jest and sometimes it is a figure of speech. Sometimes it is just tossed out into a conversation and it has not got the depth of meaning that it has when I read it out just now. Did you take John Rees seriously when he said to you: "He revealed to me his idea for having Daniel Morgan killed" because he thought there was no other way of getting rid of Daniel? Would you tell us what the circumstances were in which he said that? – A. As I said earlier, when the partnership commenced John and Daniel seemed to get on very well together as partners in their individual tasks, but as time progressed John began to dislike Daniel more and more. This dislike turned to hatred. Over a period of a couple of years John had hoped, by one way or another, that Daniel either would have been breathalysed – this would have meant that Daniel would be ineffective as a partner in the business – or that somehow or other Daniel would come unstuck in his own work. Daniel's particular task in the partnership was acting as the bailiff. In that respect he had to frequently attend premises and evict tenants. The second part of his duties was to repossess vehicles bought on hire purchase where the clients had defaulted on payment. Both of these tasks, in my opinion, required a certain tact and diplomacy. Daniel lacked both of those qualities. He frequently upset the people he was dealing with. It was not an uncommon feature in conversations that I had with John in the office that people would ring up complaining about Daniel's behaviour.

Q. You say that John Rees had arranged several times with the Police to have Daniel Morgan breathalysed. What is that statement based on? "John Rees had arranged several times with the Norbury Police to have Daniel Morgan breathalysed on three occasions to my knowledge, twice at the 'Victory' Public House in Thornton Heath, when I was present. On the first of those two occasions John Rees, Daniel Morgan and I were drinking with several other people when John Rees said to me 'When Danny drives away from here tonight, he'll be breathalysed'". – A. That is correct. The background to that is that John was very friendly with police officers in the area because his work would bring him into contact with them.

Q. Is this your idea that he was very friendly with police officers? How do you know that he was very friendly with police officers? What is that statement based on? – A. It is based on the *fact that I was present on several occasions when he introduced me to police officers in a pub. He drank and met socially and on business occasions with police officers, quite frequently.*

Q. You go on to say: "I was sure that John Rees was telling me the truth when he said that he arranged for Daniel to be stopped because he mentioned to me that the reason for stopping him would be the fact that he had told the police about damage to a rear light on Daniel's car, whereby this light was showing white light instead of red." – A. On another occasion the rear brake light of Daniel's car was broken, which would have given the police an excuse for stopping him, as this was an offence.

Q. Listen to this statement: "It was because of John Rees' frustration at all these attempts to get rid of Daniel Morgan coming to nothing that he started to talk regularly about getting Daniel Morgan killed." Can you enlarge on that? What do you mean by "regularly"? – A. By regularly I mean that that conversation regarding John Rees' attitude to Daniel Morgan took place on at least half a dozen occasions, between myself and himself.

Q. You go on to say that he kept asking you if you knew anyone who would kill Daniel. "He seemed to believe that I would know someone to do it." Why should he ask you to find somebody? You are an accountant. – A. That is right.

Q. Why does he want to ask you? Here is a private detective. Why would he ask his accountant who works for him to find somebody to kill him? – A. We were very friendly and close at this stage.

Q. Why did he ask you? – A. John also knew that I regularly moved around Croydon in pubs and clubs where he did not associate. I presume that he assumed that I would be in contact with somebody who would fit that particular task.

Q. You said: "I made it clear to John Rees that I wouldn't do this and advised him to stop considering this course of action. I have no doubt that John Rees spoke to me like this because he trusted me one hundred per cent and that he believed our conversation was in complete confidence." You then go on to say that this conversation took place on six or so separate times. – A. That is correct. I pleaded with John on each of those occasions to reconsider his course of action.

Q. I want you to think carefully about the next statement I am going to put to you. This is what you have stated in the statement: "I formed the opinion that John Rees was determined to either kill Daniel Morgan or have him killed. When he spoke to me about it John Rees was quite calm and unemotional about planning Daniel's death." Are you sure of that? – A. Yes, I am sure.

Q. Are you sure that it was not a statement that somebody would make in conversation: "I wish I could get rid of him" or "I wish I could have him killed." Are you sure that it was not a figure of speech? Was it more than that? – A. It was more than that.

Q. What do you say about that? – A. John had decided at this stage that he could no longer work with Daniel in the partnership. He had in his own mind found a replacement for Daniel. It was his objective to get rid of Daniel in order to replace him with this new prospective partner who would be, in John's opinion, a much greater asset to the business.

Q. Who was this new partner who was going to take Daniel's place? – A. At the time he was a serving police officer, Sergeant Sid Fillery.

Q. I do not think he is in the Force now. – A. No. He has retired.

Q. Mr. Fillery is due to give evidence here in this court. Did you continue working for Rees and Morgan? – A. Yes. Up until about October 1986 I was concerned with the normal duties of an accountant, preparing the books, the returns and so on.

Q. When did you finish with Daniel Morgan and Mr. Rees? – A. That was about the last time I worked for them.

Q. What date was that? – A. October 1986.

Q. Did you see them again? – A. I saw them again once or twice after that.

Q. Did you do any work for them? – A. I did not do any work for the partnership after that date.

Q. Did anybody contact you? Did Mr. Rees contact you socially or did Mr. Morgan contact you socially? – A. After that I met them once or twice for a drink.

Q. Both of them? – A. Both of them, yes.

Q. Together? – A. Not together. This was on separate occasions.

Q. Was the same conversation coming up, about wanting to get rid of Daniel Morgan? – A. At that stage John no longer discussed that conversation with me any further.

Q. You are aware that Daniel Morgan was found killed at the rear of a public house? – A. Yes.

Q. You may or may not be aware that he had a meeting that night. – A. I am aware of that.

Q. Did you know about that meeting? – A. No.

Q. Did you know about the meeting of the 9th March, the day before? – A. No, I did not.

Q. Did you know anything about a meeting, two days before that, on 7th March, in another public house? – A. No, I did not.

Q. Did you know anything about a meeting that took place in the Dolphin Public House on 5th March? – A. No.

This is an excerpt of Day 1 pages 20-23 of Daniel Morgan Inquest. Kevin Lennon is cross examined by Miss June Tweedie:

Q. You say that you had these conversations with Mr. Rees when he confided that he was planning to kill Mr. Morgan. – A. That is correct.

Q. Did he give you any details? You said that he was asking you if you knew anyone who could do it. – A. That is right.

Q. Did he tell you any details of any plans he had made? – A. At that stage he did not.

THE CORONER: May I interject here? That is not quite true, is it? I held back on this final statement. You said that it must have been some time, about May 1986, when John Rees told you about conversations and plans he had made with Sid Fillery who was then in the police. "It was late August or early September 1986. During one of these conversations with John Rees when he was discussing with me his plans for Daniel Morgan's death, that John Rees said 'I've the perfect *solution for Daniel's murder. My mates at Catford nick are going to arrange it.'" His mates are police. There were some other plans made that you have not mentioned. – A. I am sorry.*

Q. Let me finish: *"I was astounded and amazed by this revelation by John Rees and when questioned by me, John Rees said 'These police officers are friends of mine and will either murder Danny themselves or arrange for his murder.' He went on to explain to me that if they didn't do it themselves the police would arrange for some other person over whom they had some criminal charge pending to carry out Daniel's murder and in return police proceedings against that person would be dropped."* Is that true? Did he say that to you? – A. That is correct.

Q. *"John Rees continued to explain to me that Daniel's murder would be committed somewhere within the jurisdiction of Catford Police Station."* It was, was it not? – A. Yes.

Q. *"The reason for the murder being carried out in that area was because, those same Catford police officers would then be involved in the murder investigation and would suppress any information linking the murder with John Rees or themselves."* – A. That is right.

Q. Is that true? – A. That is true.

Q. Is there any embroidery about the statement you made? – A. No.

Q. None whatsoever. – A. None whatsoever.

Q. You say: *"John Rees never told me when the murder would happen or where Daniel Morgan would be killed."* You then go on to say: *"When John Rees discussed these matters with me I explained to him that if Daniel Morgan was murdered he"* – meaning John Rees – *"would be the prime suspect and the first person that police would question."* – A. I said that to John on many occasions during our conversations.

Q. You say: *"After these conversations with John Rees concerning the Catford police officers I had one more lengthy discussion with him when Rees re-affirmed the arrangements that he had made with these Catford police officers. Rees also mentioned in this last conversation that it would cost him a thousand pounds for the Catford officers to carry out Daniel Morgan's murder or arrange for it to be done."* You said: *"As far as I'm concerned that was the last time I ever discussed the matter of Daniel Morgan's murder with John Rees. This was sometime in September 1986."*

MISS TWEEDIE: why were you not prepared to tell the jury that when I asked the question a few moments ago? – A. The time you were discussing during your questioning of me earlier was the time preceding that conversation?

Q. I asked you whether any plans had been made in discussion with John Rees. I did not put any time on it. – A. Initially, no such plans had been made. It was a good time after our initial discussions that those plans were put forward to me.

Q. Why did you stop working for Mr Rees and Mr Morgan? – A. I stopped working for Mr Rees and Mr Morgan because I had my own personal problems with my business.

Q. Were you not unhappy about these conversations that you were hearing between John Rees and other people? – A. I never heard a conversation between John Rees and other people.

Q. The conversation between John Rees and yourself. – A. I was extremely unhappy about them.

Q. Did that have no bearing on your leaving? – A. It did have a bearing, yes.

Q. Did you ever think to go to the police? – A. I did discuss the matter with a police officer on one occasion.

Q. Which police officer was that? – A. Laurie Bucknall

THE CORONER: Was he with the police at the time? – A. Yes.

Q. Was he retired at the time or was he still in the police force? – A. He was still in the police force.

Q. MISS TWEEDIE: What was his reaction? – A. Unfortunately, on the occasion when we discussed it we had both had a great amount to drink. His reaction was surprise and amazement. I do not think that he believed me.

Q. Did you not think to go back to him when you were sober? – A. I considered the situation and declined to do that.

Q. A few months later Daniel Morgan was murdered. – A. Yes.

Q. Did you volunteer your services to the police at that time? – A. No.

Q. How did these statements come to be taken? – A. It was some considerable time after the murder of Daniel Morgan that I approached Laurie Bucknall who by now had retired from the police force for a couple of years. I was still very friendly with him and in contact with him. It was in June 1987 that I approached Laurie with the information that I have made public in my statement.

Q. Is it right that ex-Detective Sergeant Fillery and Mr. Rees are now working together? – A. I believe it is true, yes.

Q. Do you know any more details about that? – A. No, I do not.

THE CORONER: I have no details of that. Do you mean to tell me that Mr. Fillery is working with Southern Investigations now? – A. I was told this by a police officer.

Q. When were you told that? – A. Last night.

MISS TWEEDIE: Which officer told you that? – A. D.I. Jones.

When I heard of Kevin Lennon's testimony I could not believe my ears. I was shocked and immediately I did not know what to think. If what Kevin Lennon said was right and he believed Danny was to be killed then why didn't he tell Danny? The next thing that came to mind was the fact that ex-Sergeant Sid Fillery, now retired, was actually seen in the offices of Southern Investigations by me on Friday 8th April 1988, prior to the start of the inquest.

Kevin Lennon's testimony states it was D.I. Jones who had told him that Sid Fillery was now *working* at Southern Investigations. The same Sergeant Sid Fillery who in the first four days of the initial murder investigation had been instructed to attend the offices of Southern Investigations and remove files and documents by way of evidence gathering under the command of Detective Superintendent Douglas Campbell. To say that I was surprised as to these developments is an understatement.

Now it is only fair to point out here and now than John Rees and Sid Fillery both strenuously denied the allegations made by Kevin Lennon that a plot existed to murder

Daniel Morgan and excerpts of their rebuttals to these allegations can be seen in their witness testimony and examination by all counsel. (See Chapter The Teflon Trail)

Belmont Car Auctions and Kevin Lennon's testimony appeared to be the precursor and the background of the case surrounding the police investigations into the murder of Daniel Morgan; the foundation of some of the evidence that has been utilised in five unsuccessful police investigations over a period of 31 years.

Chapter 19
Belmont Car Auctions Robberies

A tremendous amount of contention surrounds the entire issue of the Belmont Car Auction robberies and the initial police investigation in 1987 was centred on this suggesting a motive may exist in the killing of Daniel Morgan.

It was the end of February 1986 when a client by the name of Belmont Car Auctions, Michael Thorne approached Southern Investigations via a third party. Daniel told me it was Detective Sergeant Sid Fillery who brought the security job to the attention of Southern Investigations and his friend John Rees. Belmont Car Auctions staff stated they had security concerns over large sums of money taken from buyers, on public auction events, being stolen either by robbery or theft. Belmont proprietors were desperate and required security assistance with immediate effect. I recall Daniel telling me there was a big rush on the commencement of the job. I remember things moved very quickly on this job.

(Author's note: Some of the following excerpt is repeated from chapter 18, to ease the flow in reading)

This is an excerpt from Day 1, pages 11-12 of the Daniel Morgan Inquest. Detective Superintendent Douglas Campbell is examined by the Coroner

THE CORONER: At this stage all I want you to do is to outline to the court – do not go into this in great detail – the investigation, as far as you were concerned, which has relevance – that is very important – to the case of the demise of Daniel Morgan. – A. That is in relation to Belmont Car Auctions?

Q. Yes. – A. Belmont Car Auctions is in South East London. In February 1986 an armed robbery took place where approximately £20,000 was stolen. Resulting from this, Mr. William John Rees of Southern Investigations was introduced by police officers to the Director of Belmont Car Auctions. He undertook security cover at the auctions. Security was provided on 4th, 5th, 7th, 8th, 11th, 12th, 14th, 16th, and 18th March 1986. A number of men were employed at the auctions. On

18th March William Jonathan Rees collected a sum of £18,280 in cash from the auctions. He was unable to deposit the money at the Midland Bank night safe because apparently the night safe lock was jammed. He took it to his home address in South Norwood. Outside his home address he was robbed by two men and the money was stolen. He reported the matter to the police. He attended the Mayday Hospital where he was detained for a number of days, having had some corrosive fluid sprayed in his eyes. The matter was fully reported to police and investigated. No person was ever arrested for that robbery.

About three weeks into the murder investigation I became aware that Belmont Car Auctions were pursuing a civil claim against William John Rees for the loss of this money. The solicitors acting for Belmont Car Auctions had written to three police officers who were present at the auctions at various dates whilst Mr. Rees was providing security cover. The three police officers had not notified either me or the Metropolitan Police that they were to be interviewed. On 3rd April 1987 I caused those three police officers and Mr. Rees and two other men to be arrested in connection with the murder of Daniel Morgan. It is fair to say with regard to all the men who were interviewed that there was insufficient evidence to charge any of these persons with the death of Daniel Morgan.

The three police officers that Detective Superintendent Campbell was referring to as being arrested in connection with the murder of Daniel Morgan were Detective Sergeant Sid Fillery, Detective Constable Peter Foley and Detective Constable Alan Purvis who was a cousin of Belmont Car Auctions part owner Michael Thorne. The other two men arrested along with John Rees were Glenn Vian and Garry Vian.

This is an excerpt from Day 6, pages 52-53 of the Daniel Morgan Inquest. Detective Constable Alan Purvis is examined by the Coroner.

Q. Are you related in some way to Mr. Thorne who was a part owner of the Belmont Auctions? – A. I am.

Q. What is the relationship? – A. He is my cousin.

Q. I do not wish to go into this in any great detail at all. I understand that before Southern Investigations came into the matter at all there had been a robbery or robberies at Belmont Auctions. – A. There had been an armed robbery at my cousin's business premises.

Q. Would I be right in saying that your cousin, Mr. Thorne, was quite terrified of this episode? – A. He certainly was. He was very frightened indeed.

Q. What was the frightening aspect of it? – A. Because the people had been tied up, as I understand it, and forced to lie on the floor with shotguns pointed at them, and they were robbed. My cousin was very frightened because his premises had been robbed in such a way.

Q. Had he been robbed on previous occasions? – A. I do not know. Not to my knowledge.

Q. This was a horrific type of robbery. Guns were involved. People were tied up. – A. Yes.

Q. Was it around that time that he came to you and said: "What can we do about it?" – A. He telephoned me that night.

Q. The night of this robbery. – A. The night of the robbery, I was in bed. It was about midnight.

Q. Do you know the date? – A. I think it was about the end of February.

Q. February 1986. – A. Yes.

Q. He told you about the robbery. – A. Yes, he did.

Q. What did you say? – A. Contact the police.

Q. How long after that was it that Southern Investigations enter into the matter? – A. Some days later. Again, Michael contacted me.

Q. Michael Thorne. – A. Michael Thorne. He was very, very worried because he had been let down by Securicor. He was worried about his forthcoming auctions. He asked me if there was anything I could do. I mentioned to him about the crime security convention, etcetera. He said: "I need help straight away." I said that I did not really know anybody. The only person who came to mind was a friend of Sid Fillery who, I understood, was in the security business.

Q. Did you go to Sid Fillery? – A. I told Sid Fillery about it.

Q. Who told your cousin, Mr. Thorne? – A. Told my cousin what?

Q. About Southern Investigations. – A. I told my cousin that there was a man who was a friend of Sid's, who might be able to give some advice.

Q. Was that man Mr. Rees? – A. Yes, it was.

Q. Through Mr. Fillery you introduced Mr. Rees to Mr. Thorne. – A. Not exactly. The next thing that happened was that my cousin met Mr. Rees to discuss his problem.

Q. How long after that was it that Southern Securities now started to help or took it over? – A. As I, understood it from that time onwards. From when they met each other - - - -

Q. A few days. – A. Yes.

Q. We did hear in evidence that they worked for them for three weeks before Southern Securities had a robbery. – A. Yes.

Q. Through all this, the discussion with Sid Fillery, the introduction of Mr. Rees and the suggestion later on that they were going to take it over, which is within a few days, to help with security and so forth, does the name Daniel Morgan enter into this equation at all? – A. Not at all.

Q. Was he ever brought down to the Belmont Auctions and told: "This is the place we are going to be looking after"? – A. Never while I, have been there.

Q. Not at all. – A. No.

Q. Did Mr. Thorne mention him? – A. No, Sir.

Daniel told me that the Belmont Car Auctions instructions to Southern Investigations were to carry out a security assessment and analysis. The senior staff of Belmont Car Auctions stated that they had previously instructed Securicor for security services that were on-site on a date in February 1986 whereby an armed robbery took place. Firearms were used and the employees were robbed of approximately £20,000.

The security assessment and analysis concluded that a plain clothed security team of around six operatives would be appropriate for the security requirements. An agreement was entered into and John Rees formed a security detail of plain clothed operatives to be positioned within the crowd and around the cash office. I was not privy to the entire content of the contract however; I recall Daniel being concerned as he told me that the handling of any monies would not be undertaken as Southern Investigations had no cover of insurance for any money losses in this area of operation.

Prior to the start of the operation, John Rees had attended the auction site as a reconnaissance visit on at least one occasion. A planning meeting was held on an afternoon in Peter Newby's office. Present that day were, Peter Newby, Laurie Bucknole, John, Danny and myself and others that were unknown to me. As everyone gathered and to my complete surprise, Daniel pulled me to one side and quietly told me I would not be part of this operation and I needed to leave the meeting before it started. Daniel gave me no explanation at the time other than, *"I don't want you on this job."* He looked at me and with his eyes gestured for me to leave. Had it been anyone else I would have questioned the situation however, it was Danny so I took my leave and got on with other work. Later that day, I asked Daniel, *"What was all that about?"* His response was, *"This is an operation that John is dealing with and you and I are not directly involved."*

A few days later Daniel informed me that security at Belmont Car Auctions had been agreed. Operations began and had been carried on for a period of time without incident, however this was about to change.

On the night of Tuesday 18th of March 1986, the security detail for Belmont Car Auctions consisted of John Rees, Glenn Vian and Garry Vian; DC Purvis and DC Foley were also present on site. At the time serving police officers were not permitted to undertake any work outside of their service contract. However, it seemed to be regular practice within the force to accept work (moonlighting) outside of their police contract. John, Daniel and the senior staff of Southern Investigations who were involved with this operation would have been aware of this regulation.

This is an excerpt of Day 6, page 38 of the Daniel Morgan Inquest. Detective Constable Foley is being examined by the Coroner.

Q. *There was a robbery. – A. Yes.*

Q. *Were you on duty the night it took place? I use the word "duty" because you were being seen. It was some form of duty that you were giving to Belmont Car Auctions. – A. I was at those car auctions on 18th March.*

This is an excerpt of Day 6; page 55 of the Daniel Morgan Inquest Detective Constable Purvis is being examined by the Coroner.

Q. *Let us go to the time of the robbery which was on the 18th March, a Tuesday. Were you working at the Belmont Auctions on that occasion? – A. I was not working. I visited the auctions.*

Q. *Were you fulfilling the same role as Mr Foley, making yourself known, walking around the place? – A. Yes.*

Q. *You were there. – A. Yes.*

The security detail went to work at Belmont Car Auctions and undertook their duties and at the end of the night £18,280 in cash and cheque was handed over to John

Rees to be deposited in the Midland Bank night safe. Daniel later told me that he would never have agreed to this because Southern Investigations was not insured for any loss of this type.

On returning to the office a number of days later, John told me when he arrived at the Midland Bank on Lee High Road, he was accompanied by Glenn and Garry Vian and he discovered the lock on the night safe had been sabotaged with superglue and would not operate for the deposit of the monies. He said he made a decision to take the £18,280 home. He drove Glenn and Garry home to Croydon then proceeded to his home on Cresswell Road, South Norwood - alone - a total distance from Belmont Auctions of approximately 18 miles. Travelling at that time of night on a weekday the entire journey would have taken about 40 to 50 minutes.

John Rees told me he reported to police that when he got home he could not park his car near his house. I find this a plausible account. I had called outside of John's home address for work purposes on a number of occasions over the years, at all times of the day and night, with and without Daniel and parking was always very limited on John's road especially late at night. When dropping off or picking him up I often had to pull up 30 to 40 yards down the road or even in the next street from his residence. John reported the attack taking place around midnight. He lived in a quiet backstreet that was reasonably lit; most residents would have been tucked up in bed with the street most likely full with their vehicles.

John said as he was walking to his house from his car, he was attacked by two assailants who squirted an obnoxious substance in his face. He was bundled to the ground and robbed of the £18,280 of Belmont Car Auctions money. John did not put up a struggle as his vision was impaired; he staggered to his home whereby he called police and an ambulance.

It was DC Duncan Hanrahan (and we shall learn much more about him in Chapter The Teflon Trail) a personal friend of John Rees who was on duty at Norbury police station that night who dealt with the initial investigation and report of the robbery. John was taken to hospital and it was later that he filed his police report of robbery. John initially received medical treatment at the Mayday hospital in Croydon. Returning home however he returned to the hospital the next day whereby he was hospitalised for a few days, fortunately for him he sustained no long-term injuries. It was a number of days after the assault, in the offices of Southern Investigations, that John shared these accounts with me and other staff members. Visually John looked a little tired and there was some light redness around his eyes. I believe he said that he initially had a bump on his head; I do not recall he suffered any other injuries.

The situation involving the tampering of the night safe at the Midland Bank would have placed Daniel and me on 'high alert'. I asked Daniel if a contingency plan would have been set up for circumstances such as this; Daniel shook his head and said,

"I have no idea as John should not have taken responsibility of the money in the first place due to having no insurance".

Knowing Daniel as well as I did I am sure he would have spoken to Robert West insurance brokers whom we shared a building with to take instruction regarding this matter to see if he could obtain insurance for this type of work. We discussed the possibilities that members of the Southern Investigations security team might have been followed home on previous occasions or that on the night of the robbery John was followed home by the perpetrators and the robbery undertaken. We discussed and looked at all angles of the events of the robbery. Daniel said that he had given consideration to any involvement by John with the robbery but that would make no sense.

John later said the hospital reported to him that an ammonia-like substance was used in the assault and that he was fortunate that his injuries were not more severe as either the substance was not of purity or had not completely entered his eyes.

This is an excerpt of Day 6, pages 43-44 of the Daniel Morgan Inquest. Detective Constable Foley is being cross-examined by Miss June Tweedie.

Q. Why were you not happy with what happened? – A. Because, a man does not get attacked like that. People do not just happen to attack someone outside their home address. There must have been some sort of inside information. I am not saying that against any party at all.

Q. You were suspicious. – A. Yes.

This is an excerpt of Day 6, page 100 of the Daniel Morgan inquest. Detective Sgt Sid Fillery is being cross-examined by Miss June Tweedie.

Q. When did you hear about the robbery? – A. I think at work the following morning.

Q. From whom did you hear it? – A. Mr Rees phoned me up from the hospital.

Q. What did he say? – A. I do not remember: "I have been robbed", I presume. I do not remember.

Q. Did he say anything about the robbery? – A. I went and saw him in hospital.

Q. What did he say? – A. He was fuming because he thought it was an inside job, that one of his employees had done it. He was convinced of that.

Q. One of his employees. – A. Yes.

Q. Not one of the Belmont auctions employees. – A. That is what I mean, one of the Belmont auction people, because of what the person had done. He knew a lot. He was fuming. He told me about the machine being blocked up with glue and the fact that when he went home he got mugged outside his house.

THE CORONER: Can you define what you mean by "employees"? Are you talking about people who work there? – A. Mr Rees was convinced that it was somebody he had employed at Belmont car auctions.

Q. One of the six. – A. Yes.

Q. *He changed them about. – A. Yes, he did. He was convinced at that time that it must be one of those.*

Q. *One of his employees. – A. Yes. That is what he thought at the time.*

In the office, staff members talked amongst themselves, we were all shocked about what had happened. The general consensus of opinion by the majority of the staff was that John was a partner and he made an executive decision to take the money home; consequences and responsibility that would inevitably end up having to be dealt with. While John's decision to take the money home did not prove prudent in hindsight, he would have had experience in handling large sums of cash and cheques over many years. Daniel, John, Malcolm and I would all, at some stage during our working duties, handle substantial amounts of cash.

Let's take a moment to reflect. Belmont Car Auctions employed Southern Investigations for the purpose of security to protect monies from robbery or theft. Just a few weeks earlier the auction house had reported a violent robbery while Securicor were contracted for security whereby monies were stolen by robbers wielding firearms. The threat was so real that Belmont Car Auctions entered into an agreement for plain clothes, covert security operatives supplied by Southern Investigations to protect their monies in this matter. Belmont directors were also aware that plain clothed off duty police officers were at the venue mingling with the crowd. The procedures in safeguarding the monies up until Tuesday the 18th of March 1986 were reported as going to plan.

This is an excerpt of Day 1, pages 61, 62, 63 of the Daniel Morgan Inquest. David Chapman is being examined by the Coroner.

Q. *You are David Chapman. You are a witness manager. You work at Belmont car auctions. – A. Yes.*

Q. *How did you feel about the robbery? – A. A total farce, as far as I was concerned.*

Q. *Why was it a farce, in your opinion? – A. The manner in which it was committed, having gone to the safe with our money on that occasion, having already done it on several occasions, quite successfully; he then found himself in a situation where he suggested that he could not contact us by phone. I know that I stayed there until 11.30/12 o'clock at night, so I was there.*

Q. *Do you mean after he had been coshed? – A. Yes, that is right.*

Q. *Perhaps he was not in a fit state to contact you. – A. The suggestion was that he had gone to the bank which is no more than three or four miles from our premises. He could have made a phone call back to us or could have driven back to us. He chose to go on, which is some five to six miles to South Norwood.*

Q. *Your feeling is that because one-night safe was stuck he should have gone somewhere else. – A. As Mr Thorne also pointed out, the police station is no more than 30 paces. I am sure they would have advised.*

As they say, hindsight is 20/20 and post robbery, Daniel and I discussed that other options were available to John to safeguard the monies. The night safe was only a short distance from the auction site whereby he could have returned. A police station was only a short distance away where John could have reported the sabotage of the night safe and obtained safeguarding of the monies. John Rees made a choice to go home after a long day and evening at work.

Was the superglue tampering of the night safe a random act of sabotage, vandalism or something more deliberate? Belmont Car Auctions had serious concerns over violent robbery or theft and that is why they entered into a security services contract with Southern Investigations in the first place. What has always concerned me and I know that it concerned Daniel was the robbery of John Rees outside his home and the lack of consideration into the equation that this robbery might have been connected to the armed robbery at the site of Belmont Car Auctions a mere few weeks earlier.

Subsequently from the events of John Rees being robbed what I do know is what Daniel told me and that is he gave some consideration to dissolving his partnership with John. Daniel never did act on this by instructing lawyers or formally informing John and they remained in partnership until Daniel's murder a year later.

Danny told me he did attempt to establish an out of court settlement with Belmont Car Auctions however; they filed a civil action issuing a high court writ against Southern Investigations for the loss of £18,280. He said Belmont Car Auctions claimed that insufficient action was taken by Southern Investigations staff to safeguard their money which contributed to the loss. Daniel and John instructed solicitors to act on their behalf to deal with the claim.

This is an excerpt from Day 3, pages 23-26 of the Daniel Morgan Inquest. Peter Newby is examined by the Coroner.

Peter Newby states: "Daniel has always been upset over this whole affair. At one stage he was going to lodge his own defence to the action thereby disassociating himself with the whole transaction." How did you know that? – A. He told me.

Q. Did he say why? – A. Yes. He said he felt that John had exceeded his authority as a partner and that they had originally agreed that they would never carry cash.

Q. You say: "At one stage he was going to lodge his own defence to the action thereby disassociating himself with the whole transaction." Was that the only reason he was going to start his own defence or think about it? – A. Things were unhappy at that stage and it was mentioned on more than one occasion.

Q. All right. "My understanding of our work with Belmont Auctions was that we never carried cash in transit." You have just explained that. "However, Daniel never did lodge his own separate defence. To the best of my knowledge he never attended any meetings with either Belmont Auctions or the solicitors, Clutton, Moore & Lavington, acting for us in this matter." – A. That is true.

Q. *Was there anything odd about that? Here they are, they are two partners and now they are involved in the theft of £18,000. You have to find £10,000. − A. Danny was very unhappy. That is all I can say: Danny was very unhappy about the whole of the Belmont Auctions affair. He was most unhappy about it.*

Q. *What were the main things he was unhappy about? − A. He was unhappy to start with because we had lost the money.*

Q. *Nevertheless, his partner had been mugged or his partner had allegedly been hit on the head and had been taken to hospital. − A. Yes. He was also unhappy, as he told me, because of John Rees' involvement or the involvement by John of police officers in the Belmont Auctions affair. He was most unhappy about that.*

Q. *Why was he unhappy? − A. He did tell me on one occasion that he thought it would rebound on us.*

Q. *Why? − A. Because he was using police officers while they were still police officers for security work.*

This is an excerpt from Day 8, pages 14-16 of the Daniel Morgan Inquest. John Rees is examined by the Coroner.

Q. *Would I be right in saying that you have had your arguments up and down and so forth, like all partners? − A. Yes, that is right.*

Q. *You have had your differences of opinion. − A. Yes.*

Q. *Would you use the word "hate" at all? − A. Never, not at all during the relationship or partnership.*

Q. *I am not going to ask you questions of chapter and verse about the Belmont Car Auctions, but I want to ask you these questions which I think have a distinct bearing on this inquest. Was your late partner, Daniel Morgan, entertaining the idea of a separate defence with regard to the Belmont Car Auction matter? Was he entertaining the idea? Had he started the idea? Had he talked about the idea with you? − A. Yes, sir, but we had both discussed that line of defence and we had in fact discussed it with solicitors.*

Q. *Perhaps we are at cross-purposes. I am talking about a separate defence on behalf of Daniel Morgan irrespective of you? − A. Yes, the possibility was discussed between both myself and Daniel, and we discussed it with the solicitors. In the hope of maybe halving the liability if we lost the case was that Daniel could have opened up a separate defence in that I had acted outside the partnership.*

Q. *Was that the only reason for the separate defence? − A. Yes, sir. We discussed it with solicitors and it was ruled out because the partnership was joint and several and it was not an avenue we could take.*

This is an excerpt from Day 8, page 41 of the Daniel Morgan Inquest. John Rees is cross-examined by Miss June Tweedie.

Q. *After the robbery what was Mr. Morgan's reaction to that? What did he feel about that and the court case, the court hearing? − A. As I have just said, after the event we both wished it was something we never had started in the first place. There was quite a few things that when you get involved in something and it goes wrong you wished you had never started in the first place. With regards to the legal action Daniel agreed with me we should defend with vigour that particular action because we were not in the wrong.*

Q. The original contract had been set up by yourself, had it not? – A. Yes.

Daniel saw the entire operation as a fiasco and was obviously not impressed. There were a lot of discussions between John and Danny about the stolen money however; I wouldn't say they argued about it. Danny had his doubts as to the circumstances of the robbery and said he liked to keep an open mind.

Belmont Car Auctions claim for the stolen money was settled. Half of this repayment was made by Daniel's widow, Iris, who paid a sum of around £18,000 including legal fees.

I came to realise why Daniel told me to leave the initial planning meeting and did not want me or him to be involved with Belmont Car Auctions security. It was because he could not arrange insurance cover for any loss of monies or for any personal injuries sustained by security staff. There is no doubt in my mind that a severe potential risk element surrounded this particular job. The armed robbers may well have seen the auction site as an easy target in the first instance and could easily have concocted a second plan to execute a further robbery at a later date, such as the attack on the 18th of March 1986 as reported by John Rees.

There is also the consideration of John Rees in that he told his friend and confidant Detective Sergeant Sid Fillery that he was convinced the robbery was undertaken by one of the six men that he had employed as security guards at Belmont Car Auctions.

These are questions to which we may never know the answers as in the case of both robberies no person has ever been charged or convicted in connection to these crimes. Unfortunately, both robberies remain unsolved by the police authority.

This is an excerpt of Day 6, pages 48-49 of the Daniel Morgan Inquest. Detective Constable Foley is being cross-examined by Mr Goldsworthy.

Q. Had you in fact been moonlighting at the Belmont? How bad a matter is that as far as the police are concerned? Do you understand? – A. If I can take this opportunity of pointing out, there seems to be some concern in the press that it is a heinous offence. You are talking about something that is not a criminal offence whatsoever. There is no element of dishonesty in it, unless of course the police officer should have been somewhere else.

THE CORONER: Whatever you did there, was it in police time? – A. It was not in police time and I know, or I think I know, that the police force will treat that, with the evidence they have, if they decide that someone has been moonlighting they will treat you fairly. It depends on the circumstances. It is not a criminal offence and you are not likely to get sacked. To suggest that you would kill someone to hide it is laughable.

Is it possible from any of the events that took place on the 18th of March 1986 or any other events surrounding the Belmont Car Auctions robberies that a motive might exist that lead to the murder of Daniel Morgan?

Chapter 20
Something Doesn't Add Up

t was early in my relationship with Daniel and Southern Investigations when he first introduced me to Kevin Lennon, the business bookkeeper. I recall meeting Kevin on a Saturday morning at the offices of Southern Investigations; a time when Daniel held a respect for the man and his role within the business.

My immediate impression of Kevin Lennon was he was civil but not an amenable individual by way of approach, not someone I found to be friendly, a man somewhat stands offish and aloof, I didn't take to him. I told Daniel of my opinion and his response was, *"Sometimes it takes a little while to get to know someone".*

Daniel told me that Kevin had been his accountant since the initial company formation of Southern Investigations. Kevin was an out-source bookkeeper; Southern Investigations was one of a number of Lennon's clients. He would liaise with the office staff accessing the company accounts and files, etc. I would meet him from time to time when he visited the office or local pubs. We would exchange pleasantries but that was as far as our association went and the way things remained.

One-day Daniel happened to mention that he found out Kevin Lennon was experiencing personal problems and another more private matter was troubling him and as a father of a large family these concerns were proving problematic.

Daniel said that Kevin was spending more time in the pub and he had become a different person due to the stress from the upheaval in his personal life and was a worried man. Daniel expressed to me that he felt concern for Kevin but in the same breath I could see his sympathy was limited.

On more than one occasion in the months prior to Daniel's murder I accompanied him to public houses in the Thornton Heath area where we met Kevin Lennon. On one occasion Kevin was visibly upset and was clearly 'well into his cups'. From talking with Kevin, Daniel was of the opinion that Lennon's personal and business dilemma was becoming dire; Kevin relayed his concerns about his family and what might happen. Danny gave Kevin some cash which I saw Kevin was very appreciative.

What was most apparent from when I first studied Daniel's interaction with Kevin and to what I was seeing now was that Daniel's opinion of Kevin Lennon was no longer the same.

After Daniel's murder things dramatically changed with many shocking revelations but it was not until day one of the Daniel Morgan Inquest, on the 11th of April 1988, that the most shocking revelation of all came to public knowledge the witness testimony of Kevin Lennon.

This is an excerpt of Day 1, page 38 of the Daniel Morgan Inquest. Kevin Lennon is being cross-examined by Mr Nutter.

Q. At the time you made any of the statements which you have read out to the jury were you on bail pending certain hearings in some court? – A. Yes, I was.

Kevin Lennon made three statements to police in 1987 on the 2nd of April, 4th of September and the 15th of September. These statements were read out in open court and they can be found in their entirety on Day 1 pages 26-37 of the Daniel Morgan Inquest transcript.

I will briefly summarise what Kevin Lennon has said in these statements.

Kevin Lennon said that he became the bookkeeper of Southern Investigations and would socialize with John and Daniel about once a week on average. They drank mostly in the Victory or the Harp pub. He said he met Iris Morgan on a few occasions but he didn't know her very well. He further said the last time he saw Daniel was in February 1987. He said he had known Jonathan Rees for at least six years and that he knew him socially from drinking in public houses in the Croydon area. It was about six months after meeting John that he first met Daniel and over time he became friendlier with John than Daniel. He and John became friends having home visits with each other's family.

Lennon said that as time went on John grew to hate and despise Daniel and that John's rage was fierce toward Daniel. In conversations Lennon said John made it perfectly clear that nothing would please him more than for him and Daniel to go their separate ways. Lennon goes on to say that Rees broached the subject of getting rid of Daniel; usually being said in the Victory when both men where alone with each other. Lennon said Rees would like to 'kill him' and that Rees was not drunk on the day that he told Lennon that he wanted Daniel killed.

At first Lennon did not take Rees' remarks seriously as he had said it before in general conversation. Lennon said the realization that Rees was serious was reinforced when Rees informed him of attempts to get Daniel caught for drink driving. This was because getting him banned meant he couldn't drive and this would render Daniel ineffective as a partner as he would have no driving license. These attempts failed for a variety of reasons and during a meeting with Rees, Lennon said when the subject came up again to kill Daniel, Rees asked Lennon to find someone to kill him. Lennon said this happened on at least two occasions and Rees was under the impression that Lennon knew people who could or would be willing to kill Daniel.

Lennon goes on to say he attempted on each occasion to dissuade Rees from such a course of action. But Rees was adamant that he wanted Daniel killed. It was an evening in the Victory whilst Lennon and Rees were alone that Lennon reports Rees said words to the effect of, forget about arranging Daniel's death I've got it fixed. Lennon said that Rees explained that police officers who were friends of his based at Catford nick were capable and willing to organize it. They would either do it themselves or they would get someone else (they had something on) to do the killing for them in return being let off for whatever they had over them. Lennon said this conversation was some time around seven or eight months prior to Daniel's death; definitely over six months but not as long as 12 months.

Lennon goes on to say that it was around this period that a police officer, Sid Fillery, stationed at Catford was mentioned by Rees and that Fillery was to take Daniel's place after his death. Lennon said Fillery was to get an ill-health pension and medical discharge from the police. Lennon said there was no talk when the murder would take place but it would be undertaken in the Catford area and be sorted out by Catford police to cover up the murder. Lennon said Rees treated him like a close confidant and would speak about this knowing that Lennon would not divulge his secret. Lennon said a few days after this conversation he asked Rees again about what was going to happen to Daniel as he said it took some believing; but he states Rees confirmed the arrangements for the killing stood as he had stated and it was never discussed again.

Lennon says that in November 1986 he stopped seeing Rees and Morgan on a regular basis partly because of his own personal problems but mainly because of what John Rees had told him. Lennon goes on to say that to his knowledge there were two other people along with Fillery that Rees had told him were aware of the plot to kill Daniel.

The two-other people that Kevin Lennon told police had knowledge of a plot to murder Daniel Morgan were Sharon Rees wife of John Rees and Michael Goodridge solicitor and friend of Daniel and John.

This is an excerpt of Day 6, pages 27-28 of the Daniel Morgan Inquest. Detective Superintendent Campbell is further cross-examined by Miss June Tweedie.

THE WITNESS: *The two people whom Kevin Lennon said John Rees had spoken to were his own solicitor, Mr Michael Goodridge, and his wife.*

MISS TWEEDIE: *Sharon Rees. – A. Sharon Rees.*

THE CORONER: *What did you understand him to mean by "he had spoken to"? – A. He had discussed wanting someone to kill Daniel Morgan with his solicitor and his wife.*

MISS TWEEDIE: Did you then go on to speak to Sharon? – A. I tried to speak to Mrs Rees. She refused to speak to me. In fact, I was hoping to have another chance here on Monday, but since I arrested her husband she has refused to have any conversation or contact with me.

Q. When did you first put this matter to her? – A. I tried to arrange to see her shortly after Mr Lennon told me, which I think was somewhere about October of last year.

Q. She refused to ---- -- A. She refused to see me.

This is an excerpt of Day 5, page 74 of the Daniel Morgan Inquest. Detective Superintendent Campbell is cross examined by Miss June Tweedie.

Q. We heard from Kevin Lennon that he has told you the name of two people who might have known about Mr. Rees' plan to kill Mr. Morgan. – A. Yes.

Q. Have you investigated those people? – A. I have spoken to one.

Q. What about the other person? – A. I have not spoken to that person.

THE CORONER: ---- Q. It is a point that Miss Tweedie has made that he has spoken about two people, two people who may have killed Danny Morgan. – A. I can clearly say one. One, it was suggested, was his solicitor, Michael Goodridge. I put that to Michael Goodridge and in his statement, he says he knew nothing of it. That is in his statement.

MISS TWEEDIE: Did you ask him subsequent to Kevin Lennon's evidence this week. – A. No.

This is an excerpt of Day 3, page 74 of the Daniel Morgan Inquest. Michael Goodridge (Solicitor) is examined by the Coroner.

Q. --- On the 20th October 1987: "further to my statement of 14th March, I have been asked to clarify a number of points: --- I have no knowledge of threats being made to kill Daniel Morgan either by John Rees or others." – A. That is correct.

Sharon Rees was due to attend the inquest and give evidence however she was reported by her GP to be medically unfit to give any testimony in person at the hearing. Certainly, questions would have been put to her as to any knowledge she may have to Daniel Morgan's murder and she would have been scrutinised in cross examination by all counsel. Sharon Rees made two statements to police on the 17th and 20th of March 1987 which the Coroner read out in open court.

The significance in the Coroner reading the statements was to demonstrate to the court that Sharon Rees made no mention or awareness of any plot to kill Daniel Morgan and two weeks before the inquest police contacted her again to ask if she wished to change or update her witness statements which she replied no. Due to Sharon Rees' GP evidence regarding her medical condition she never attended the court and therefore was never examined by the Coroner or cross examined by counsel.

This is an excerpt from Day 8, pages 9-11 of the Daniel Morgan Inquest. Detective Superintendent Campbell is examined by the Coroner.

The Coroner: I have two statements here. Ladies and Gentleman of the jury, I am now going to read the statements of Mrs Sharon Rees. --- Her first statement is made on the 17th day of March, 1987 ---- This is the second statement ---- dated the 20th day of March 1987. -----

If I remember right, according to my notes (I was looking this up before I entered the court this morning) I had the impression from Det. Supt. Campbell that some two weeks before the beginning of the inquest Mrs. Rees was contacted by telephone to see whether she had anything to add to the statement she had already made. I believe the answer was no.

DET. SUPT. CAMPBELL: *That is correct, sir.*

THE CORONER: *I was looking at my notes. I found it on the tape but it was a bit vague on the tape.*

DET. SUPT. CAMPBELL: *That is right, sir she was contacted by one of my officers to see if there was any information at all that she wanted to add to these two statements. A lot of other witnesses were similarly contacted, but Mrs Rees had no further information for police at that stage.*

Sharon Rees' statements of the 17th and the 20th of March 1987 make no mention of any plot or involvement of John Rees in the murder of Daniel Morgan, however Kevin Lennon's statement of the 15th of September 1987 says Sid Fillery was quite aware that Daniel Morgan would be killed. Kevin Lennon further stated there were two other people with whom John Rees had spoken about the possibility of murdering Daniel Morgan in which Lennon replied, *"I have discussed that matter with police and I have given them the names".*

This is an excerpt of Day 6, pages 31-32 of the Daniel Morgan Inquest. Mr Nutter makes a submission to the Coroner.

MR. NUTTER: *This man has given evidence that my client has made admissions to him of a planned murder, the murder of the man whose death the jury are currently concerned with. Those admissions were made only, according to him, to this man, not in the presence of anybody else. He has also given evidence that my client – this is, of course, hearsay – has made admission to his wife and also to his solicitor. The only evidence to that effect comes from Mr. Lennon. It has been reported in the press that those admissions are said to have been made ---*

Kevin Lennon's first statement of the 2nd of April (consisting of three pages) made a full 23-days after Daniels's death, makes absolutely no mention of Lennon having any knowledge whatsoever of a plot by anyone to murder Daniel.

It was a full six months after Daniel's murder in Kevin Lennon's second statement (of the 4th of September consisting of seven pages) in which Lennon first reports he has knowledge of a plot to murder Daniel Morgan.

He said, *"I have told Laurie Bucknall about what was going to happen to Morgan but I don't think he realised what I had said to him because he was drunk when I said it. Since the murder I have told Mr Bucknall and I know what I said would be passed onto police".*

If any knowledge of any threats to kill had been relayed to any police officer as Kevin Lennon states, other than what he has alleged he told Laurie Bucknole, perhaps Daniel Morgan might still be alive today.

Kevin Lennon's third statement of the 15th of September consisting of 33 pages states:

"John Rees had planned all this well before Daniel Morgan was killed and he told me that Sid Fillery was quite aware of what was going to happen to Daniel Morgan, that he would be killed. it must have been sometime about May 1986 when John Rees told me about his conversation and plans that he had made with Sid Fillery ----- I think it was possibly April 1986 whilst I was having a meal with Laurie Bucknall in the Mythos Restaurant in Thornton Heath, that I mentioned to Laurie what John Rees had told me and his intentions towards Daniel Morgan. This conversation with Laurie Bucknall took place well before John told me about his dealings and plans that he had made with Catford police officers". *"Both Laurie Bucknall and I had been drinking that night"*

What I find significant are the inconsistencies in Lennon's statements. Lennon's third statement said Bucknole had been *"drinking"* and not the emphatic *"drunk"* stated in his second statement where he said:

"I have told Laurie Bucknall about what was going to happen to Mr Morgan. I don't think he realised what I had said to him because he was drunk when I said it. Since the murder I have told Mr Bucknall and I know what I said would be passed onto police".

Lennon says that Bucknole acknowledged to him that he understood what he had said however it was not until June 1987 when he again spoke with Bucknole when he realised that Bucknole had not understood or fully realised what he had said to him about a plot to murder Daniel. Yet it is not until Lennon's second statement that he makes reference to these claims.

Lennon goes on to say that at first, he did not want any part and under no circumstances did he want to get involved as a witness and he said it was out of conscience that he contacted the police.

It is from Lennon's third witness statement where he further said it was after June 1987:

"About two or three weeks later I had another meeting with Laurie Bucknall; I met him in a pub which I think is called the Horseshoe on Thornton Heath Pond. After one drink there we both went to the Mythos restaurant for a meal. Over the meal we had a further conversation during which Laurie Bucknall questioned me about what I had told him concerning John Rees and Daniel Morgan. What I said to Laurie Bucknall during our meal was in confidence and "I still do not want to become involved as a witness".

This meeting between Kevin Lennon and Laurie Bucknole lends more controversy to the police investigation. Detective Superintendent Campbell made it clear to the Coroner that he had at his disposal the ability to undertake covert undercover recordings of conversations.

This is an excerpt of Day 6, page 29 of the Daniel Morgan Inquest. Detective Superintendent Campbell is further cross-examined by Miss June Tweedie.

Q. *There was another person Kevin Lennon spoke to at a later date, and that was Mr Bucknell. – A. Yes.*

Q. Have inquiries been made of Mr Bucknell as to whether he knew about it? – A. Yes. Mr Bucknell is a retired Detective Chief Inspector who served for a number of years at Croydon. I do not think he ever served at Catford. Mr Lennon told us that he discussed the matter with Mr Bucknell in 1986. Mr Bucknell has no recollection of that conversation.

Q. Have you also asked Mr Bucknell about his involvement in the setting up of Belmont Auctions, the security? – A. Yes.

Q. What did he say about that? – A. He went with Mr Rees to advise on certain security aspects regarding the safety of money.

Q. Was he a serving officer at the time? – A. No.

DSI Campbell informed the court Laurie Bucknole had no recollection of any conversation with Kevin Lennon (in 1986) regarding a plot to murder Daniel Morgan. I cannot believe if Laurie Bucknole had an awareness of this information, he would not have told Daniel or done something to prevent the murder.

I pose the question, why was Ex-Detective Inspector Laurie Bucknole's evidence or witness statements not heard or read to the Coroners court in its entirety pertaining to Kevin Lennon's claims regarding a plot to have Daniel killed. Bucknole was a key witness and his evidence or examination may have had the potential to reveal so much more.

It was two years before Lennon met Rees that he first met (then serving) Detective Inspector Laurie Bucknole who was assigned to Croydon police station. It was Bucknole who introduced Lennon to Rees.

Lennon said John Rees arranged several times with Norbury police to have Daniel breathalysed on three occasions; twice at the Victory pub when he was present and once at the Blue Anchor Pub when he was not in attendance, yet none of this happened.

(Author's note: The following excerpt is repeated from chapter 18 to ease the flow in reading)

This is an excerpt of Day 1, page 15 of the Daniel Morgan Inquest. Kevin Lennon is being examined by the Coroner.

Q. You cite three individual cases here. You say that John often spoke to you – this is hearsay evidence, obviously – about arranging to get Daniel breathalysed or arrested for drinking and driving. Did he tell you that or is that something you found out for yourself? – A. John told me that.

Q. Did this surprise you that somebody was going to try and get him arrested for drinking and driving? – A. At this stage the relationship had deteriorated from John's point of view, where he would have liked it if Daniel could no longer operate as an effective partner in the business. As Daniel needed his driving licence to perform his particular duties, if he were breathalysed this would have meant that he could no longer perform as a partner.

Lennon goes on to say that, *"on the first of these two occasions Rees, Daniel Morgan and I were drinking with other people when John Rees said to me, when Danny drives away from here he will be breathalysed. When John said this, I formed the opinion he had arranged for Daniel to be stopped by the police however, Daniel was not stopped that night but I don't know why."*

The second time Lennon said they were at the Victory pub Rees said to him, that he had arranged for Norbury police to stop Daniel after he left the pub; again, nothing happened. Lennon was sure that John Rees was telling the truth and that he had arranged for Daniel to be stopped by the police. Again, Lennon said that Rees told him that arrangements had been made after a function at the Blue Anchor Public House in Croydon; Lennon went on to say that he did not attend the function however once again Daniel was not stopped or breathalysed by police.

The field operation staff of Southern Investigations were all regular alcoholic beverage drinkers and talk regarding drink driving was regularly discussed in the office and the pub; as we all needed our driving licenses to do our jobs.

Drink driving was common place in the 1980s and public information ran regular TV advertising campaigns, especially in the weeks running up to Christmas, informing drivers that police were out to prosecute offenders. More resources were in place to combat the situation with posters and beer mats in most pubs telling people 'don't drink and drive'.

Daniel and I had previously discussed that if Daniel was ever stopped and failed a breath test and lost his licence I would accompany him and undertake all the driving duties whilst he served any disqualification period. Daniel would often telephone me and say we have work to do tonight but I have had a drink so come and pick me up. We both had an acute awareness of the drink driving law.

I am very surprised Kevin Lennon has stated that John Rees told him Daniel losing his licence would *"render him unable to be an active member of the partnership"*. As far as Danny and I were concerned that was clearly not the case and I can't believe John Rees would not have been aware of this.

I do not recall any incident of Daniel being breathalysed by the police at any time that I knew him. Nor do I recall Danny ever telling me that he had been prosecuted for any motoring offences.

During my tenure at Southern Investigations and throughout my entire driving career I have never been disqualified for drink driving. I hold both full car and motorcycle licence. Nothing occurred during the years I spent with Daniel that would have prevented me from driving a car with Daniel as a passenger.

Lennon said Rees mentioned to him an incident that happened in the offices of Southern Investigations on the same day Daniel had repossessed a motor vehicle that belonged to a well-known south London criminal and that this man had phoned Southern Investigations twice and spoke to John Rees and threatened to break Daniel's legs. Lennon said John Rees was elated to learn that someone wanted to cause Daniel harm.

I do recall an incident such as Kevin Lennon refers to. An individual had contacted the office and threats to Daniel's person had been made. I recall John spoke to Daniel and said words to the effect, your behaviour has finally caught up with you regarding repossession and your winding up of defaulters which has now lead to these threats. I had previously spoken to Daniel about his behaviour in winding up debtors. (See Chapter Repo Man)

I come to the part of Kevin Lennon's statement where he said a plot existed to kill Daniel and Sid Fillery knew about this and that he was to replace Daniel at Southern Investigations once Danny was killed. Now we do know that Sid Fillery did indeed begin a working relationship with John Rees at Southern Investigations sometime after Danny's murder. This may not be immediately sinister as some may be led to believe.

I had a working relationship with Daniel whereby I answered only to him. It is my opinion that If Rees wanted to have Sid Fillery working with him, he could have done so at any time as long as Fillery generated wealth for the business.

Prior to the inquest John Rees and Sid Fillery together with four others had been arrested in connection to the murder investigation of Daniel Morgan; subsequently they were all released from police custody without charge.

It was at the inquest that we found out about Kevin Lennon's evidence of an alleged plot by Rees to murder Daniel Morgan which he said he learned of six months before, where Lennon testified Rees said Catford police were involved. However, all may not have been as it seemed.

I recall colleagues speaking in the office when Kevin Lennon was on remand in Brixton prison and the topic of his bail was being discussed and that he was looking at a lengthy jail term for a crime that had no connection to his work at Southern Investigations; also, it was said his personal problems had worsened.

Over time the staff at Southern Investigations learned that Kevin Lennon had been released from prison on bail and that he subsequently did not receive a custodial prison sentence for his crime; he received a suspended sentence. I did wonder at the time had indeed a deal been struck between the police and Lennon as suggested by John Rees at the inquest.

There was further talk in the office (after Kevin Lennon received his suspended sentence for his crime) of a conversation supposedly seen and heard by a member of staff by chance in a pub or a café, where Rees and Lennon were present; Lennon it was said was heard apologising to Rees for what Lennon had said about Rees at Daniel's inquest.

I don't know if what I heard in the office regarding a meeting between Rees and Lennon actually took place as I did not witness it and on that basis, I can only treat it as gossip or hearsay.

Lennon has said he told police, that Sid Fillery, Sharon Rees, Solicitor Michael Goodridge and Ex Detective Inspector Laurie Bucknole were all aware or had prior knowledge of a plot by John Rees to kill Daniel. However, after extensive police inquiries into establishing any third-party knowledge of a plot, this remains uncorroborated, which I find an absolute mystery if indeed a plot to murder Daniel actually existed.

It does pose the question - would you tell four other people you were actively planning a murder where you would most likely become the prime suspect?

Kevin Lennon has said there was a plot to kill Daniel; my first question would immediately be why on earth would he not tell Daniel? If Kevin believed a genuine threat to life existed why did he not tell his friend? Or go running and screaming at the top of his lungs into a police station?

Or is it possible that Daniel was aware?

Sir Montague Levine in his summing up on Day 8, page 129 of the inquest said: *"What about the startling and frightening evidence by Mr Lennon? This damning evidence which dropped like a bomb-shell in this court early on in the inquest, I think on the first day. His allegations that Mr Rees had asked him "Find somebody to kill Daniel Morgan". What could be more stark, more horrific, more poignant, more dramatic than that single statement that the press took up? All those allegations regarding that matter have been denied by Mr Rees. There were no other witnesses that we have heard in this hearing who heard those statements that Mr Rees is purported to have made. So, there is a very big conflict of evidence. It is Mr Lennon against Mr Rees. I make no further comment on that, because there is no evidence I have heard that is able to corroborate that".*

Something doesn't add up regarding these allegations, one man says one thing and another man says something else. The ultimate decider in situations such as this is the British judicial system.

Chapter 21
Daniel's Desk Diary

ince Daniel's murder a great deal of mystery surrounds the whereabouts of his 1987 desk diary. In all the time I knew Daniel he always used a large day to day annual desk diary which was enclosed in a genuine leather black diary case. This was kept on the top of his desk or in the desk drawer and only occasionally he would travel with it. In the last few months of his life Daniel shared his office with me and Tony Pearce however it was I who actually shared Daniel's desk.

Danny liked to hear what was going on in the rest of the building so his office door remained unlocked and open and access was not restricted to any member of staff.

Although the diary was clearly private it was not stored under lock and key therefore when Daniel was away and his office unattended any interested party could gain access and examine the diary's content and the entries. Danny was very trusting.

This is an excerpt of Day 1, page 47, of the Daniel Morgan Inquest. Iris Morgan is cross examined by Miss June Tweedie.

Q. Do you know whether your husband carried an appointments diary? – A. Yes.

Q. Did he carry it around with him? – A. No, it was in the office.

Q. Can you describe it? – A. I gave him a diary for Christmas. I cannot remember the colour.

Q. Can you remember how big it was? – A. It was small.

Q. Was it bigger than that? – A. It was slightly bigger than that.

Q. Did he have an appointments diary that he carried around with him, so far as you knew? – A. No.

I recall Daniel telling me that Iris had purchased him a desk diary for Christmas. When we returned to the office in the New Year he asked me, whilst I was out on my travels, if I could pick him up a larger diary as the one Iris gave him wasn't sufficient. I said to him that was a Christmas present from Iris and he said, *"I know and whatever you do, if Iris asks, don't mention that I have changed it".* Danny told me that he wanted a large Letts Diary. Over the next few days I did locate and purchased what he asked for.

On numerous occasions I witnessed Daniel undertake the usage of his diary. He almost always did this at his desk, with his feet up and the diary in his lap. He would spend quite some time methodically penning his entries or studying the diary. Danny's diary was important to him.

Daniel was fastidious and always knew how he had last left the items on his desk. He would often ask me if anybody (other than me) had been at his desk if he thought the diary or other desktop items had been moved.

Over time Daniel's desk became a site of organized chaos with numerous files being stacked and piled high over the surface of his desk.

This is an excerpt of Day 3, page 60 of the Daniel Morgan Inquest. Peter Newby is cross examined by Miss June Tweedie.

Q. Do you know whether Mr. Morgan had an appointment diary? – A. Yes, he did.

Q. Can you describe it? I am not talking about a large desk diary. I am talking about a smaller diary. – A. Yes. If I can get my briefcase, I can show you the sort of diary.

THE CORONER: Have you got the actual diary? – A. Not the actual diary.

Q. I see. – A. That was the sort of diary. That was the holder. Inside, was an ordinary diary.

Q. He would carry that about with him. – A. Yes.

Q. Was that diary ever found? – A. I do not know.

This is an excerpt of Day 3, page 61 of the Daniel Morgan Inquest.

Detective Superintendent Campbell is recalled and further examined by the Coroner.

Q. Mr. Campbell, was that diary ever found? – A. To the best of my knowledge a 1986 diary was found, but not a 1987 one.

Q. Was the actual diary 1987 inside or was it the outside that had leather insets and the leather 1986? Do you see my point? – A. Yes. The diary that was found was that type of diary, and it was 1986 and to the best of my knowledge, it was found in his vehicle.

Q. Was there anything you found in there with reference to the meetings and so forth? -- A. His desk diary, personal diary and anything relating to Mr. Morgan was checked thoroughly and anything that was material or that we considered material was acted upon.

Cross-examined by MISS TWEEDIE

Q. You say that the inside part of the 1986 diary was found, but there was no leather case at all. – A. To the best of my knowledge, no.

Q. And there was no 1987 one. – A. To the best of my knowledge, no, but if you would like to ask me later, I will check and find out exactly.

MISS TWEEDIE: I would be grateful.

This is an excerpt of Day 3, page 61 of the Daniel Morgan Inquest.

Peter Newby is recalled and further cross-examined by Miss June Tweedie:

Q. Returning to that very briefly, Mr. Newby, the diary that you held up did have an insert for the year. – A. Yes.

Q. And a leather outer part? – A. Yes. Daniel did carry it.

Q. He carried it with him. – A. Yes.

From time to time, when Daniel was out of the office he would ring from his car phone and on only one or two occasions he asked me to access his diary and obtain from it the information he requested, however this was not common practice. If Daniel and I were out of the office together he would contact Peter Newby to access his diary for the requested information. This was more in the early part of Peter's tenure and I recall Daniel told me that Peter had said to him that he needed to carry it with him more often as accessing the diary was interrupting with Peter's daily routine.

I was not privy to the entire content of the diary and I do not recall any specific information whatsoever but what I do know is that the diary held information containing: names, addresses, telephone numbers, dates and times and personal notes penned in Daniel's hand.

On the morning of March 10th 1987 I saw Daniel's diary open on his desk as he was using it. I thought nothing of it as this was normal. That was the last time I saw Daniel's diary.

However, things were to change dramatically over the next 24 hours and the significance of Daniel's 1987 desk diary and other Southern Investigations files and documents would cause controversy that remains unresolved to this day.

It has been reported that on the night of the 10th of March 1987, Daniel made notes on pieces of paper at the Golden Lion Public House. That would not be an unusual practice for Daniel. He would constantly write down snippets of information on scraps of paper; anything from a petrol receipt to a beer mat; notes that only Daniel could understand. Mostly these were phone numbers, names, addresses, etc. He would keep these notes in his wallet or pocket; sometimes leaving them in his car; all for use at a later time. This was part of Daniel's filing system. When returning to the office I often watched Daniel add these notes of information to existing files or his desk diary.

I arrived at the office around lunchtime on the 11th of March 1987 unaware of the horrific events that took place the night before. It was Peter Newby who told me that Danny had been killed.

Peter Newby said that sometime after 9:30 am that morning, Detective Sergeant Sid Fillery and a Detective Constable had visited on behalf of the murder squad investigating Daniel's death. Peter mentioned that Fillery had a black sack and the officers started removing files from the office including the Belmont Car Auction file. I was not the only person Peter said this to as I know he told others.

This is an excerpt of Day 3, page 36 of the Daniel Morgan Inquest. Peter Newby is being examined by the Coroner.

Q. *"Since the death of Morgan, police have taken away certain files. To my knowledge, on the Wednesday 11th, D.S. Fillery and a crime squad officer attended the office and saw Rees."* – A. Yes.

Q. *Were you there at the time?* – A. Yes.

Q. *"He came to me for the Belmont auction file."* Who actually came to you for the Belmont auction file? – A. John.

Q. *"....and the Ross Clarke file."* What is the Ross Clarke file? –A. That was a long drawn out divorce.

Q. *So this had nothing to do with Belmont auctions.* – A. No.

Q *"I looked up the number to the first one but I had the location of the second. I got out the Clarke file and Rees got out the Belmont file and these were handed to D.S. Fillery. Subsequently, files have been taken by investigating officers. To my knowledge, neither file has been returned to my office...."* – A. Yes.

Peter went on to tell me that he noticed that Daniel's desk diary was missing. I asked Peter if he was given an inventory as to what had been removed by Sergeant Fillery. Peter said no. (Police procedures at the time did not warrant any receipt was necessary unless it was asked for)

We were both in shock regarding Danny's murder however this did not make us impotent in our thought process; and it was very clear to me that Peter was not happy about what took place regarding the evidence gathering by police in the offices of which he was the manager.

Peter was no stranger to police procedure being a special constable for many years within the police service and he was adamant as to what had happened however his witness testimony was questioned.

This is an excerpt of Day 3, pages 59-60 of the Daniel Morgan Inquest. Peter Newby is recalled and further examined by Miss June Tweedie.

Q. *Mr Newby, you said in your evidence earlier on that on 11th March, the day after the death, D.S. Fillery and someone from crime squad came into the office. What time was that?* – A. Half nine, 10 o'clock, something like that.

THE CORONER: *Is this 11th March?*

MISS TWEEDIE: *Yes, the day after the death. Half past nine or 10 o'clock.* – A. I cannot recall exactly.

Q. *Who was in the office at the time?* – A. There was myself, John was in his own office, I think Mr Pearce was in his office and Mrs Thorne, the secretary, she was in the office, I think.

Q. *Did you speak to either of the officers?* – A. Yes, I said "good morning" to them.

Q. *I was referring to any matters that you told us about this morning, about taking files from the office.* – A. I think they said that they would like some files, but I referred them to John and he came down.

Q. *Were you there when they were having that conversation?* – A. No I went back upstairs.

Q. So your only involvement was an initial request which you passed over to Mr Rees. –
A. Yes.

Q. Have you any idea why they would have taken those particular files? – A. I do not think they just took those files. They took others as well.

Q. Do you know which others? – A. No, I do not. They had a great big bag of files.

Q. You say "a great big bag of files". – A. It was a big bag; a bin liner.

Q. Do you know what was in there? – A. No. As I understand it, they were all subsequently put into the property book.

Q. That is your understanding. – A. Yes.

Q. Who told you that? – A. I have seen the book because they also return files to me and they were listed in the book.

Q. At the time when the files were taken, were you given a list of files they had taken? – A. No.

Q. Do you have any way of knowing whether all the files that were taken were listed? – A. No, I could not say.

Peter was further questioned as to his recollections and accuracy regarding what he actually witnessed on the 11th of March 1987 and what he had said in relation to Sergeant Fillery removing files.

This is an excerpt of Day 3, pages 64-65 of the Daniel Morgan Inquest. Peter Newby is being cross-examined by Mr Goldsworthy.

Q. Can I briefly ask you about the situation when police officers came to the office on 11th March and took possession of various documentation? I think you said that there was a dustbin bag full. Is that right? – A. No. I said there was a bin liner with files.

Q. That being the smaller version. – A. It was a black bin liner, but I did not say it was full.

Q. Did you actually see the quantity of files that were taken? – A. No.

Q. You said earlier that the Belmont file was kept in Mr. Rees' briefcase? – A. Yes, the best part of it was.

Q. The best part of it. When a request was made for specific files to you, you referred it to Mr. Rees. – A. Yes.

Q. Do I understand you correctly as saying that thereafter, the matter was no concern of yours. – A. Once they had been given the files, yes.

Q. Which files? – A. The files they asked for.

Q. You said that it was your responsibility to supply the second file, which was a matrimonial file. Is that right? – A. I supplied one of them and Mr. Rees went into the filing cabinet and supplied the other one.

Q. Were you there when that happened? – A. Yes.

Q. Did you see the file that he took out? – A. Yes.

Q. Did you see the label on it? – A. Yes.

Q. Were you able to identify that file that he took out as being the Belmont file? – A. No. I assumed that when Mr. Rees said: "I have got it", I assumed that he knew he had got it.

Q. So what it comes down to is that in response to a request for the Belmont file, Mr. Rees handed over a file which you are unable to identify? – A. If you put it that way, yes.

Q. And in any event that file that was in the filing cabinet, as I understand you to describe it, would not have been the entire Belmont file - - - - - - - A. As I later found out, yes.

Q. Because the best part of the Belmont file was kept in the briefcase. – A. Yes. I did not find this out until much later.

Q. No, but that is your testimony now. – A. Yes.

It would seem from Peter Newby's initial statement to police and his subsequent witness evidence at the Coroner's Inquest, (some one year later) the accuracy of his previous statement could be seen as a misunderstanding of what actually took place.

Peter's evidence is further examined by way of the testimony of Sergeant Sid Fillery and John Rees.

This is an excerpt of Day 7, page 7 of the Daniel Morgan Inquest. Detective Sergeant Sid Fillery is being cross examined by Mr Gompertz.

Q. Let me move on to something else that you may be able to help us about. After the killing you went, on Wednesday the 11th, to the offices of Southern Investigations. – A. Yes.

Q. And you, with the assistance of another officer, took possession of a considerable number of documents which were listed in Mr Rees first statement. – A. That is right, yes.

Q. You did not take possession, as I understand your evidence, of the Belmont Auctions file from Southern Investigations. – A. No, I did not.

Q. Did you ever see it at those premises on that day? – A. No.

Q. Did you ask for it? – A. No. I am adamant about that, I remember, because it was put to me on that day. I remember, and as far as I was concerned that was the main cause for my arrest. I could not believe it when they came knocking on my door and saying "you have got this file". I didn't even know at first what file they were talking about. I have never had possession of that file.

Q. I am not concerned in this cross examination to ask you about your arrest, because that would be trespassing into an area that I am not entitled to go into. Do you understand? But what I do want to know is whether there was any conversation between yourself and Mr Rees at the premises of Southern Investigations when he was present in the building, at any rate, and you were taking possession of these documents; any conversation about the Belmont Auctions file. – A. No, there wasn't. None at all.

Q. So you never asked for it? – A. No.

Q. And he never mentioned it? – A. No.

Q. And you never saw it? – A. I definitely never saw it.

Q. If it had been in Daniel Morgan's desk you would have taken it into your possession. – A. Not necessarily, because I relied on Mr Newby as to what was recent on Daniel Morgan's desk. There was so much there so I relied on what Mr Newby told me was his recent caseload.

Detective Sergeant Sid Fillery states and he is adamant he never asked for nor did he mention or even saw the Belmont Car Auction file on the 11th of March 1987. John Rees goes on to elaborate the situation surrounding the storage and handling of the Belmont Auction file and this is what he said.

This is an excerpt of Day 8, pages 50-51 of the Daniel Morgan Inquest. John Rees is being cross-examined by Mr Gompertz.

MR GOMPERTZ: Mr Rees, there are very few matters I want to ask you about. When you were conducting business as security guards at Belmont Auctions you kept a file of that business did you not? – A. No.

Q. No file at all? – A. No, no file.

Q. No documents? – A. No documents.

Q. Nothing at all? – A. Nothing at all.

Q. Do you not normally keep documents in relation to work? – A. Yes, we do. When we receive instructions from a particular client then a file is prepared. On that particular matter we did not receive any written instructions from Belmont Auctions and it wasn't until a later date that a file started to exist as we know it today. At that time there was no file.

Q. What do you mean by "a later date"? – A. The later date being after the robbery.

Q. So at some stage prior to the death of Daniel Morgan there was a file on Belmont Auctions? – A. Yes.

Q. Where is it? – A. It is in my briefcase.

Q. You are prepared to produce it to the police? – A. The police have had it.

Q. Are you prepared to produce it to the police? – A. The police have had it already and they are welcome to it again.

THE CORONER: The question is, are you prepared to let them have it? – A. Yes, sir.

MR NUTTER: He has just said so.

MR GOMPERTZ: you are saying that is the entirety of the documentation of Belmont Car Auctions? – A. Yes, I am.

It was on or around the 12th of March 1987 at lunchtime that I witnessed Sergeant Sid Fillery and a DC attend at the offices of Southern Investigations. I recall Peter Newby and John Rees were in the office and I believe Malcolm Webb was also present.

Sid Fillery accompanied by a Detective Constable walked up the stairs and entered Peter's office. They did not talk to me however they started speaking to Peter. Peter looked apprehensive and spoke to Fillery in a manner which I perceived to be that of concern. Fillery said he had inquiries to make and wanted more access to the Southern Investigations files; he then walked up to John's office.

On entering John's office Fillery started examining Southern Investigations files and documents; this went on for approximately 20 minutes. Fillery and the DC then went into different offices examining and removing files from there. During this time John, Peter and Fillery exchanged words regarding the removal of the files and it was mentioned that some of the files were ongoing active inquiries. A disagreement almost took place between Rees and Fillery with Peter in support of John. Peter seemed to become most frustrated when Fillery picked up a particular job file that Peter said was new work that had only just come in. Fillery backed off and placed the file back on John's desk and did not remove it.

John Rees actually looked perplexed as to what was going on. Shortly after this dispute I witnessed Sid Fillery and the DC leaving the offices of Southern Investigations with a bundle of files and documents.

After Fillery left the office a conversation ensued between Peter and John as to what had gone on and how Peter would be unable to run the office with job files disappearing; being removed by police every other day. I believe existing files that were not removed by the police and were still active were duplicated on the off chance they might be removed later.

What was clear to me was this was becoming a difficult situation which both Peter and John were most concerned. The removal of active files was beginning to interfere with working procedures in the day to day running of the business. The general consensus of the staff was the head of the murder investigation team should be contacted and informed of the situation. However, I am unaware if any actions were actually taken.

In relation to Detective Sergeant Sid Fillery I do not wish there to be any question or inconsistency regarding my knowledge of him. For absolute clarity it is important to explain that while, at that time, I had not been formally introduced to him; I had an awareness of who he was.

This is an excerpt of Day 4, page 6 of the Daniel Morgan Inquest. I am being examined by the Coroner.

Q. Do you know an officer called Detective Sergeant Fillery? – A. His name had been mentioned in the past by Mr Morgan and Mr Rees, but the first time I ever met Sergeant Fillery was last Friday.

This is an excerpt of Day 4; page 13 of the Daniel Morgan Inquest. I am being cross-examined by Miss June Tweedie.

Q ---- A. The first time I ever met Sid Fillery was on Friday. He introduced himself to me.

Q. Where was that? – A. He was sitting and having a meeting with John Rees.

Q. Where? – A. In John Rees' office.

Q. Do you know whether he is working with John Rees? – A. No, I do not.

I had seen Sergeant Sid Fillery interacting with John Rees and Daniel over time however I was not acquainted with him nor was I ever formally introduced to him until around April 1988.

To further this matter, in relation to Mr Fillery, I have made a number of witness statements to the police in connection with the murder of Daniel Morgan and I now refer to my witness statement of the 2nd of March 1989 which is transcribed here in its entirety.

I have made a number of statements in connection with the murder of Daniel Morgan.

I have now been asked about the Christmas function of the Solicitors, Coffey, Whittey, that took place at il Carreto Restaurant, Streatham High Road, London SW16 in December 1986. The function was just before Christmas but I cannot remember the exact day. Danny Morgan was not at the function, he was in Scotland with his wife and children. John Rees who attended the function nominated me as duty driver for the day.

I do recall that Margaret Harrison and Tina Jones attended and Tony Pearce from Southern Investigations, I cannot now remember who else attended but in all about twenty persons attended.

I dropped John Rees and Tony Pearce at il Carreto at about 1:30 pm and then I returned to Southern Investigations. About 4:30 pm I received a call to return to the restaurant and collect Tony Pearce because he was drunk, I then drove him to his home address at Mitcham. I then returned to il Carreto and picked up John Rees, Margaret Harrison, Tina Jones and one other male Richard Nicholson, a solicitor's clerk. I have a recollection that Detective Sergeant Fillery was also in the car. I drove these persons to the Cavendish Club in Croydon. I then returned to il Carreto and picked up the Solicitor, Michael Goodridge, and some of his party and took them to the Cavendish club.

I went into the Cavendish club where I had one drink. John Rees then told me that he wanted his car as he was thinking of going on to another club. He gave me £20 to get back to Southern Investigations where I had left my car.

Sid Fillery was one of a number of people that I drove that day. I did not know him or have an acquaintance with him. I merely ferried him in the car that day in my role as Southern Investigations designated driver.

There is a significance and connection associated to the Belmont Car Auction security job, Southern Investigations files and Detective Sergeant Sid Fillery which cannot be ignored – let's explore this.

It was Detective Sergeant Sid Fillery who was associated in bringing the Belmont Car Auctions security job to the attention of Southern Investigations and his friend John Rees whilst being a serving police officer.

We know that off duty serving police officers were present, including Detective Sergeant Sid Fillery, at the site whilst public auctions were taking place, as a presence within the crowd. John Rees, Glenn Vian and Garry Vian and other Southern Investigations casual staff formed a plain clothed security detail.

It is known that prior to the security operation taking place John Rees had attended the Belmont Car Auctions site as a reconnaissance visit on at least one occasion.

We know that security was required on site to protect the auction house 'takings' from a possible threat of armed robbery.

A planning meeting was held in Peter Newby's office. Present at that meeting were: Peter Newby, Laurie Bucknole, John Rees, Danny and others. All those present at the planning meeting should have had some, if not all, knowledge of the assignment requirements.

I was not privy to any of the content of the Belmont Car Auction file however that does not mean I can't make an educated supposition as I worked on hundreds of files each year and knew what type of information might be included, it's meaning and any implication.

A file would likely have included the names of all the personnel working on the job, costing, invoicing, wages, time sheets and operational planning. All of this I could imagine would have been recorded in the file at some stage by way of good management.

It is reported that John Rees was robbed of £18,280 on Tuesday the 18th of March 1986 outside his home in South Norwood. (See Chapter Belmont Car Auctions Robberies).

It is also known that Belmont Car Auctions had litigation pending against Southern Investigations. Was a file created that may have included any possible witness statements as to the robbery or letters of communication pertaining to any pending litigation. It is stated solicitor's letters had been sent out to police officers that were known to the Directors of Belmont Car Auctions as being present on public auction nights as part of the litigation into the loss of the money.

What other relevant information could the file contain? If the file held any sensitive or incriminating intelligence then why would it be in the office or even exist in the first place? John Rees has stated that initially a file did not exist because Southern Investigations did not receive any written instructions from the Auction house. I am of the opinion that may well have been the case as the security arrangements were undertaken at a breakneck speed due to the fears of the Belmont Directors as to further robberies. If anyone had any sinister intention to dispose of the Belmont Auctions file, they would have had ample opportunity to do so well before the 11th of March 1987; however, John Rees has said that he kept the file in his briefcase and that the police were welcome to it.

Since the morning of the 11th of March 1987, one of two days that Detective Sergeant Sid Fillery was witnessed removing files and documents from the offices of Southern Investigations, detectives from the Daniel Morgan murder investigation have stated that Daniel's 1987 desk diary has never been entered into evidence and has not been seen by any of the investigating officers.

I am adamant and absolutely 100 percent sure I saw Daniel's 1987 desk diary on his desk the morning of March 10th 1987.

This is an excerpt of Day 6, page 88 of the Daniel Morgan Inquest. Detective Sergeant Fillery is examined by the Coroner.

Q. What did you take from the office? – A. His blotter, his diary.

Q. What sort of diary was it? – A. A desk diary.

Q. Did you find any personal diaries there? – A. I do not think so, no.

Officers of the initial police investigation squad and Peter Newby have stated conflicting accounts as to what actually took place at the offices of Southern Investigations on the morning of March 11th however, what is obvious is that Daniel's 1987 desk diary is missing. In fairness it must be taken into consideration that the diary was mislaid or otherwise somehow lost albeit negligently. Detective Sergeant Fillery has stated that a desk diary was taken from the office, however he goes on to say no *personal* diaries were found; unfortunately, he did not inform the Coroner of the year of the desk diary which was taken.

It would seem someone may have thought Daniel's 1987 desk diary might have held sensitive information or even incriminating evidence and was significant enough that it should be removed and not form part of any police investigation.

I find the omission of Daniel's 1987 desk diary to be a seriously menacing aspect surrounding the Daniel Morgan murder. Only a few people would have had access or opportunity to remove the 1987 desk diary from Daniel's desk if it was indeed still there after the last time I saw it on the morning of the 10th of March 1987.

I must mention that I do not recall, over the last 31 years, one police officer or murder squad investigator ever asking me if or even when I last saw Daniel's diary.

Since Daniel's murder no proof of guilt has been established upon anyone as to any theft or loss of the missing 1987 desk diary.

Should this be seen as a worrying situation; is it plausible that the missing diary could be party to a possible conspiracy to his murder. This is another situation that I feel the Daniel Morgan Independent panel will have to give concise consideration when reporting their findings.

Chapter 22
Ladies' Man

D aniel was a habitual offender when it came to extra marital affairs. I have no doubt he loved his wife and children however his womanising was his failing, an area of his life where his moral compass was flawed.

He thought he was God's gift to women. He was never shy in approaching members of the opposite sex; at times it became embarrassing being in his company as he was almost constantly on the make. He saw womanising as a sport. Danny was an opportunist.

Daniel had a keen eye and only slender beauties of a particular vintage need apply. He had a taste for the sophisticated well-presented businesswoman type or what may resemble that and it wasn't about quantity although he had his fair share. Married, divorced, widowed or single, it made little difference to Danny. Daniel liked the hunt, the pursuit and the risk was almost like a drug that he found immensely exciting; his nickname was 'The Stud'.

Daniel was alluring with a charming persona, women were drawn to him and he flashed the cash. Danny was a naughty boy.

I am not proud to say that I was aware of Daniel's extra marital relationships. From first meeting Daniel and becoming friends with not just him but his family; I was never comfortable from the moment he started telling me of his exploits. I did not appreciate being entrusted with having awareness of the moral betrayal of his family. I was placed in a difficult position by Daniel with this knowledge; however, he clearly trusted me to know that I would remain, at the time, tight lipped.

I remember an occasion when Daniel and I were in the Victory pub around lunchtime. We were sitting at a table in the public bar when a young couple entered and sat at a table near us. Daniel's gaze immediately landed on the woman; I could tell he liked what he saw. Daniel was keen not to avert his gaze. He said to me, *"Isn't she a darling"*. Daniel is eyeing her up for about 20 minutes and the woman is looking back at Daniel with side long glances. The man gets up and goes to the gents and before his seat cushion has fully returned to normal Daniel is on his feet and approaching their table.

Daniel starts chatting to the woman and she is not rejecting his attentions and just a few seconds before the man returns, Daniel returns to our table. I said to Daniel, *"I don't believe you, that was a bit ballsy, wasn't it? Do you know her?"* And with a smile on his face Danny replied, *"I do now"*.

In the early evening a couple of days later I noticed Daniel's car parked on Gillette Road which, meant he was either still in the office or at the Victory pub. I walked into the public bar and there is Danny with this bird from the other day snuggling and getting friendly. I was going to have a pint but on seeing this I just walked out saying, *"Hey Dan, see ya later."* This was just one of a number of examples of how Daniel interacted with women.

Daniel would meet girlfriends at wine bars and pubs in and around the Thornton Heath area. He shared with me and clearly enjoyed talking about his female conquests to the point where I would say to him, *"It is not necessary to tell me who you were shagging last night"*.

During the inquest into the murder of Daniel Morgan and on giving my evidence, the Coroner Sir Montague Levine instructed me to the following: *I do not want you to particularly mention the name of girlfriends, especially if they extend back one or two years. I think this would be unfair. The court is not to be used for that. These people may now have stable marital relationships and I think it would be wrong to bandy names about. I do not want you to throw any names willy nilly. These people are married with children and this is a long time ago. This would not be in the public interest -- it would be wrong -- and I do not wish you to do that.*

I feel, to this day, that the Coroner was correct to instruct me not to divulge names and I have not done so nor do I intend to. However, there was one exception to this.

This is an excerpt of Day 4, pages 10-12 of the Daniel Morgan Inquest. I am being examined by Miss June Tweedie.

MISS TWEEDIE: Q. Do you know anything about the relationship between Daniel and Margaret Harrison? – A. I knew he was seeing her. I do not know what he was doing, but I knew he was seeing her and was spending time with her.

Q. When was this? – A. I believe it was September 1986 till just after Christmas, January 1987.

Q. Did he ever talk to you about that? – A. He would have a laugh and say: "I've got another bit of skirt, and I am doing this, that and the other." We used to get on that well that we could talk about these things, and not worry about it too much.

THE CORONER: Was Mr. Rees seeing her at the same time? – A. Daniel, John, Margaret and another lady used to go around in a foursome for a while.

Q. Did you have any reason to believe that Mr. Rees was also having a relationship with her? – A. Maybe not at the time, but possibly just after or around about the time that Daniel finished.

MISS TWEEDIE: Do you mean around about the time of Daniel's death? – A. Yes.

Q. You say that you went to the Golden Lion on one occasion. – A. Yes.

Q. Was that in January 1987? – A. I believe so, yes. I made a point in my statement. I cannot remember the month I put down in the statement.

Q. It was around that time. – A. Yes, it was around that time.

Q. Can you describe what happened? – A. I came into the office about half past two. Paul Goodridge was just coming down the stairs. He looked very upset about something. I went upstairs. Daniel was muttering to himself. He looked a bit upset, and he said: "Right we are going for a drive." I said: "Where are we going?" He said: "Just get in the car. We are going for a drive." I said: "What's up?" Daniel used to be thinking about things in his mind. He would just say: "Look, be quiet, I am thinking." He would be like that.

Q. Did he seem upset? – A. Yes, you could say that.

Q. Where did you go? – A. We drove up to Crystal Palace and we drove down Sydenham Road and opposite the Golden Lion is a car front. We had a look round the side turnings and I said: "What are we looking for?" He said: "I'm looking for John's car."

Q. Who did you understand by "John"? – A. John Rees.

Q. He was looking for John Rees' car outside the Golden Lion? – A. I said to him: "Why are you looking for it for?" He did not say anything. He was upset. We stayed around there for about five minutes. We did not go into the car park of the Golden Lion. Then we drove on down and turned right at Bromley Road. There was another pub up there he had a look at then, found nothing and then came back to the office.

Q. Did he say to you what it was about or did you ask him what it was about? – A. I asked him what it was about. I said: "What's up, Danny? Is it something to do with Paul Goodridge?" He just looked at me. I said: "Is John up to something?" He just smiled at me. I said: "Is John seeing some woman or something?" He did not say anything, he just smiled at me. That was basically his way of saying: "Yes".

Q. Is it right that you got the impression that you were looking for John Rees about a woman? – A. Yes.

Q. Do you know which woman it was? – A. Margaret.

Q. Was Daniel Morgan seeing Margaret Harrison at that time? – A. Yes. I would say that he had either just finished his relationship with her or was just about to. I cannot be exact of that fact.

Q. You said earlier that you thought John Rees might have been seeing her after that. It is right, is it not, that you said you stopped working for Southern Investigations about four months after Daniels' death. – A. Yes, that is right.

DANIEL MORGAN SOUTHERN INVESTIGATION

Daniel Morgan and John Rees both knew Margaret Harrison well. Danny told me that Margaret was an estate agent working for Furmstone Estates having met her at a Christmas party. I had limited interaction with Margaret Harrison and this was only through either Danny or John at their respective offices or in public houses and restaurants in the Thornton Heath area. I was aware that she was a married woman and a mother. I recall that her daughter, Karen, came to work for Southern Investigations as a secretary for a time. Margaret Harrison was considerably older than me and we would exchange pleasantries when meeting or passing on the high street. Daniel was clearly attracted to her.

(Author's note: Some of the following excerpts are repeated from chapters 1 and 6 to ease the flow in reading)

These are excerpts from Day 2, page 2-3 and 6-17 of the Daniel Morgan Inquest. Margaret Harrison is examined by the Coroner.

Q. In December 1985 you attended a Christmas party. This party was held by a firm of solicitors that worked for your firm and you were invited to the party by Peter Goodridge who I understand is a solicitor. – A. Michael Goodridge. .....

Q. That should be Michael Goodridge. – A. Yes.

Q. At this party it was the first time that you met Danny Morgan. – A. Yes, that is right.

Q. I understand that he came and sat next to you and you had a friendly conversation with him. – A. I had.

Q. After that meeting Danny would phone you up at work at irregular times. – A. Yes.

Q. You go on to say "I think he knew the staff quite well. I last saw Danny on Tuesday 10th March 1987." –A. Yes, that is right.

Q. "He rang me in the office at about 6 p.m. He asked me what I was doing. I explained I had some cleaning up to do and if he wanted a cup of coffee to pop over. He more or less came straight over as his office Southern Investigations is situated opposite our estate agents." – A. More or less, yes.

Q. "When he arrived he asked me if I wanted a drink and suggested going to Regans Wine Bar which is just down the road from our premises. I think in Brilstack Road. I agreed and we walked to the wine bar arriving at 6:20 p.m." – A. It must have been approximately that, yes.

Q. "We had a bottle of wine between us." – A. Yes.

Q. "He told me he had to meet his partner John Rees." – A. Yes.

Q. "I think he said he was meeting him about 7:30 p.m." You knew John Rees. – A. Yes.

Q. Would I be right in saying that your relationship with John Rees was perhaps a little more complex than it was with Danny? – A. No.

Q. Did you go out with John Rees? – A. Again, he used to be in some of the groups whenever we went round to the pub and luncheon clubs.

Q. Are you telling me then that you never went out with John Rees on his own? – A. Not at that time, no.

Q. *"We left Regans together at about 7:15 p.m." Did you have any more to drink? – A. No. I went straight home.*

Q. *"I last saw Danny about 7:15 p.m. The last time I saw him before Tuesday was sometime last week when we went for a drink at Uno Plus Wine Bar in London Road."*

Q. *"I cannot remember what day it was or whether it was lunchtime or early evening. I would describe my relationship with Danny as being good friends although we have had a sexual relationship but not so much in recent times." – A. That was the first couple of weeks I met him but it really fizzled out from there.*

Q. *"Our meetings were mainly for lunch time drinks, occasionally in company of other people. The meetings were not normally pre-arranged. He would normally ring up in the morning. We would normally go to the Uno Plus Wine Bar but sometimes we went to other pubs." – A. As I say, it was no that often.*

Q. *It was not that often. – A. No.*

Q. *"As I have said, sometimes I would see him twice in one week. Other times I would not see him for two or three weeks. From what I've heard from things Danny has probably said that we've been having an affair however it was not as serious as that. It was a very loose relationship." – A. Yes.*

"When I said I have had a sexual relationship with him this was in December 1985 after our initial meeting...." As you have just said. – A. Yes.

"... and only lasted a few weeks. As far as I am aware my family do not know of my relationship with Danny, however I have spoken to my husband about it but only since his death. My husband understands this to be a business acquaintance. I have been asked if I know of any threats that have been made against Danny. He has not told me about any threats although I was aware of the dangers that his job involved. Over the past few weeks I know he has been tired because of work." – A. Yes, he appeared to be tired.

Q. *"I learnt of Danny's death on Wednesday, 11th March 1987. Mike Goodrich", who is Michael Goodridge, "came into our office as a result of which he told me what had happened. I would describe Danny as being a fairly generous person. I had a very friendly relationship with him. On the Tuesday evening, 10th March, when he paid for the wine at Regans I know he had quite a large bundle of bank notes in his possession." – A. Yes.*

Q. *.... "Further to my statement dated 13th March 1987, on Tuesday 10th March" – remembering that was the day that he was killed – "after leaving Regans Wine Bar with Danny Morgan we walked together around the High Street, Thornton Heath." – A. Back to my car. Well, back to my office, yes. It is the same thing. It is the same route.*

Q. *"I left him by the zebra crossing near my office. I crossed over the road here and Danny carried on walking towards his office." – A. Yes.*

Q. *"I never went into my office at all or spoke to anybody after leaving Danny and arriving home. I got home at 7:30 p.m. My husband, Leonard, was there and my daughter Karen with her boyfriend, Ian Benford." – A. Yes, that is correct.*

Q. *"My husband, Leonard, is a chauffeur for a director of British Gas. He sometimes works overtime in the evenings. On Tuesday, 10th March, my husband had to go out again in the evening back to work. I don't know where exactly he went but it will probably be in his works diary. I think he had something to eat first before he left the house. I can't remember what time he left but when he returned I was in bed asleep."* – A. Yes.

Q. *"I don't know what time he returned."* – A. No.

Q. *"My husband always wears a plain dark grey suit, with a grey peaked cap and a British Gas tie"*, which you described. *"He travels to and from work in his own car which is a yellow Vauxhall Cavalier"*, and you give the index number.

Q. Have you ever met Danny's wife? – A. No.

Q. Now we jump to Friday. *"Friday 13th March 1987 after I had received the telephone call from Detective Sergeant Fowles wishing to speak to me, I went over to Danny Morgan's office because I was worried. I was panicking and wondering where police had got my name from."* – A Yes, I was just worried.

Q. Did you pop over to see John Rees and speak to him in his office? –A Yes, I went over there.

Q. *"Because I was panicking he told me sit down and have a cup of coffee. I did this and went to Norbury police station where I made my previous statement."* – A. Yes.

Q. *"I can't remember when or even if I actually gave John Rees my home telephone number. He has rung me at home about three or four times. I am very friendly with John Rees. We have never had a sexual relationship but when I have been in his company I got the impression that he was chatting me up."* – A. Again, we all got on very well. There was a group of us and we all got on well.

Q. *"We are very friendly, he is good company, always telling lots of stories and has a good sense of humour. I'm sure he only telephoned me at the office and the odd occasions at home because he just wanted to chat, nothing more than that."* – A. Again, I cannot recall that.

Q. *"On one occasion I answered the phone to John Rees at home (and) I put the receiver straight down again because my family were at home."* Was it unusual that you would have to put the phone down when a man phoned up? It could have been a man having business with you. You were an estate agent and estate agents do get calls about property and all sorts of things. – A. Yes.

Q. Was this because you were having a relationship with John Rees and you wanted to make sure that the family did now know? – A. No.

Q. *"I can't remember when that was but it was a few weeks ago, before the time he telephones me on that Friday night. I was a bit cross that he phoned me home but didn't say anything to him when I saw him."* – A. I cannot recall that.

Q. *"I have been asked whether I received two telephone calls from John Rees on 7th January 1987 .... I was off that day from work. This is the occasion I have described when I put the telephone receiver down when I recognised John's voice."* – A. I cannot remember making that statement.

Q. "*Again I didn't tell police about receiving calls at my home from John Rees because I was frightened. I have been asked about receiving a telephone call from John Rees on Tuesday, 13th January, at 9:53 a.m. I do not remember this call. I have checked my diary and I am not shown as being off work on that day. My diary shows me having half day off on Friday, 16th January 1987.*" *I would not expect you to log in your mind every single call you had with any accuracy.* "*I have been asked whether I received a telephone call from Danny Morgan on Tuesday, 6th January. By reference to my diary I can say that I met Danny for a meal early that evening and I used his car telephone to ring home to say I was on my way.*" *May I ask you this? If Danny Morgan had rang you at home, would you have put the phone down if your family were in?* – A. No, I more likely would have chatted.

Q. "*We went to the Ming Garden Chinese Restaurant in London Road, Thornton Heath. I met Danny at the restaurant after work.*" – A. Yes.

Q. "*I have never used John Rees' car telephone to ring home.*" – A. Yes, I have.

Q. *Here you say, "I have never used John Rees' car telephone".* – A. I have.

Q. *You have.* – A. Yes.

Q. *Would you like me to change that in your statement?* – A. Yes.

Q. "*Today at Sydenham Police Station, Detective Superintendent Campbell showed me an axe. I have never seen an axe similar to the one I was shown. I have never seen an axe in either John Rees' or Danny Morgan's cars. My husband does not have an axe. My company supply me with a company car which is a white Ford Fiesta …. which I have been using for business purposes since last June 1986.*" – A. Yes, that is right.

This is an excerpt of Day 1, page 8 of the Daniel Morgan Inquest. Detective Superintendent Campbell is examined by the Coroner.

DS Campbell reports: *In the course of the inquiry I directed that details of all outgoing calls made by Daniel John Morgan and William John Rees, his partner, from their individual car telephones be made available. The period covered in respect of Mr. Morgan was from 1st January 1987 until 10th March 1987, and in respect of Mr. Rees from 20th November 1986 to 13 March 1987. From details available I can say that during these periods Mr. Morgan made one telephone call to Margaret Harrison's home address and two calls to her business premises. Mr. Rees made four calls to her home address and 60 calls to her business premises. I have a set of the print outs of the two vehicles and marked are the respective calls relating to each other.*

This is an excerpt of Day 3, page 72-73 of the Daniel Morgan Inquest. Mr. Michael Goodridge is examined by the Coroner.

Q. *How many years had you known Morgan?* – A. From the moment that he came to Thornton Heath until his death.

Q. *Do you think he had a number of affairs?* – A. More than two.

Q. *You say that over the past two years you had been told by Rees that Morgan had a number of affairs. You know of no names of women or where or how they were involved except on one occasion when Morgan brought a woman to the Victory some six to nine months ago. You think that she was in the middle of an expensive and complicated divorce and that he was* involved. *"I am guessing, but I think she was in her early thirties with long blond hair."* You are not sure, but there could have been a connection with a Porsche at that particular time. – A. That is correct, yes.

Q. *"I have knowledge that Morgan had a"* (<u>inaudible</u>) *"and because of his involvement and liking for women, he was known as 'The Stud'"*. Was that name locally known amongst all his friends? – A. Amongst a number of friends.

Q. *"His other women were not in the Thornton Heath area."* You were making a reference to more than two there. – A. Yes.

I knew that Daniel's nickname was 'The Stud, Studley' this was most constant between Danny and Mike Goodridge. I would often accompany Daniel to Mike's office when we were undertaking the swearing of affidavits. Mike would welcome Danny into his office with a rousing *"Stuuudd, Studley"* they would laugh and Daniel would share with his friend whatever the next instalment was of his philandering. Mike Goodridge was a nice guy and he was well liked by most everyone who knew him. He enjoyed a laugh and a joke. I never found Mike to be anything but honest and professional as a solicitor and a person.

At a time after Daniel's murder I visited with Iris Morgan and it was I who discussed with her the truth of what had been reported about Daniels personal life. I paused for a moment and as tactfully as possible I told her everything I knew. I explained to her that I never wanted to be involved with the deception but that Daniel had placed me in an impossible position.

Since the murder of Daniel Morgan, John Rees and Margaret Harrison subsequently separated from their respective partners; they have cohabitated and sustain a relationship to this day.

Is it possible that Daniel's womanizing or any events surrounding his extra marital affairs might have established a motive that led to his murder?

Chapter 23
Conflict of Evidence

The Daniel Morgan inquest supplied a tremendous amount of information from witnesses. Much of this information included hearsay and gossip. There were a number of circumstances where the Coroner ruled *"a conflict of evidence"*. I am of the opinion that the following witness evidence is most significant. This is the entire inquest witness testimony of Alastair Morgan.

This is an excerpt of Day 5, pages 1-27 of the Daniel Morgan Inquest. Alastair Morgan is examined by the Coroner and all Counsel in turn.

Q. You are Alastair Roderick Morgan? – A. Rodri.

Q. I will change that then. Your address is flat 2, 34 Station Road, Petersfield, Hants. – A. That is incorrect. My address is flat 1, 64A Station Road, Liss.

Q. Thank you very much. I am told, although you were not on the list of witnesses, that you have some information to give to this court which will help in the inquiry into the demise of your brother, Daniel Morgan. – A. I hope so.

Q. I hope it is relevant. May I say this? If there are ladies or families that have been associated with your brother in the past I would wish you not to mention these names. I do not want this inquest to be responsible for the breakup of stable marital relationships. That is not the function of this court. – A. No, I understand.

Q. I would rather you be relevant and to the point on the point you are going to make. – A. I was expecting to be questioned.

Q. Yes, I will question you in a moment but you have something to tell me that is very important in this hearing. – A. I have a lot of information which I believe to be extremely relevant.

MISS TWEEDIE: Sir, I wonder if it would be a better course if I went through the items with Mr Morgan now.

THE CORONER: Yes, if you can keep to the relevant items that have a definite bearing.

MR NUTTER: Sir, a matter of law arises. It is certainly a matter which need not concern the jury.

(The jury left the court)

MR NUTTER: It is my usual concern about this being an adversarial set of proceedings.

THE CORONER: We have not heard anything yet.

MR NUTTER: No. That is why I stand up now before we do.

THE CORONER: Now, look, there is no need to remind me of that. I reminded you and the jury of that at the beginning of the session. I think that is a little unnecessary at this particular stage and you have heard the comment I have made.

MR NUTTER: If you will hear me, all I have to say is this. In the ordinary course this gentleman would be expecting to make a statement to your officer. In the ordinary course, having made a statement to your officer you will know what is relevant and you will examine this witness and then invite, if you choose to do so, all of us to cross-examine.

THE CORONER: Mr Nutter. This is my court. I have the prerogative as to how I question and what I do with regard to this witness.

MR NUTTER: I know it is.

THE CORONER: So far, we have not said a single word yet.

MR NUTTER: We have not said a single word yet. The reason that I am on my feet is this. In the ordinary course he would make a statement to your officer and you would know that which he was about to say before he was examined upon it.

THE CORONER: There is a good deal of extraneous matter in this report. I was told that he had something very important to give this court which was relevant. I am asking counsel in this particular case. I would like to hear what you have to say.

MISS TWEEDIE: Mr Morgan does have various pieces of information which are relevant. Some are more important than others.

THE CORONER: Are these pieces of information, information that is new; completely new to the hearing and new to statements that he made initially to the police?

THE WITNESS: They are.

THE CORONER: Are you going to tell me something this morning that has not been said before to anyone?

THE WITNESS: I believe so, Sir. The information that I have was brought to mind by the witnesses, particularly DC Hanrahan's testimony.

THE CORONER: In view of that I shall take you through some of the statements I have and will give you the opportunity of adding to them. I have the impression that you have something new to tell this court.

THE WITNESS: I do, Sir.

THE CORONER: Something not mentioned previously before?

THE WITNESS: Yes. I would not come up into the box otherwise.

THE CORONER: I shall examine you together with the statements that we have already had.

THE WITNESS: Certainly.

(The jury returned into the court)

THE CORONER: Mr Morgan, I understand that you live in Petersfield which is a bit of a distance away. – A. Yes.

Q. How often did you see Daniel Morgan, your brother? – A. I would say possibly on average I saw him three or four times a year, perhaps for a week; sometimes for longer periods of time.

Q. That was the first question. The second question I would like to ask you is on the occasions you saw him did he discuss his business affairs? – A. Not in great depth, Sir.

Q. Did you ever meet Mr Rees? – A. I did on many occasions.

Q. On many occasions. – A. I worked at Southern Investigations.

Q. Can I take you back to the time of your brother's demise, which is 10th March 1987? Go back a few months before that. We are going to go back to the end of 1986. You would be seeing him at sporadic intervals. – A. Yes.

Q. Were you aware that there were some problems beginning in that partnership? – A. I was always aware that there were certain tensions in the partnership.

Q. Tensions? – A. Yes.

Q. When you use the word "tensions" can you perhaps define it? – A. When I was with my brother, usually alone because it is possibly relevant to point out that I actually worked in the offices of Southern Investigations -----

Q. When did you actually work there? – A. I was actually in the office for about a fortnight in February 1987.

Q. Actually working there, doing a job? – A. The job I had been given to do was compiling an index of property companies for my brother.

Q. I am not really concerned with the exact work you are doing. You met all the various people in the office. – A. Yes, I knew all the people.

Q. You have made a statement here. You say you know on some occasions Danny mentioned that he had some girlfriends but you did not pay particular attention to that. – A. The only time I ever .... Daniel only pointed out a woman to me -----

Q. I do not want you to tell me this woman's name. – A. No. ----- on one occasion.

Q. When he mentioned this woman did he suggest anything, that he had been threatened by the husband or anything of that nature? – A. No, he did not.

Q. So there was no cause for alarm as far as that was concerned? – A. I felt it uncomfortable for my brother to tell me about things like that. I did not really want to know about them.

Q. At that particular time when you were working there for these two weeks were you aware there were any problems in the office. – A. I knew that Daniel disliked certain aspects of Mr Rees' conduct and things like that.

Q. Were you working in the office at the time it was alleged that police and some of the members of the Southern Securities were helping at Belmont Auctions? – A. No, I was not.

Q. Did you know about a meeting that your brother was to have with Mr Rees on the night of 10th March? – A. I did not, no.

Q. Where would you be at that time? – A. On that evening I was in Petersfield, Hampshire.

Q. When were you in London around that period? – A. As I said, Sir, in February I was there for two weeks.

Q. So you were not there for March. – A. No, but on 11th March, the morning after ------

Q. I have not got there yet. In the period just before 10th March you were not there, you were in Petersfield. – A. No, I was not there.

Q. Were you in telephone communication with either Mr Rees or Mr Morgan during that time? – A. I was.

Q. May I ask you if there was anything relevant in those conversations you had? – A. I do not think so.

Q. We go now to 11th March. You were informed of the demise of your brother. – A. I was.

Q. Is that the earliest time you were involved. – A. I had heard about the Belmont Auctions robbery and I was concerned about that. I heard about that very soon afterwards and I was rather concerned about that.

Q. Hold on a moment. If I remember rightly the Belmont Auction robbery took place on 18th March. – A. The previous year, that is right.

Q Why were you concerned about that at that particular stage, on 11th a year later. – A. If I can explain, I heard about the auction robbery by chance. I was in Petersfield I believe it was possibly on 20th or even 19th. I was doing nothing particular at that moment and I thought, "I will give Danny a ring just to see how he is." We were in regular contact, he was my brother.

Q. But you heard about it. – A. Danny told me briefly about the robbery on the telephone. When he told me my first concern was I asked him, "Was John hurt?" I was concerned. I thought he had been robbed of £18,000 and I had visions of him being shot or clubbed or something like that. Danny said, "No, it is all right. He got some ammonia sprayed in his eyes but he is all right."

Q. Did he express any feelings about that robbery? – A. No, he did not. I was worried. "Dan, what is this going to do to your company, a drastic thing like that?"

Q. Let me leave that for the moment. You heard of Danny's death on Wednesday, 11th March, having contacted your mother as a result of a call from the police. – A. That is correct.

Q. As soon as you heard this you made haste for London? – A. I did, yes. I took a taxi. Before I actually went to London, my mother did not know what had happened to Danny. All she had heard was that he was dead. Before taking the taxi up to London -- I did not drive, I was not in a state to drive, I was too shocked -- I rang Daniel's office.

Q. Who did you speak to? – A. I spoke to Jonathan Rees.

Q. What did he tell you because this would be the morning of the 11th. – A. That is right. It was about 09.30.

Q. What did he tell you? – A. I rang up and I said, "what has happened, John? What has happened?" He said to me, "I had a meeting with Daniel last night in a pub in Sydenham." He said, "do you know where that is?" I said, "no, I do not" because I did not really know where Sydenham was. He said, "it is a seedy area of town and there are a lot of junkies and things around that area." He said that Daniel had been mugged and that he was dead.

Q. That is all he said? – A. As far as I can remember.

Q. Did he say how he was killed? – A. I asked him and I am not sure …. I was in a state of absolute shock.

Q. That is understandable, of course. – A. I got the impression -- whether it was whether John said it -- it was something like an ice pick that had been used.

Q. An ice pick. Are you sure of that? – A. All I am sure of is that is the impression that was in my mind when I put the telephone down.

Q. You made post haste for London and arrived in London. Also, according to the statement you made around that time, apparently, he told you that your brother had his car keys in his hand when he died. – A. I made that statement very shortly afterwards and if I said that it is possibly correct because it is a long time ago.

Q. Indeed. You made your statement on 13th day of March -- two days after you heard about it. It was fresh in your mind, was it not? – A. Yes.

Q. You made some comment about John Rees making some reference to your brother's wife. – A. I am afraid you will have to refresh my memory of that.

Q. You are suggesting here that John Rees did not get on very well with your brother's wife. – A. That is true.

Q. Why did you make that reference at that particular time, two days after the death of your brother? – A. There were various reasons, Sir. I had met John Rees on countless occasions before that and I suppose I had formed certain impressions of the man's personality and character and he had said things to me on various occasions which it made me feel uncomfortable about certain aspects of his personality. It made me wary of him as a person, if you like. If you would like me to elaborate, I will.

Q. You were making references that John Rees had made some overtures to your brother's wife. – A. This is what Iris had told me.

Q. I will not go into that in any great detail. Anyway, you had a drink with John Rees and Iris' brother -- Iris of course is your sister-in-law, her brother. – A. No, her brother-in-law.

Q. And during the course of the conversation it transpired that there was a woman in the Sydenham area whose husband might have a grudge against ----- A. I had two meetings with John Rees in the immediate days after Daniels' killing. I met him on two occasions. Which occasion is this one?

Q. You mentioned something about David. You suggested somebody had been arrested for the murder of your brother. – A. That is right. On that occasion...... Can I tell you the sequence of events around this?

Q Yes, you can. I do not want you to bring in too many names. – A. I will try and be as brief and to the point as I can. I arrived in London probably around I should think 11.30. I took a taxi from Petersfield shortly after 9.30. About 11 o'clock, I suppose, I arrived at Iris' house. Everybody was devastated. Her parents had come down from Scotland; my mother was on her way from Wales and shortly after my mother had arrived John Rees came to Iris' house and he came in and he came in very quickly into the house with some money for Iris for expenses for her. He did not say anything to anybody there, any of the relatives. He hardly even acknowledged my presence. He immediately wanted to go off with Joe Harty, Iris' brother-in-law, to discuss the business. Joe had come down from Scotland to, if you like, look after Iris' financial and business interests.

Q. This is understandable. – A. Joe wanted to go off with him within, I should think, a minute or two minutes of arriving at the house. He did not want to stay there at all or answer any questions. I knew that he had been with Danny at around the time of Danny's death and I wanted to find out.

Q. Did you ask him? – A. I did. I said, "John, I want to come with you now because I want to ask you what has happened." He said to me, "it is going to be nasty, Alastair." I said, "Daniel has just been hacked to death. I know it is going to be nasty but I want to find out what has happened."

Q. Understandable. – A. He, reluctantly .... I insisted that I came with Joe and he to the meeting that they were going to have. I insisted. I said, "my brother has just been murdered, John, you were one of the last people to see him I want to ask you what happened." We then went to a pub which I believe is called The Maypole Tree, although I am not absolutely certain. Joe and John and I sat down with a drink.

Q. Did he tell you about what had happened that night? – A. He was doing most of the talking and I just sat and listened to what he had to say. One of the first things he said was that he had just identified the body and that he had been questioned by the police. He was very derogatory about the police investigating the case.

Q. The police had only just started. – A. I know.

Q. He was derogatory about the police on the morning of the 11th when he had allegedly been killed the night before? – A. Yes.

Q. In what way was he derogatory about the police? – A. He mentioned that he had been questioned by the man who was leading the investigation. He did not mention any names, but I have since learnt it is Supt. Campbell who was leading the investigation. He said that Supt. Campbell was a drunk.

Q. Said he was a drunk on the morning of the 11th? – A. Yes.

Q. This must have surprised you. – A. I did not know.

Q. You do not know any of these police at all. – A. No, I did not know anyone.

Q. Did he tell you something else that suggested your brother was very promiscuous? – A. I met him, I believe, on the night of the 12th and on those occasions. Perhaps I should go into that later.

Q. After making that statement the following morning that the man who was investigating was a drunk -- what time would that be? – A. It was during the lunchtime opening hours. I would say that it was midday, 1 o'clock; something like that.

Q. Did he give you any idea as to who might have murdered your brother or how he could have been murdered? – A. Did John give me any idea?

Q. If you are not sure, please say so. – A. What he said to me was the police had certain ideas about it. He said to me (I will try and recollect exactly what he said) -- and I assume he meant Mr Campbell because he was talking of him -- "that man keeps going on about a jealous husband, but I don't think it is a jealous husband".

Q. Why? Who did he think it was? – A. He did not give any indication.

Q. In the next few weeks that elapsed now because the investigation is at its peak -- your brother has been killed in an horrific manner and so forth -- did you stay in London or did you return to Petersfield? – A. No. Daniel and I were quite close. We were loyal to one another and I know that if something had happened to me my brother would have turned over heaven and earth to find out who had done it.

Q. Who told you that there might be an Australian who might have murdered your brother? – A. Jonathan Rees did this but he mentioned this to me in November last year. This was on a much later occasion.

Q. After a period of time your feelings seemed to change with regard to Mr Rees. Why? – A. If I am to be perfectly honest -------

Q. I want you to be honest. – A. When the Belmont Auctions thing happened, I spoke to Daniel and Daniel told me briefly what had happened. My first instinct was to think, "God has John Rees been hurt; has he been shot?"

Q. Yes, you mentioned that. – A. When I heard that he had just had some ammonia sprayed in his eyes and it happened outside his house the thought crossed my mind -- I will not say any more than that -- that he might have done it himself. Because I did not have any further details of the case (our conversation was brief) I thought, "I am not going to say anything to Daniel -----

Q. Why should he do it himself? – A. He had said on other occasions when I had met John ...... I do not know.

Q. A feeling, perhaps? – A. Yes. I did not really trust him.

Q. What happened to the relationship between you and Rees in the ensuing few months, as time went on. You became a little disillusioned with Mr Rees. – A. I did.

Q Why? – A. To me it seemed that if Daniel had been killed by a mugger or anybody at all other than somebody inside his company, if you like -- or other than Mr Rees if I am going to be perfectly blunt -- I would have thought that as I knew Mr Rees was a suspect and I knew this -----

Q. How could you know? – A. Simply because as time went by I gleaned certain facts about the surrounding circumstances of the murder and I thought in the light of circumstantial evidence it looked bad for him.

Q. Is it right that during this period of time Mr Rees was expressing to you in no uncertain terms that he thought the police were grossly incompetent in the way they were handling the investigation. – A. I only spoke to him on a couple of occasions. I only spoke to him on a couple of occasions over the whole year. Because he did not ring me and he did not say anything to me -- he said absolutely nothing to me -- I thought, "if the man is a suspect and he is innocent, why does he not say something to me? I worked in their offices. I am Danny's brother. Why does he not say to me, 'Alastair, I swear I did not do it' or something like that?"

Q. Is there anything specific that you have not mentioned up to now that you would like to tell me that might have some bearing and is relevant to the demise of your late brother; something specific that you know about. – A. I believe that the conversations I had with Mr Rees ----

Q. Which were not many, you say. – A. No. ---- both indicate certain things.

Q. What things did they indicate? – A. If I am going to be blunt, I believe they indicate that he was guilty of being a party to it. That is for the court to decide.

THE CORONER: That is not for this court to decide. Miss Tweedie.

MISS TWEEDIE: It is my right to question this witness last.

THE CORONER: You are quite right because he is here at your instance. I think I will ask Mr Nutter.

MISS TWEEDIE: If I may say at this stage, Mr Morgan has mentioned to me various other matters and I do not know whether, if I question him about those matters, I would have the right of questioning him at the end.

THE CORONER: Yes, you can, if you have some other matters that we do not know about.

Cross-examined by MISS TWEEDIE

Q. Mr Morgan, firstly about cars -- your brother and his relationship with cars. Did he ever make any specific remarks to you about car parking? – A. Yes.

Q. Can you tell me what they are? – A. I will elaborate. When Danny was in Malta I, as I mentioned earlier was working in his office. He said, "You can use my car."

THE CORONER: Was that the BMW? – A. Yes. On one occasion on one evening there was a church in Forest Hill in London and there was somebody going to speak there that I wanted to listen to. I drove over there in the evening. The thing was going to be held in a school building and I parked the car in a big school yard. I suppose there must have been 100 other cars in that yard. I went in, listened to what was said, I came out and I found the back windscreen of the car had been shattered. The loudspeakers from the stereo system had been taken out. I felt pretty stupid. It was my brother's car and I thought, "Somebody has just bust into it." Danny was in phone contact from Malta practically every day or every other day and when he rang up on one occasion I said, "I am sorry, Danny, I parked your car in a car park the other night and the *window got smashed." He said, "Oh dear". He was a little bit irritated and he said, "Do you not know that you never ever park an expensive car in a dark car park in London."*

Q. That is the point. – A. Yes.

MISS TWEEDIE: Mr Morgan, you described a meeting on 11th March between John Rees and Mr Joe Harty. – A. Yes.

Q. You said in answer to the learned Coroner that Mr Rees was talking about having identified the body. – A. Yes.

Q. What did he say to you about that? – A. When he told me, one thing he said was, "It was still in his head." "I have identified the body", he said, "and it was still in his head."

Q. What did he say "it" was? – A. I asked him. I said, "what did they do it with John? What did they do it with?" And he was vague. He said it was a machete or a cleaver, something like that – Japanese. He said the word "Japanese". In my mind that conjured up a very vague picture. I thought it was some sort of oriental martial arts instrument that he was talking about. That was the mental picture I went away with from that.

Q. He definitely used the word "Japanese"? – A. He definitely used the word "Japanese."

Q. Did he describe the police coming to see him the previous evening? – A. Yes.

Q. Did he say who had come to see him? – A. He did not mention any names. What he said was something like this. "They came from the police last night. I was just having a meal with Sharon. We were eating. I was eating with Sharon when they arrived" and he said that one policeman had come in and was pretty brusque with him. John seemed irate about that. The policeman had said, "Are those the clothes you were wearing tonight?" He said the policeman who was accompanying the first policeman (I know their names) had said, "Take it easy, I know Mr Rees" and then Rees said something about, "Who do you think I am, the mad axe man of Catford?" Or something like that.

Q. But he did say to you he had known one of the police officers who came to see him? – A. That was the impression that he gave.

Q. You had an interview I think on 13th March with the police? – A. I had an interview with the police on 11th March first.

Q. Was this the interview with DS Fillery? – A. No. The first time I came to the police station .... When I was at the meeting with John Rees in the pub where I had asked him about what they had done it with, Dave Bray came in and said that they had arrested somebody. I thought, "I wonder who it is?" So that afternoon I went over to the police station and said, "Is it true that somebody has been arrested for the murder of my brother?" I spoke to, I believe, DI Jones who said, "No, it is not true."

Q. Mr Morgan, can I take you to the interview you had with Fillery and Mr Jones. – A. Yes.

Q. Did you tell them anything about your suspicions in this case? – A. I did.

Q. Can you tell them that you said, briefly? – A. I just had a feeling that somehow the Belmont robbery had something to do with my brother's death.

THE CORONER: It was just a feeling. – A. Yes; no more than that.

MISS TWEEDIE: *Did you tell the police about this feeling?* – A. I did.

Q. *Who was there?* – A. DS Fillery and DI Jones.

Q. *Did either of them comment on your feeling?* – A. Fillery commented on my feeling.

Q. *What did he say?* – A. He said to me, "We all have gut feelings and if we were to follow our gut feelings in this investigation we could be running down blind alleys" or words to that effect.

Q. *Did he indicate to you he knew nothing about the Belmont Auction?* – A. Not in any way, no.

Q. *In the days following that where were you staying?* – A. I spent a lot of the time at Iris' home.

Q. *Were there any phone calls made?* – A. I was staying with friends round the corner.

Q. *Can I ask you were there any phone calls made to Iris' home?* – A. Yes, there were.

Q. *Who were they from?* – A. I learnt, much later on, that these calls were made by DS Fillery.

Q. *What was the content of those phone calls?* – A. The content of the phone calls was that I was getting under the feet of the investigation department.

THE CORONER: *Could you hear somebody speaking on the telephone?* – A No.

Q. *How do you know what Fillery said?* – A. Because my family were giving me a very hard time about it.

Q. *Yes, but you do not know what Fillery said.* – A. That was the - - -

Q. *This is what somebody has told you Fillery said.* – A. That is correct.

MISS TWEEDIE: *What did they tell you?* – A. All I heard was that the police had rung me up and were saying that I was getting in the way of the investigation; I was being a nuisance they said and I should go home to Petersfield.

Q. *How did you discover the phone calls were from D/S Fillery?* – A. I spoke to my sister, Jane, who lives in Germany. It was only a few months ago that she pointed this out to me. She said that those phone calls were made by D/S Fillery.

Q. *Had she herself spoken to him?* – A. Presumably she had or somebody who had answered them had said that Sergeant Fillery was saying it.

Q. *You also had a meet with Mr. Rees. Was there a time on 10th November when you saw him?* – A. I did not see Mr. Rees, I spoke to Mr. Rees on the telephone.

Q. *Did he say anything to you about the investigation at that time?* – A. He said to me that he was very bitter about the way the investigation had gone.

THE CORONER: *Bitter in what way?* – A. He said the police were concentrating almost exclusively on him (or something like that) and they were ignoring all the other possibilities in the investigation basically.

MISS TWEEDIE: *Did he say anything about the actual people involved in the murder squad?* – A. No, he did not mention any names, it was just the police in general.

Q. *Did he say anything about them specifically?* – A. No. Only that they were, as he claimed, ignoring other possibilities.

Q. Has John Rees ever said anything to you either before or after the murder about "fitting anyone up"? – A. Yes.

Q. When was this? – A. When Danny came home from Malta. Danny, I believe came home from Malta on February 10th and after work he came in the afternoon, (he had driven all the way back from Malta through Italy and France, he got home, had a shower and changed and came to the office - - - - -

Q. Could you just stick to the point.

THE CORONER: Yes, could you get to the point. – A. Yes. We went to the pub after work and there were a crowd of us in the pub. John Rees was there and Tony Pearce. We were sitting talking. We were talking about work. I did not have an awful lot of experience of being a private detective - - - I had worked in the office on a few occasions - - -

Q. Can you get to the point. – A. Yes. On one occasion I had worked in East Anglia, working for Southern Investigations. I brought this particular incident up in that conversation. On that occasion I had not found anybody whom I believed to be guilty of any crime. Rees sort of winked at me and said, "If I had not found anybody I would have fitted somebody up."

MISS TWEEDIE: Finally, Mr. Morgan, you said – and the learned Coroner has pointed out that he does not want any names mentioned other than the names that have already been mentioned - - -

THE CORONER: Yes, because I think we are going to drag a lot of people in and I do not think it is a function of this court unless we have something very very specific.

MISS TWEEDIE: I want to ask you one thing that you did tell the learned Coroner in your evidence. You said that Danny pointed a woman out to you on one occasion. Was it someone who has been mentioned already? – A. It was.

Q. Can you say who it was? – A. It was Margaret Harrison.

Q. What did he say about her? – A. It was in the pub that night that Mr. Rees made that last statement that I mentioned.

THE LEARNED CORONER: What date was that? – A. 10th February.

Q. 1980 what? – A. I believe, I am almost certain - - - - -

Q. 1987? – A. That is correct.

MISS TWEEDIE: What did he say about her? – A. I was standing perhaps a little bit apart from the rest of the people with Daniel and he sort of nudged me and said, "That's my girlfriend." Those were the only words he said.

THE CORONER: Mr. Nutter.

MR. NUTTER: No, thank you. (Pause). I said, "No, thank you" but perhaps I can take some instructions.

THE CORONER: You want five minutes? All right five minutes but not more.

(A short adjournment)

MISS TWEEDIE: I do apologise at this stage, but Mr. Morgan pointed out I omitted to ask him about one short incident.

THE CORONER: Yes.

MISS TWEEDIE: Mr. Morgan, you had a meeting with John Rees after you had spoken to D/I Jones. – A. Yes, I did.

Q. Did you tell him why you wanted to see him? – A. Yes.

Q. What did you say to him on the phone? – A. I said to him on the phone that I had not mentioned to D/I Jones the identity of the woman who had been pointed out to me in the pub. I wanted to ask him about women in Daniel's life, if you like.

Q. What was Mr. Rees' reaction to that? – A. He was very interested to hear what I had not told D/I Jones.

THE CORONER: What you had not told or what you had told? – A. What I had not told D/I Jones.

MISS TWEEDIE: You then met Mr. Rees. What did he say about this issue? – A. I said to John, "What about women in Daniel's life, John?"

THE CORONER: Can I just get back to "what I have not told D/I Jones." Could you explain what you mean by that? – A. I had been interviewed on 11th March by D/I Jones.

Q. I see, it is about omissions. – A. Yes.

MISS TWEEDIE: What was John Rees' attitude? What did he say? – A. "Women" - - he said - - "that was the only thing Daniel ever talked about." According to what Mr. Rees said he had women everywhere; Daniel had women absolutely everywhere.

Q. What impression did you get from John Rees about what he was saying? – A. I thought Daniel worked very hard and I could not fathom out how Daniel had the time, quite frankly.

Q. What was your impression of the way John Rees was speaking as to why there was any reason for saying this? – A. This was purely my own thought. I thought if he were guilty of being involved in Danny's death then he would be very keen to encourage me in the belief that Daniel had lots of women.

MISS TWEEDIE: Thank you.

Cross-examined by MR. NUTTER

Q. In the past, Mr. Morgan, is it correct to say that you have been addicted to certain drugs.

MISS TWEEDIE: Sir, I - - - -

THE CORONER: Hold on a moment. What bearing has that got?

MR. NUTTER: It has great bearing on this case and I am prepared to argue it.

MISS TWEEDIE: It may be a point of law arises. I am objecting to my friend - - - - - -

THE CORONER: Are you suggesting at the time of the incident he was under the influence of drugs?

MR. NUTTER: No, Sir.

THE CORONER: What does it have to do with this?

MR. NUTTER: The jury are here. I do not want to be put in the position of making speeches to this jury. If you want to hear what I have to say perhaps the jury ought not to be concerned with this.

(The jury left the court)

MR. NUTTER: In a nutshell it goes to this. The area of Sydenham is an area which is known to be one of the parts of Croydon where readily available drugs are sold on the streets and in pub car parks and behind this public house in question. My instructions are that this man has in the past been a drug addict as far as serious drugs are concerned, he was weaned off that and he was now occasionally and certainly during the lifetime of his brother, getting drugs off his brother and that might be a reason why Daniel Morgan was parked in the darkened car park on that night.

THE CORONER: Why his brother was parked there?

MR. NUTTER: Yes, Daniel Morgan. If we are looking for reasons for a killing, there has been a great deal done and said as to things pointing towards Mr. Rees. That is one reason and that is something I have very firm instructions about. If this gentleman was in the habit of receiving drugs from his brother of course that is a matter of relevance to this jury as to whether or not that is a possibility on that night.

THE CORONER: The possibility that Daniel Morgan was getting drugs, you mean?

MR. NUTTER: Yes, for his brother.

THE CORONER: I will bring the jury back but I am going to warn you you are not obliged to answer any questions if they might lead to a criminal charge as far as yourself is concerned. That is most important.

MISS TWEEDIE: Sir, may I say at this stage I am doubtful about the relevance of questions relating to the present at the time of the death but certainly questions about Mr. Alastair Morgan's past are totally irrelevant.

THE CORONER: I will allow questions relating to the car in the car park and the point you are making with regard to him but I will say -------

THE WITNESS: I am under oath -----

THE CORONER: No, I must have the jury back.

(The jury returned into court)

THE CORONER: Mr. Nutter, put your question but do not reply in case I need to caution you.

MR. NUTTER: Am I permitted to repeat the question I asked before?

THE CORONER: About his past?

MR. NUTTER: Yes.

THE CORONER: No, not at all.

MR. NUTTER (To the witness): Is it the case that at the time of Daniel Morgan's death you were occasionally receiving soft drugs which Mr. Morgan obtained for you in the London area and you would collect when you saw him?

THE CORONER: Do not reply to that question until I have cautioned you. You are not obliged to answer that question – it is your privilege – unless you wish to do so if you think it tends to incriminate you. – A. Sir, I have nothing to hide, I am perfectly happy to answer that question. That allegation is completely and totally and utterly false.

THE CORONER: *So be it. I do not think it is relevant to discuss this man's previous history. He is a witness in this court. There is no need to discuss his previous history once he has replied to that statement on that point.*

MR. NUTTER: *Sir, with respect a great deal has been brought out about whether or not Mr. Rees is a nice person. We have even had whether or not Mr. Rees is wholly irrelevant issues to this case has talked of "fitting people up" --- it has all be admitted. In fairness I out to be able to ask question of this witness.*

THE CORONER: *Put your question.*

MR. NUTTER: *My question is this. Have you ever taken hard or soft drugs.*

THE CORONER: *You are not obliged to answer -----*

MISS TWEEDIE: *I am afraid I do object.*

THE CORONER: *He has a question. You have already heard the question. I am putting the caution to you. You are not obliged to answer that question if you feel it will tend to incriminate you. – A. The way I see it, Sir, I swore an oath before I came into this box.*

THE CORONER: *You are privileged.*

THE WITNESS: *No, I am not.*

THE CORONER: *You are privileged. You are not obliged to answer that question and I have put that to you.*

THE WITNESS: *I am not obliged to answer the question. About 15 to 20 years ago I did, on certain occasions, take drugs. I am not going to lie.*

THE CORONER: *Leave it at that.*

Cross-examined by MR. GOLDSWORTHY

Q. *You have told Her Majesty's Coroner and the jury that you were interviewed by D/I Jones and D/S Fillery in relation to the death of your brother? – A. That is true.*

Q. *Are you sure you are right about that? – A. I am absolutely certain about that.*

Q. *Because what I have to suggest to you is that there has never been any interview of you by those two officers. – A. That is untrue. They did interview me.*

Q. *You realise if such an interview has taken place there will be record of it. – A. I do not know about what the police would do.*

Q. *What date was this interview? – A. I believe it was on 12th March.*

THE CORONER: *That is two days after the murder. – A. Yes.*

MR. GOLDSWORTHY: *What in fact amounts to the only contact you have ever had with D/S Fillery is this, is it not. On the day after the death of your brother or the day after that, you were in a room at Sydenham police station with D/S Fillery and an officer by the name of Davidson for two or three minutes during which no interview of any sort took place. – A. That is incorrect.*

MR. GOLDSWORTHY: *Sir, I invite the police to put the record straight whichever way it be.*

THE CORONER: *Is it your point that he did not have an interview at all.*

MR. GOLDSWORTHY: *That is right. No interview at any time with Fillery.*

THE CORONER: *The statement we have got is dated 13ᵗʰ, the next day, of March 1987.*

MR. GOLDSWORTHY *(To the witness): This would suggest you had had an interview on the day before as well. – A. I did.*

MR. GOLDSWORTHY: *I am not suggesting no interview, Sir, I am suggesting no interview conducted in the presence of D/S Fillery. If there was such an interview there would be a record of it and I invite the police to clarify.*

THE CORONER: *Yes. If you would like to step down a moment.*

DETECTIVE INSPECTOR JONES, *Recalled*

Further examined by THE CORONER

Q. *Mr. Jones, you have heard the statement that there was an interview with D/S Fillery the day before the statement, is that true? – A. On 11ᵗʰ, which was the first time I saw Mr. Alastair Morgan, I do not recall that Sergeant Fillery was present when I spoke to Alastair Morgan. I did not speak to him for long but the officer I was with I do not recall now. It may well be D/C Davies continued the conversation. I left Alastair with the officer who I believe was D/C Davies.*

Q. *But D/S Fillery was not there? – A. I do not recall D/S Fillery being there.*

Q. *What about 12ᵗʰ. Was there any interview on 12ᵗʰ? – A. I do not know whether anybody saw him on 12ᵗʰ. There was an interview on 13ᵗʰ.*

DETECTIVE SERGEANT DAVIDSON, *Recalled*

Further examined by THE CORONER

THE WITNESS: *If I can assist you, Sir, I saw Mr. Morgan on 12ᵗʰ. D/S Fillery was present.*

THE CORONER: *He was present? – A. He was present, yes. I do not know how long the interview lasted. It was not an interview as such. It was an informal conversation. Part of the arrangement was that Mr. Morgan would return at a later date in order to make a statement.*

Q. *Would that be 13ᵗʰ, the next day? – A. That was 13ᵗʰ.*

Q. *So what are you saying to me is that D/S Fillery was present at the interview on the Friday. – A. Yes.*

MR. GOLDSWORTHY: *Sir, there was no interview on 12ᵗʰ.*

THE WITNESS: *As I said, Sir, people are getting confused between an interview and an informal conversation. There was an informal conversation between myself and Mr. Morgan where Mr. Morgan was expressing certain things. The ideal thing to do was to take a statement off him. I had no officer available to take a statement that day. Arrangements were made for him to return the following day when I asked D/C Davies to take a statement from him.*

THE CORONER: *With all fairness you cannot expect Mr. Alastair Morgan to know the difference between an interview and a casual chat that you are having. – A. That is correct.*

Q. *So in actual fact as far as he was concerned he did see D/S Fillery and talk to him, with you, on 12ᵗʰ. – A. That is correct.*

MR. GOLDSWORTHY: *That is what I put to Mr. Morgan. That is my case, that there was an informal chat lasting two or three minutes in the company of Mr. Fillery and Mr. Davies.*

There was never any interview as such and there was no conversation at all in the presence of D/I Jones. That, I think, has been confirmed.

THE CORONER: It was you. – A. It was myself and D/S Fillery. I cannot honestly recall what was discussed.

Q. D/I Jones was not there? – A. Mr. Jones was not there.

THE CORONER: That was your point.

MR. GOLDSWORTHY: Yes.

THE CORONER: We will recall Mr. Morgan.

MR. ALASTAIR RODRI MORGAN, Recalled

Cross examination by Mr. GOLDSWORTHY (cont)

THE CORONER: You have heard what was said, Mr. Morgan, that D/I Jones was not there but the officer you have just seen was and D/S Fillery. – A. I saw D/S Fillery in the company of D/I Jones on 12th March.

THE CORONER: There is a conflict of evidence.

MR. GOLDSWORTHY: You are wholly unprepared to admit that you may be wrong about that, are you?

THE CORONER: How many times have you seen Mr. Jones? – A. On, I should think, half a dozen occasions.

Q. Could you have been wrong on that day? – Not about Fillery, absolutely not.

Q. But what about D/I Jones? – A. Because I particularly asked D/I Jones the day before if I could speak to him.

Q. I understand. Could you be wrong about D/I Jones? – A. I do not think so.

THE CORONER: We will leave it at that. It is a conflict of evidence.

MR. GOLDSWORTHY: There is one matter I am afraid I have to put which I am reluctant to put.

THE CORONER: Please.

MR. GOLDSWORTHY: It may be understandable in the circumstances. When you were in the company of D/S Fillery at Sydenham police station – and I have suggested to you it was Mr. Davidson and not Mr. Jones – were you under the influence of alcohol? – A. No, Sir, I was not under the influence of alcohol.

Q. The other thing I want to ask you about is this, Mr. Morgan. You have told the Coroner and the jury that messages were left to you through Mrs. Morgan, your sister-in-law, to go back to Petersfield and stop being a nuisance, or words to that effect. Is that right? – A. Yes. Not through Mrs. Morgan. The messages came to me from my mother, my brother-in-law and my sister who were also there at the time.

Q. Where? – A. At Iris' house in London.

Q. Who received the telephone call or calls? – A. Who took them exactly I do not know. All I now is the messages I was given. I was told by members of my family and Iris' family that messages had come from police saying to me that I should get out of London because I was getting in the way of the investigation. I later learnt from my sister that these telephone calls were either from Mr. Fillery himself or junior officers under the direction of Mr. Fillery. This is what my sister said to me.

Q. The first thing I want to ask you about is this. At the time you received the messages no suggestion was ever made that they emanated from D/S Fillery? – A. At that time, no.

Q. Or any other police officer in particular? – A. No. I was just told it was the police.

Q. The allegation that it was D/S Fillery was made by your sister recently? – A. My sister lives in Germany. She stayed in England for about a week after Danny's murder and since then, for most of the time, she has been in Germany. She told me that she particularly remembered that it was either Mr. Fillery or junior officers who said "Mr. Fillery had said to us to tell Alastair to go home to Hampshire because he is getting in the way."

Q. Was she one of the people who was said to have received such a message. – A. I believe that she actually took a call or several calls herself. I am not sure about that. I do not know.

Q. If she was such a person she failed to disclose the source of such a message at the relevant time? – A. I do not think at the time that she would have understood there was any relevance. It was only later when D/S Fillery was arrested she assumed there was any significance.

THE CORONER: The point is that until that time you did not know it was D/S Fillery. – A. No, I did not know.

MR. GOLDSWORTHY: It was only after that unfortunate officer was arrested that that suggestion was ever made. Is that right? – A. It was not a suggestion. It was a statement.

Q. Was it speculation? – A. No. It was a statement. My sister is an honest woman. She would not say something like that to me unless she believed she was telling the truth.

Q. Mr. Fillery does not know and never has known the telephone number of Mrs. Morgan's home. What do you say to that? – A. I believe that that would have been obvious data in the case from the beginning.

MISS TWEEDIE: My learned friend is asking this witness to comment on police operations which he cannot do.

THE CORONER: No.

MR. GOLDSWORTHY: With respect, the rules of evidence and admissibility have been treated with a certain amount of latitude in the course of this inquiry.

THE CORONER: That is a point taken, I agree.

MR. GOLDSWORTHY: The fact of the matter is – and I want to make it quite clear to you – that no such thing has ever happened. You could only comment by virtue of what might be called either hearsay or gossip. Is that right? – A. I would not say that was hearsay or gossip. My sister told me that those calls came from D/S Fillery.

Q. As a matter of law it is in fact hearsay but I am putting to you in fact really what it amounts to is gossip.

THE CORONER: Let us leave it as a conflict of evidence.

Cross-examined by MR. GOMPERTZ

Q. Mr. Morgan, you will no doubt be glad to hear that I am not going to suggest to you that you are either under the influence of drugs or alcohol or have been at any material time. I only want to ask you about two things. I just want to get it clear that as early as 11th March Mr. Rees was attacking the character of the police investigating the murder. Is that right? – A. That is correct.

THE CORONER: That was in actual fact at 9:30 the following morning, you say. – A. I spoke to John Rees first at 9:30. We later met at the pub.

Q. And he made disparaging remarks about the investigation when the alleged murder of your brother took place round about 12 hours previously. – A. Yes.

MR. GOMPERTZ: The second matter I want to ask you about is this. Is it right that you wrote a letter to the Daily Telegraph. – A. That is correct.

Q. I think it was published on 3rd March of this year? – A. Yes, that is right.

Q. The prime purpose of the letter was for you to express your views as to the right of persons who were being questioned by the police to maintain silence. – A. That is correct.

Q. Of course you are perfectly entitled to your views but perhaps this inquest is not concerned with your views on the topic. What I do want to ask you about is a little bit of that letter. Did you say this after some introductory remarks: "Throughout the investigation I have made every effort to stay in close liaison with the Murder Squad. Their job has proved to be extremely complex. Hundreds of people have been interviewed and almost as many statements taken."

Then you refer to the right of silence and say: "The investigating officers have exerted themselves to resolve the matter." – A. They have.

Q. Thank you. "Indeed, one senior office who worked himself to a point of medical exhaustion in his efforts to convict my brother's killer informed me today" --- and this is a reference to the right of silence ---"that a suspect can again refuse to answer questions put to him." – A. That is correct.

Q. Thank you. "Without exception, every policeman to whom I spoke has expressed frustration and disillusionment." Is that right? – A. Yes, correct.

Q. Then you refer to your views of whether in fact there should be a right of silence. So, you were, in passing in that letter, expressing the view that the police had worked extremely hard on this investigation. – A. That was the impression I had.

MR. GOLDSWORTHY: Thank you.

MR. NUTTER: Sir, I wonder if, arising out of that ----

THE CORONER: Please.

MR. GOMPERTZ: I wonder how many bites of the cherry one is allowed to have.

THE CORONER: Is it something new?

MR. NUTTER: It arises out of the letter which my learned friend has put in. I had no notice it was going to be put in.

MR. GOMPERTZ: Sir, with the very greatest respect, there is a right to cross-examine once. You can, of course, renew that right. But merely because I raised something which my learned friend did not anticipate, and if he did not anticipate it with the greatest respect to him that is his fault (because it was mentioned to Mrs. Morgan at a much earlier stage of this inquest) does not mean that he should have a second bite of the cherry.

THE CORONER: You are right, of course, but I will make an exception in this case.

MR. NUTTER: Thank you. Why on earth things mentioned to Mrs. Morgan which has nothing at all to do with my client should have any bearing upon my knowledge, I have no idea.

MR. GOMPERTZ: You could have asked to see it.

MR. NUTTER: I did not know what Mrs. Morgan's - - - -

THE CORONER: Let us not get excited.

Further cross-examined by MR. NUTTER

MR. NUTTER (to the witness): Only this. Is it your impression that the police, from a relatively early stage, had had an idea who the killer is? – A. I do not think it would be proper for me to comment on that. I cannot answer for what the police have thought or have done. I just received impressions that they worked diligently to try to get to the truth. What their thoughts and suspicions and ideas on the matter have been is not my place to comment on.

Q. You have not a clue about that? – A. I would say it is not my place to say anything about that. You should ask the police about that matter.

Q. The police have made it plain to you, have they not, that they are trying to nail Mr. Rees for this? – A. No, they have not.

THE CORONER: Answer the question. Is it "yes" or "no"? Have the police said to you they are trying to nail Rees for this? – A. No.

Further cross-examined by MISS TWEEDIE

Q. Just to clarify, Mr. Morgan. Counsel for Mr. Fillery has asked you whether you are sure about that conversation you had with D/S Fillery on the morning of the 12th. Irrespective of who was with D/S Fillery, are you sure it was Mr. Fillery you spoke to? – A. I am absolutely certain. I even wrote a letter to that effect to the police which I believe they have probably still got in their possession.

Q. Who did you write to? – A. I addressed a letter to D/C Brian Davies because he interviewed me and he asked me to put down all the information that I had in my mind about the incidents surrounding the case - - - all information that I had about it - - - and to put it in a letter and address it to the police. I believe in that letter, which I wrote some time in November last year, I mention the interview with D/S Fillery.

Q. Have you any doubt that it was D/S Fillery? – A. I have absolutely no doubt whatsoever.

MR. GOLDSWORTHY: I am sorry to interrupt. I do so in order to clarify the issue. I have said twice now there is no challenge whatsoever that D/S Fillery saw this man at the police station.

THE CORNER: Yes, we have accepted that.

MISS TWEEDIE: My question was whether the conversation (and I am sorry if I have not made myself clear) - - - not whether he saw D/S Fillery - - - was as Mr. Morgan said it was; in *other words, he expressed doubts about the Belmont Auction involvement and D/S Fillery had said to him, "We cannot go charging down blind alleys" or words to that effect. – A. That is correct.*

Q. It was definitely D/S Fillery? – A. Absolutely correct.

Q. Just to clarify one point which may have become confused, the derogatory remarks which John Rees was making about the police. When were they, on 11th March? – A. That was at lunch time in the pub.

Q. Not at 9.30 in the morning? – A. No, not at 9.30 in the morning but lunch time in the pub.

THE CORONER: Can I just say one point to you. The remarks that you make about Mr. Rees, most of them are gut reactions that you had; feelings about Mr. Rees at that particular stage. It was no particular

facts you had gleaned? – A. No, it was just on the basis of things that he had said.

Q. It was a gut reaction? – A. It was a gut reaction.

THE CORONER: Thank you very much indeed.

(The witness withdrew)

The evidence here is self-explanatory these statements were responded to by the witnesses for the police in the following way.

This is an excerpt of Day 6, page 103 of the Daniel Morgan Inquest. Sid Fillery is being cross-examined by Miss June Tweedie.

Q. Alastair Morgan mentioned to you, two days after the death, that he thought the Belmont Auctions business was in some way involved. – A. May I mention this meeting with Alastair? It was in the room downstairs. We were waiting to start an office meeting. Somebody 'phoned up and said: "There is an Alastair Morgan downstairs." The conversation in front of Davies lasted two or three minutes. That was it. We went back up to the meeting and I never saw Alastair Morgan from that day.

Q. During that conversation, call it an interview or what you will, mention of the Belmont Auction was made. – A. If it had been made, I am sure that Davidson would say: "What is all this about the Belmont Auction?" It was not mentioned.

Q. You told him: "We cannot go charging down there, Alastair, on gut instincts." – A. Nothing of that nature was said. It was a two-minute conversation with Alastair Morgan.

Q. In fact, you suggested that if at any time Alastair Morgan wanted a chat you would meet him for a drink. – A. I am not saying that I would not have said that. I felt sorry for the man. His brother had been killed. He was in a sad state. I do not remember saying it but I do not deny it.

This is an excerpt of Day 6, page 112 of the Daniel Morgan Inquest. Sid Fillery is being cross-examined by Miss June Tweedie.

Q. You also made 'phone calls to Alastair Morgan. – A. I have never made those 'phone calls. I would not do such a disgusting thing. I have never 'phoned that family.

Q. Or asked anyone else to 'phone. – A. What would be the point of me saying: "'Phone up because I do not want them to recognise my name." I never made those 'phone calls.

Q. Did you think that Alastair was getting in the way of this investigation? – A. I only saw him once. I did not think he was getting in the way. He was the man's brother. Of course, he would make sure that he knew what was going on and so on.

Q. You have no knowledge of these 'phone calls at all. – A. Absolutely none.

This is an excerpt of Day 6, page 6 of the Daniel Morgan Inquest. Detective Sergeant Davidson is further cross-examined by Miss June Tweedie.

Q. You say that you considered it to be an important part of the investigation to take a statement from Mr. Rees. Do you actually have a list of the instructions you gave to Sergeant Fillery and at what time? – A. There are one, two ---

Q. ----- – A. ----- There are two on the 12th March. One was to obtain information from Mr. Rees as to Southern Investigations working on a particular project which does not concern the inquest, and the other one was to obtain a background statement from Mr. Alastair Morgan.

This is an excerpt of Day 6, page 13 of the Daniel Morgan Inquest. Detective Inspector Jones is further cross-examined by Miss June Tweedie.

Q. On 12th March you were present at a conversation, interview or whatever, with Alastair Morgan. – A. Was that the first time he came in?

Q. I am not sure whether it was the first time. It was the second time that he came into the station. Yourself and Detective Sergeant Fillery saw Mr. Alastair Morgan. – A. You asked me this before. I said that as far as I recall there was no such conversation with myself ----

This is an excerpt of Day 6, pages 15-16 of the Daniel Morgan Inquest. Detective Inspector Jones is further cross-examined by Mr. Goldsworthy.

Q. If Alastair Morgan had made an allegation to you at the Golden Lion on 10th March 1988, to the effect that Detective Sergeant Fillery had been attempting to put him off stimulating the inquiry, would you have reported that? – A. It depends in what context you are putting that in. If Alastair Morgan had said to me: "I was threatened by Sergeant Fillery not to make", I would probably make something of it. Perhaps Alastair had rung up during the course of inquiries and he said: "Don't keep interfering with us. We are busy."

Q. Were you in court when Alastair Morgan made the allegation that he made? – A. I was in court for some of the time. Whether I was in court all of the time I do not know.

Q. It was an allegation that a number of the members of the family had been told, either by Mr. Fillery or on behalf of Mr. Fillery on the telephone, not to interfere in the inquiries. If that allegation had been made to you in the public house would you have reported it? – A. There are two ways of interpreting: "Don't interfere." It could be: "Don't interfere; you are being a nuisance" or "Don't interfere because you are treading on dangerous ground."

Q. I take it that we are to understand these alleged telephone calls as being an attempt to interfere with the inquiry. If an allegation had been made to you that there had been an attempt by a police officer to interfere with the inquiry, would you have reported that? – A. Yes.

MR. GOLDSWORTHY: That is all I ask.

(The witness withdrew)

THE CORONER: Detective Sergeant Davidson.

DETECTIVE SERGEANT DAVIDSON, Recalled

Further cross-examined by MISS TWEEDIE

THE CORONER: I wonder if you could help with Miss Tweedie's questions. – A. I think that I can help Miss Tweedie with two things here. I misunderstood your question about: Did I know who had made the telephone call to the Morgan residence regarding Mr. Fillery?

MISS TWEEDIE: Are you talking about the telephone calls after the death? – A. Yes. I said that I could not say because I cannot say, but I have been told at a subsequent conversation by Alastair Morgan that it was Sergeant Fillery, but I have no – – – –

THE CORONER: Let us get this clear. Sergeant Fillery made these 'phone calls. – A. No. I am not saying that. What I am saying is that – – –

Q. Alastair Morgan said that. – A. Alastair Morgan said that.

MISS TWEEDIE: I think that counsel for Mr. Fillery is suggesting that this is a recent invention, that Alastair Morgan – – – – – – – A. Discussed it with me, yes. What he has alleged to me is that Sergeant Fillery in some way spoke to his relatives in an effort to stop Alastair interfering with the inquiry.

Q. When was this conversation? – A. This may have been roundabout October of last year.

Q. Did you make inquiries into these 'phone calls? – A. I took the view that Sergeant Fillery was no longer on the inquiry. Alastair Morgan was keeping me supplied with information. There was no damage that Sergeant Fillery could do to the inquiry at that stage. It was just something that I understood Alastair Morgan had told me.

This is an excerpt of Day 6, page 19 of the Daniel Morgan Inquest. Detective Sergeant Davidson further cross-examined by Mr. Goldsworthy.

Q. You have told my learned friend that Alastair Morgan made an allegation about something Mr. Fillery was said to have done, the allegation being made in around October 1987. – A. I cannot be exact about when he told me. We have had many conversations. During the course of these conversations he has made that allegation.

Q. You refer to that period. Did Mr. Alastair Morgan give you any reason for a six-month delay in make the allegation? – A. No, Sir. I think that what was happening was that the family were getting worried about the way the investigation was going. I had a long conference with himself, that is Alastair, and his mother, at Bromley Police Station to discuss many things; in particular, the role Sergeant Fillery had played. That is when he told me about it. I do not think he saw it as a delay. He just told me. I did not ask him why he delayed telling me. It was just something that came up in conversation. I did not attach anything sinister to it.

Q. You did not. – A. No. It is a thing I have done myself in the past. In the past I have asked relatives to speak to other relatives who are bereaved because they are interfering and causing problems in the investigation.

Q. At the time that it was raised to you it was not a suggestion that Mr. Fillery was unlawfully interfering. – A. I certainly did not see it as that. I listened to what he said but I did not see it as an obstruction. It was not put to me in that way. It was put to me that a member of the family had spoken to Alastair having spoken to Sergeant Fillery. That is how it was put to me.

This is an excerpt of Day 6, page 10 of the Daniel Morgan Inquest. Detective Sergeant Davidson is further cross-examined by Miss June Tweedie.

MISS TWEEDIE: There were questions that I was going to ask Mr. Jones. One of them was whether there was authority from anyone to telephone Iris Morgan's home address. – A. Officers do not have to seek authority to make those inquires. If they feel it is necessary to speak to the widow they will do it of their own volition. If they think it is a delicate matter, they would speak to either WDS Poles or to Detective Constable Davies who were set aside to liaise directly with the family.

Q. I am asking you about the telephone calls that we heard about on Friday. It may be that Inspector Jones is the person to ask. – A. Are you speaking of the telephone calls to the address where it was alleged that somebody told Alastair Morgan not to interfere with the inquiry?

MISS TWEEDIE: Yes.

THE CORONER: Can we have the answer to that question? – A. As far as I am aware, no telephone call has been made with authority from any person on my particular inquiry. I do know that Mr. Morgan has spoken to me, that somebody --- I think it was his brother-in-law --- had been told by a member of the police force that Alastair was making a nuisance of himself and that he should leave it to the police. Alastair told me that his brother-in-law said: "Alastair, leave them alone. They are the police and they know what they are doing." I can to that extent confirm what Mr. Morgan was trying to tell us.

Q. You cannot be sure who said it. – A. I cannot be sure who said it and I do not know ----

THE CORONER: Can we leave it at that, without pursuing it any further?

The Morgan family alleged telephone calls were made to Iris Morgan's home from someone who they believe was representing the police. The name Sid Fillery or his subordinates was mentioned. I was around the family at that time and I can confirm the events stated were discussed. However, it has always been denied by those who faced the allegations that the events ever took place; this clearly established a conflict of evidence.

This Document contains Parliamentary information licensed under the Open Parliament Licence v3.0. This is an excerpt of the actual parliamentary statement made by Mr Tom Watson Member of Parliament on the 29th of February 2012.

Investigation No. 1 was severely compromised by police corruption. For 20 years the Met failed to admit that, despite the repeated pleas of the Morgan family. Indeed, it was not until 2005 that the Met's then commissioner, Sir Ian Blair, admitted that the first inquiry involving

Detective Superintendent Sidney Fillery had been compromised. If that admission had come earlier, the subsequent inquiries might not also have failed.

As part of the first investigation, it is now known that DS Sid Fillery—a member of the original murder squad—failed to reveal to his superiors that he had very close links with Jonathan Rees when he became part of the inquiry. I am told that Fillery took a statement from Rees, but it did not include details that both he and Rees had met Daniel at the Golden Lion pub the night before the murder, nor did it include details of a robbery of Belmont Car Auctions a year earlier. Had those details emerged at the time, they would have revealed that those incidents brought both men into direct conflict with Daniel.

In the aftermath of the murder and just as predicted by the evidence of Kevin Lennon seven months before at the inquest in 1988, Fillery took early retirement with an enhanced sick pension. Alastair Morgan has also told me how, at the inquest, members of the Met disputed the fact he had ever spoken with Fillery directly as part of the investigation. He believes that they were trying to cover up for Fillery.

Detective Sergeant Sid Fillery retired from the police force with an exemplary record and was not the subject of any police internal disciplinary action regarding any of these allegations. Sid Fillery has faced an allegation of perverting the course of justice which the crown prosecution service dropped in 2011. Sid Fillery brought a successful claim for malicious prosecution over the charge that he perverted the course of justice and, as a result, has been awarded substantial damages.

Chapter 24
Morgan Rees & Co

A lot transpired in the life of Daniel Morgan in the late autumn and early winter of 1986. It was around November when Daniel first said that he and John had agreed to establish a new business called Morgan Rees & Co. The business was devised to undertake the very lucrative and expanding area of commercial bailiff work and was to incorporate the existing bailiff work clientele of Southern Investigations.

This was also around the time that Daniel had taken a trip with Bryan Madagan to the Algarve in Portugal which was part business and part pleasure; for the purpose of a possible merger between Southern Investigations and Madagan's. (See Chapter The Algarve Trip)

Since John Rees was robbed of the Belmont Car Auctions monies in March 1986, Daniel's relationship with John had certainly been tested. (See Chapter Belmont Car Auctions Robberies) Although their interaction had been awkward and concerns may lay on the horizon, Daniel said starting a new business, Morgan Rees & Co, would be a reasonable course of action by which to safeguard the Southern Investigations business clientele against any possible repercussions from the robbery which Daniel said was a 'fiasco'. Morgan Rees & Co would operate out of Southern Investigations offices at 53 High Street, Thornton Heath.

Tony Pearce was recruited into the new business and was appointed as consultant. His duties were to undertake the legal administration and the day to day running of the business. Malcolm Webb joined the business as a bailiff and he along with Daniel undertook the field work with John assisting when required. Daniel would also instruct other independent bailiffs around the country to act as his agents. All bailiffs coordinated with Tony Pearce in the office.

Daniel told me that Tony Pearce's consultancy role could change dependant on his level of commitment, reliability and productivity. The door was left open for him to establish himself as a shareholder or partner.

Daniel said that one of Pearce's responsibilities was to approach known business clients of Madagan's; existing commercial property and land portfolio managers in an attempt to entice them to transfer their bailiff assignments from Madagan's to Morgan Rees & Co. These were clients with extensive wealth; the bailiff fees alone from just one of these clients had the potential to run into five figures per annum. I am sure any bailiff company would have wished to attract these businesses as clients.

I formed the opinion this was a premeditated and organised attempt in poaching clients from a friend and business associate - Bryan Madagan. However, from what Daniel said transpired during his trip to the Algarve this did not come as much of a surprise.

From a business perspective, almost immediately, Morgan Rees & Co seemed to be proving a great success steadily expanding in this most rewarding market. I watched the business grow and participated in all aspects of associated bailiff work; this was a remarkable endeavour.

Morgan Rees & Co had a great potential to become one of the largest bailiff entities of its kind.

The mid 1980s was a time when there were only a handful of businesses in the commercial bailiff industry that were able to handle the well-paying corporate market. The employees of Morgan Rees & Co were all experienced players in every area of operational bailiff procedures. Daniel had a proven track record in getting clients their money.

Daniel said that it was he who encouraged Tony Pearce and Malcolm Webb to join the enterprise however this was discussed between both Danny and John; the recruitment had financial implication and responsibility in cost of manpower to both men.

The significance of this venture is that Danny and John had agreed to agree. Just a few months prior to Danny's death they had decided to further their business partnership and expand. These actions suggest that the business development between all parties involved would have been a long-term commitment. Even though just after John was robbed Danny told me he gave consideration to ending his partnership with John Rees.

This is one of many features of the relationship that Daniel Morgan had with his business partner John Rees.

Chapter 25

The Teflon Trail

The Daniel Morgan murder and the subsequent police investigations have been shrouded in controversy particularly surrounding the actions or inactions of police officers, serving or retired. Many witness statements have been taken or made pertaining to allegations of threats *to* police officers or wrongdoing *by* police officers by witnesses or persons of interest involved in the murder investigations.

In my opinion the statements of witnesses that are of most interest are those of Mr Kevin Lennon, Southern Investigations bookkeeper, Detective Sergeant Sid Fillery initial police investigation detective and friend of John Rees, Detective Constable Duncan Hanrahan and Mr John Rees, Southern Investigations partner. The outcome of some of the allegations from the statements actually made by these individuals has shown some amazing coincidence and consequences over the years.

There are many other witnesses and persons of interest; however, it is Lennon, Rees, Hanrahan and Fillery that in my opinion have made some of the most intriguing statements in the entire history of the murder investigations.

To examine all of the situations of witness testimony where controversy may exist over a period of 31 years is a momentous task. At the time of writing this book a vast amount of the police murder inquiry evidence remains unavailable to the general public. Only time can reveal if certain witness statements taken early on in an inquiry may actually have been much more accurate or inaccurate (by the persons making the allegations and statements) than the first impression might have seemed.

Research and review of witness testimony can sometimes establish a pattern of circumstantial behaviour by witnesses or persons of interest who have made statements, allegations or threats in the prelude to or immediately after the murder of

Daniel Morgan. Allegations being made that have subsequently been denied by those persons that the allegations were made to or about.

What the passage of time does is it gives an opportunity to reveal if some of these allegations or threats made in early witness statements had any relevance in meaning or might show some pattern in actual behaviour of some of those individuals.

What is revealed in the study of the witness statements and testimony seems ultimately to be culminating in corroboration, vindication or criminal prosecution. In my opinion, these are some of the instances that are of most interest.

△ △ △

Kevin Lennon
Southern Investigations Bookkeeper

The most contentious witness statements are the three made by Kevin Lennon in 1987 referred to in the Daniel Morgan Inquest transcript. How they are perceived and why they were made remains debateable to this day. Public knowledge is that Kevin Lennon was charged with and was on police bail during the inquest for an unrelated matter which he was later convicted of fraud, a criminal offence which had a long custodial sentence in the offing.

Kevin Lennon made three police witness statements which were recorded and signed *after* Danny was killed. The first statement made no mention whatsoever he knew of a plot to kill Daniel Morgan.

This is an excerpt of Day 8, page 15 of the Daniel Morgan Inquest. John Rees is examined by the Coroner.

Q. You may have been in court – and I am sure you have heard – that a Mr Lennon, a former accountant working in your firm, has made various statements about the relationship and various allegations as to what you have said. Would you like to make any comment about that? Take your time. – A. Firstly, Sir, he is not a qualified accountant. He is a book-keeper. He has got no qualifications at all. I think the reason, I am sure Mr Lennon has 72 good reasons ---
-

THE CORONER: Sorry? – A. Mr Lennon had 72 reasons for stating what he did state, and that would be the months in prison that he is looking forward to on the series of frauds that he has been charged with.

Q. That does not answer my question really. Mr Lennon made various statements regarding you. – A. Yes.

Q. Are they true or are they not true as far as you are concerned? – A. They are absolutely not true, sir.

Q. Are you then saying that everything Mr Lennon said in the witness box regarding your relationship of hate, of your desire to get him killed are not true? – A. That is right, sir.

Q. Have you any reason why Mr Lennon should have singled you out to make these statements about? – A. I can understand as I just stated Mr Lennon's reason for wanting to maybe do a deal with certain police officers. I can understand that.

Q. How do you mean "a deal"? Can you explain that? – A. Again, Sir, Mr Lennon is looking at a very lengthy custodial sentence. I am sure it would be in his interests if he could avoid doing that custodial sentence.

John Rees has stated that everything Kevin Lennon has said regarding him having a desire to get Daniel Morgan killed was absolutely not true. (See Chapter Something Doesn't Add Up)

△ △ △

Detective Sergeant Sidney Fillery

There has been great speculation and controversial witness testimony surrounding Detective Sergeant Sid Fillery who, at the time of the murder, was an acting regional crime squad detective stationed at Catford. He was a good friend of John Rees and an acquaintance of Daniel Morgan and it is only fair to say Fillery held an exemplary record in the police service.

This is an excerpt of Day 6, pages 75-76 of the Daniel Morgan Inquest. Detective Sergeant Sid Fillery is being examined by the Coroner.

Q. For how long have you known Mr Rees? – A. I have known Mr Rees some five to six years. I cannot be exact.

Q. You got to know him about 1983. – A. Something like that, five or six years ago.

Q. In what capacity did you first get to know him? – A. I was on one of the Scotland Yard departments called the regional crime squad. Mr Rees, and the man whose name you heard before Mr Bucknell, who was then a serving officer, saw me and my supervising officer. He was dealing with a very large-scale fraud in the Essex area. I will not mention the name of the firm unless you want me to. They had some drivers who were allegedly being dishonest. Because it was so widespread and so busy the local police could not deal with it, so we were approached and took on the job.

Q. It was obviously in connection with some job. – A. Yes.

Q. Can you tell me when the relationship between you and Mr Rees, from being on a purely professional basis changed to a more friendly relationship, whereby you saw each other quite often socially? I know that most officers when they get to know people, they do see them occasionally socially. I mean something more than that. You became very friendly and started to see each other on a very friendly basis. – A. That job went on for some months. I had to see him regularly because he had an undercover man. It was Rees' own firm. He had a report and so on. I saw him more and more while that job went on. Then, of course, we had to wait until the case came to court because people were charged. It just developed from then on. We were like minded people, I suppose.

Q. When did you get to know Daniel Morgan? – A. Quite early on. I remember meeting him a couple of times during the Essex job. I knew him from quite early on. I knew that they were partners.

Q. The relationship between you and Mr Morgan never got on to the same sort of level as the relationship you had with Mr Rees. – A. No.

Q. Can you tell me why? What was the basic difference? Here are two men. They are two partners. They are both in the same profession, although they do different jobs. You never really got friendly with Daniel Morgan. – A. I got friendly with him. I never met him as often in those days.

I do recall the Southern Investigations job to which Sid Fillery is referring and I would say that his comments are as accurate as can be regarding the interaction he had with John Rees and Fillery's acquaintance with Daniel Morgan.

Fillery goes onto to tell the Court of his service within the police and his consideration into the character of his friend John Rees and his concerns at being involved in the police investigation into the murder of Daniel Morgan.

This is an excerpt of Day 7, pages 16-17 of the Daniel Morgan Inquest. Detective Sergeant Sid Fillery is being cross-examined by Mr Goldsworthy.

MR GOLDSWORTHY: Mr Fillery, I do not want to ask you many questions. I think most of them have been dealt with. Tell her Majesty's Coroner and the jury this: you were a serving police officer, I think, for 23 years. Is that right? – A. Yes, all but.

Q. Did you leave the police force with a spotless record? – A. Yes.

Q. Having three commendations? – A. Yes, I think so.

Q. And having the police service good conduct medal? – A. Yes.

Q. So far as your friendship with Mr Rees is concerned, to your knowledge is he a man of good character? – A. Absolutely, yes.

Q. Not a shady character in any sense of the word? – A. In no sense of the word at all, no.

Q. Is it right that in the recent past he has been awarded the Binney award for courage in assisting the police? – A. Yes. It was the police in the Croydon area, I think.

Q. To deal with the details of one of two facts, the encounter that took place between you and Detective Superintendent Campbell on the Sunday following the killing, at the public house has been referred to, I would like to deal with a little of the detail of that, if you please. I think it has been confirmed that that took place at the Bricklayers Arms opposite Sydenham police station? – A. Yes.

Q. And it has been confirmed also that the persons present were you, Mr Campbell, Mr Jones and a police officer by the name of Kimberley Davies? – A. Yes.

Q. Had you gone into the office that day as a result of a summons from Mr Campbell? – A. No, but having said that, to be fair to him, he may have phoned my home and missed me. I went in earlier of my own accord.

Q. How early? – A. An hour earlier, and as I say, of my own accord.

Q. Up to that time had you suffered from progressive misgivings about your involvement in the murder inquiry? – A. Yes.

Q. Had you spoken to Detective Sergeant Davidson about that? – A. Yes.

Q. On how many occasions? – A. My recollection is two, perhaps three.

Q. It was accepted by Detective Superintendent Campbell that it was you who initiated the fact that you were taken off the squad. – A. Yes. On that point Mr Campbell did say to the court that I said I wanted to come off the squad because it may ruin my friendship with Rees. He is not quite correct there. What I said was I was in a no win situation, because Rees may say something to me which a policeman should feel suspicious about, and it would go right over my head because I had dealt with him on a different basis. Also, if Rees became a suspect and found out something about the murder squad, everybody is going to start looking at me straight away.

Q. Again it has been confirmed that it was thought desirable, because of your relationship with Rees, that you should be involved in the inquiry at the outset. – A. Yes. As I have said, normally a crime squad were running on these things for three days, but it was intimated to me that because I knew both parties that I would be on it for a lot longer.

This is an excerpt of Day 6, pages 5-7 of the Daniel Morgan Inquest. Detective Sergeant Davidson is further cross-examined by Miss June Tweedie.

MISS TWEEDIE: The next question is as to when the murder squad was first formed and when Mr Fillery was first notified. – A. Yes, I was the officer who was engaged in recruiting the staff for the murder inquiry. A few officers, probably one or two, I managed to contact that evening.

Q. Did that include Mr Fillery? – A. No, not Sergeant Fillery. Sergeant Fillery was in charge at that time of a crime squad of officers whom I wished to utilise on the inquiry. It was I who suggested to Mr Campbell that (a) we would require a crime squad and (b) it would be practical to have Sergeant Fillery who knew the deceased and his partner to work on the inquiry team. ---

Q. Did you know at the time that Sergeant Fillery was a friend of Mr Rees? – A. Yes, I did. I specifically suggested to Mr Campbell that as Sergeant Fillery was a friend of the Morgan family it would be a good idea to have him working on the inquiry.

Q. With hindsight, do you say that was probably not a good idea? – A. With hindsight it proved not to be a good idea, but at the time we appreciated that he had a working relationship with Mr Rees and not a deep personal friendship.

Q. You say that you considered it to be an important part of the investigation to take a statement from Mr. Rees. Do you actually have a list of the instructions you gave to Sergeant Fillery and at what time? – A. There are one, two ----

Q. I am interested in the earlier instructions. – A. The earliest written instruction I think you will find is on the 12ᵗʰ March. There are two on the 12ᵗʰ March. One was to obtain information from Mr. Rees as to Southern Investigations working on a particular project which does not concern the inquest, and the other one was to obtain a background statement from Mr.

Alastair Morgan. That was also issued on the 12th March. I also know from personal recollection that I did ask him to go straightaway to see Mr. Rees to obtain a statement concerning Daniel Morgan and the workings of the Company.

Q. Was that statement taken at the offices of Southern Investigations? – A. Yes, it was.

Q. You do not know whether he twice attended the offices or whether it was one occasion. – A. He may have attended the offices several times to obtain a statement.

MISS TWEEDIE: And your instructions were to go and take a statement. Did you give him instructions to remove files from the offices of Southern Investigations? – A. Sergeant Fillery is an officer with some considerable experience. He does not need instructions from me to tell him what or what not to do as far as removing exhibits or property is concerned. If he felt it was necessary to remove them he would have removed them. When he is sent to do an inquiry like that he brings back everything that he feels will be of use to my inquiry office. No, I would not specifically have had to say to him: "Will you get these documents" or "will you get those documents?" I would expect an officer of that service to do that automatically.

Q. Would you expect an officer to leave a receipt of the documents that he has taken? – A. No. We do not leave receipts for any documents that we take. When we collect property from anywhere we log it at the police station. A record is kept at the police station and it is for inspection. We do not normally leave receipts.

Q. Who would log those files, or whatever, at the police station? – A. The stuff is first brought into myself or to the exhibits officer. On this occasion I can remember property being brought back by Sergeant Fillery which I examined. I handed it to the exhibits officer and he records it in these books.

Q. There is absolutely no way of telling whether everything that left the offices of Southern Investigations that morning actually arrived at the police station. – A. In this case, when he took the statement Sergeant Fillery incorporated on Mr Rees's statement a list which says: "On Wednesday, 11th March, 1987, I handed to police certain documentation" and then listed it. That is listed in Mr. Rees's statement.

Q. Who was present when that statement was taken? – A. I cannot help you on that. It may have been a member of the crime squad.

Q. My question is whether, if there had been any collusion between Sergeant Fillery and Mr Rees, it would have been possible -- it sounds as though it would have been possible -- for Mr Rees and Mr Fillery to make the statement listing the documents that they said had been taken to the police station and not include any documents that have since disappeared. – A. It is certainly right that if Sergeant Fillery and Mr Rees did not wish to bring certain documents to the attention of the inquiry team, they would have had ample opportunity to do so.

Fillery has said that he was a known good friend of John Rees and an acquaintance of Daniel Morgan which is accurate. The men knew each other and Fillery had involvement in introducing John Rees to the security assignment at the ill-fated Belmont Car Auctions; a year before the murder in February 1986.

Fillery has said he socialised with Rees and Danny on the night of the 9th of March 1987 at the actual pub where 24 hours later Danny was found murdered.

Kevin Lennon has given testimony that John Rees told him that a plot existed which Detective Sergeant Sid Fillery was aware of and that Rees had stated his mates at Catford nick were to be involved or arrange the murder of Daniel Morgan and part of the alleged plot involved police at Catford undermining the police investigation once the murder had taken place.

Lennon said that once Daniel was dead Fillery would leave the police service by way of pension and join his friend John Rees at Southern Investigations. Detective Sergeant Fillery did indeed join John Rees at Southern Investigations sometime after April of 1988.

Sid Fillery was part of the initial murder investigation team for a number of days, being appointed certain tasks by Detective Superintendent Campbell, the lead police investigator of the initial Daniel Morgan murder investigation.

Tasks that closely involved Fillery were the undertaking of initial witness statements from Rees in relation to assisting the police with their inquiries and in the gathering of evidence in the pursuit of the assailant. Rees was one of the last known persons to see Danny alive and these interviews were undertaken at a time when the police have said John Rees was not a suspect.

As far as Kevin Lennon's testimony involving police at Catford deliberately undermining the police investigation once the murder had taken place, I would find this questionable on the basis of police protocol and procedures. To establish such a complex situation might not be as readily achievable as one may be led to believe.

This is an excerpt of Day 5, pages 63-65 of the Daniel Morgan Inquest. Detective Superintendent Campbell is cross examined by Miss June Tweedie.

Q. When was D/S Fillery first notified, that he was to be on the team? – A. Possibly Tuesday night, the night of the murder.

Q. Why would he have been notified on the night of the murder? – A. Because you ring officers as soon as you have got a murder to warn them to be at certain station the next morning.

Q. So you would have rung him along with a number of other officers? –A. I would not have rung him but one of my officers would have rung him.

Q. Within how long after the body had been found? – A. Possibly an hour.

Q. Is this something that information could be found. – A. It is just general practice, madam, that once a victim has been found a murder team is set up.

Q. --- A. I explained earlier that I have a detective sergeant who works with me exclusively on murder investigations.

Q. Who is this? – A. Detective Sergeant Davidson. He would have been the officer, I imagine, who was responsible for calling the staff out. In my absence he would direct the staff to whatever actions he considered necessary.

My opinion is that an experienced police detective such as Sergeant Sid Fillery being sanctioned or by allowing himself to become associated with the murder investigation at all was a catastrophic error of judgement by him and the Metropolitan Police Service. Fillery being a known acquaintance of the murder victim and having a close friendship with John Rees, the business partner and one of the last known persons to see the murder victim alive, Fillery should never have been involved at any stage of the murder investigation under any circumstances whatsoever.

Detective Superintendent Campbell goes on to inform the Coroner's Court of his opinion of what could have transpired pertaining to the actions of Detective Sergeant Sid Fillery. With shocking revelation as to a decorated police officer whom he or his sergeant subordinate had appointed as a member of the initial murder investigation squad and this is what he said.

This is an excerpt of Day 5, pages 66-68 of the Daniel Morgan Inquest. Detective Superintendent Campbell is being cross-examined by Miss June Tweedie.

Q. *Do you feel, with hindsight, that DS Fillery's involvement in the murder inquiry, given that he was then taken off the inquiry because of his involvement with John Rees, hampered the initial investigation in any way?* – A. *Possibly.*

Q. *In what way?* – A. *It might well have been that DS Fillery was possibly keeping John Rees abreast of the investigation.*

Q.--- *You did say it is possible you thought there was some hampering of the inquiry at an early stage by having DS Fillery on that inquiry.* – A. *I might as well tell you exactly what happened. On the Sunday, John Rees was spoken to at Sydenham police station. Having left the police station, he immediately used his car telephone.*

Q. *This is the Sunday following the murder?* – A. *That is right. I caused -- DS Fillery was off duty -- an officer to ring his number and the phone was engaged. I thought that he was too close to John Rees and I called him in. I spoke to him and at that stage, that is four days after the murder, he said to me, "I was going to suggest to you that I came of the investigation anyway" because he classed John Rees as a friend and he felt like we were asking him to get John Rees and he felt he was losing a relationship between a friend. In fact, either the day before or the day before that, he had spoken to my DS Davidson and suggested that he came off the inquiry. He was going to take a week's leave the following week and suggested that he came off the inquiry.*

Q. *By which time, if he had suggested coming off the inquiry a couple of days earlier, that would have been the Friday.* – A. *The day before, I think, the Saturday. I am not sure. As I say, he spoke to DS Davidson.*

Q. *And to your knowledge that was the only time he spoke to anyone?* – A. *As far as I am aware. He certainly only spoke to me on the Sunday and expressed his desire.*

Q. *As far as you were aware the only other time was to DS Davidson the day before.* – A. *As far as I know.*

Q. *Not three or four times, but only once.* – A. *Not to my knowledge.*

Q. By the time, to your knowledge, he first expressed anxiety about being on the team, he had already been on the team for a good three or four days. – A. Yes.

Q. If there were any sinister reasons, as has been put forward by Mr Lennon at the beginning of the week -- do you remember Mr Lennon's evidence that the murder should be carried out in the Catford area so that officers could deal with any evidence? He could have already done that by then. – A. He could already have achieved that.

Q. You agree with that? – A. Yes.

Superintendent Campbell actually agrees that Fillery could have already achieved some type of indiscretion in dealing with evidence or in hampering the earliest part of the investigation into the murder of Daniel Morgan, the first three or four days, as alleged by Kevin Lennon's testimony. It was Campbell's investigation and it is he who was calling the shots and allows Fillery to act under his instructions and command as part of the investigation team. Campbell then informed the court when he first became aware that police officers at Catford knew both Daniel Morgan and John Rees and this is what he said.

This is an excerpt of Day 5, pages 72-73 of the Daniel Morgan Inquest. Detective Superintendent Campbell is being cross-examined by Miss June Tweedie.

Q. We have heard evidence from PC Gibbs and PC Lathan that they were friends of Mr John Rees. – A. Yes. They met him socially, yes.

Q. I think it was PC Zdrojewski that Sergeant Fillery and John Rees were friends as well. – A. Yes.

Q. Was it generally well-known in Catford police station? – A. I subsequently found out it was.

Q. You subsequently found out it was well known. – A. That John Rees and Sergeant Fillery were friends, yes. But it was made known to me on the Wednesday that they were friends.

Q. Did you not see any conflict? – A. On the Wednesday morning, if I did not suggest it myself, I certainly agreed that to obtain a statement from the partner and background information on Daniel Morgan, Sergeant Fillery was an ideal man to do it.

Q. You did not really think at any time that there might be some conflict, even at those early stages, given that John Rees was the last person to see Daniel Morgan alive? – A. No.

Q. Do you know, after DS Fillery was taken off the inquiry I understand that he had health problems? Is that right? – A. Yes.

Q. When did those health problems occur? – A. I have details of those. I think it was shortly after his arrest. He was off sick.

Q. Shortly after his arrest? – A. Yes.

Q. When was he arrested? – A. 3rd April.

Q. When did he go off sick? – A. Shortly after that. Then he went sick again in September and remained sick until 19th March when he left the police force.

Q. What was the nature of this illness? – A. Stress.

Superintendent Campbell stated that he became fully aware of a relationship between Fillery, Rees and Morgan on Wednesday morning the 11th of March 1987; yet initially he saw no conflict of interest. He also became aware at that time of many other serving police officers being known to Rees who were currently stationed at Catford. I find it intriguing that almost everyone else at Catford police, apart from Superintendent Campbell, was well aware that an established relationship existed between Catford police officers and John Rees and an acquaintance in Daniel Morgan.

One of the largest bones of contention in this saga seems to be when Sergeant Sid Fillery takes his friend John Rees' initial witness statement on Wednesday 11th March 1987. The question relates to why there was no mention of the Belmont Car Auctions incident by either Rees or Fillery. Rees and Morgan were being sued by Belmont Car Auctions for the loss of the money from John Rees being robbed on the 18th of March 1986. Fillery had been involved in the introduction of Belmont Car Auctions and Southern Investigations for the purpose of security services. It is my opinion had this been mentioned in its entirety when Fillery was taking Rees' initial witness statement it would have shown that both Fillery and Rees had a previous relationship that also involved a crime having taken place in the robbery of John Rees. I believe this would have established an immediate conflict of interest to the police investigation into the murder of Daniel Morgan. This was Fillery's evidence to this at the inquest.

This is an excerpt of Day 7, pages 8-9 of the Daniel Morgan Inquest. Detective Sergeant Sid Fillery is being cross-examined by Mr Gompertz.

Q. ------ *You had taken a statement from Mr Rees himself on the 11th of March, the day you went to his premises.* – A. *Yes.*

Q. *I will be corrected, I am sure, if I am wrong, by the Coroner, but I don't think there is any mention in that statement of Belmont car auctions.* – A. *There is indirectly. If I remember, Rees gave me his reason for being in the pub that night was to arrange this loan. Somebody eventually -- I mean what you are suggesting, are you, is that I left something out of the statements?*

Q. *I am not making any suggestion of the moment, Mr Fillery, and I doubt very much whether I am permitted to make any suggestion. All I am asking you is what your recollection is. Are you saying that the Belmont car auctions saga was dealt with by Mr Rees in his statement?* – A. *No, because at that time Rees was not a suspect. Belmont car auctions were a thing of the past as far as I am concerned, but I will say this, it is worthy of mention, that Mr Rees on the first day, when I took a statement off him, explained that he was in that pub to obtain £10,000. If and when the Belmont car auctions became relevant, somebody is going to say "Well what is the £10,000 for?" Somebody is going to answer "They were being sued". Somebody else is going to say "By whom?" And so forth. So indirectly Belmont car auctions were mentioned, weren't they?*

Q. *What was said by Mr Rees -- and I am looking at page 54 of the statement bundle -- was this: "We met in that pub as a result of an arrangement made between us at about 11 AM that day. We chose that pub as we had arranged to meet Paul Goodridge who was going to introduce us to a third party in the hope of securing a loan. However, Mr Goodridge failed to appear because his wife had had an accident"* and so on. *You see all that is mentioned is the hope of securing a loan. – A. Yes.*

Q. There is no mention at all of Belmont car auctions, is there? – A. I suggest to you it is indirectly mentioned in as much as eventually, if it became relevant, somebody is going to say "A loan for what? What is the loan for?"

Q. My next question -- and let me make it perfectly plain I am not making any accusation, I am merely asking you, but if there is an objection, perhaps you will pause before you answer it -- there was no attempt, I suppose, to cover up the Belmont car auctions saga, was there? – A. No.

Q. That is your evidence? – A. That is the answer to the question.

I pose the question, how was it possible that Superintendent Campbell saw no conflict of interest; together with the evidence that only 24 hours prior to the murder of Daniel Morgan, Fillery, Rees and other police officers from Catford were all known to have been drinking together with the murder victim at the murder venue.

Had Sergeant Sid Fillery failed immediately to reveal to his superiors that he had very close links with Rees when he became part of the murder inquiry? Fillery took a statement from Rees, it did not include specific details of a robbery of John Rees and Fillery's association with both Rees and Belmont Car Auctions a year earlier, yet Fillery argued at the inquest that indirectly it was mentioned and there was no cover up. Fillery was not a novice in police investigation, far from it, he was a 23-year seasoned veteran and it is my opinion a man of experience someone who would not make schoolboy errors. Had those details emerged at the time it may well have brought both Rees and Fillery into direct conflict with the murder investigation of Daniel Morgan.

Superintendent Campbell with time to reflect from making his decisions, a year prior to the inquest, and then on viewing witness testimony before and during the inquest, Campbell says that Fillery could *"possibly"* have hampered the investigation. Detective Superintendent Campbell had it in his power from the moment he took control of the investigation to pick and choose the members of the murder squad.

I am of the opinion when Campbell learned on the morning of the 11th of March 1987 of a police connection between these men and especially a closer association between Fillery and Rees he should have isolated any doubt or consideration of conflict by interviewing, filtering or removing any investigation staff who knew the deceased or anyone associated with him, especially Fillery. The initial police investigation should have been seen as contaminated by way of prior association alone.

Sergeant Sid Fillery was arrested on 3rd April in connection to his actions whilst undertaking his duties as a police officer in the Daniel Morgan murder investigation. (See Chapter Daniel's Desk Diary). This is what he said transpired.

This is excerpt of Day 7, pages 18-20 of the Daniel Morgan Inquest. Sergeant Sid Fillery is being cross-examined by Mr Goldsworthy.

Q. I want to ask you, please, about the details of what occurred when you went to the office of Southern Investigations to uplift documentation, to go through his desk and so forth. – A. Yes.

Q. You have already told the court that the desk was piled high so you left that. – A. Yes.

Q. The court has heard that the majority of the Belmont Auction files in any event were in Mr Rees' briefcase. – A. So, I understand, yes.

Q. Which I understand has been taken by the police and returned. Is that right? – A. That is my understanding, yes.

Q. You have already told the court that you knew nothing of any file in relation to Belmont at that time. Who physically uplifted what documents were taken on that day? – A. One of my juniors P.C. Thorogood.

Q. Did you in fact physically touch any documentation there at all? – A. It would be unfair of me to say I never actually touched anything, but on this point, he was picking up and putting them in the plastic bag, with the assistance of Mr Newby, because it was just a mass of papers. I mean, as I said to Mr Newby "what of this is recent?"

Q. When the documentation had been transported, with, I believe, Mr Rees, is that right, to the police station? – A. I am not sure if he came with us or if he followed us in his own car.

Q. I see, but around the same time? – A. Yes.

Q. And at the police station Mr Rees, of course, made a statement. – A. Yes.

Q. In the course of making that statement was the documentation that had been uplifted listed in the statement? – A. Yes. The police procedure is that the documents have to be formally produced by somebody, so he said "well, this is the blotter which I identify as a blotter of Daniel Morgan's desk, exhibit so and so". That sort of thing.

Q Then, I think you went through the documentation at the police station. – A. Piece by piece, yes.

Q. Who was the officer who was with you? – A. Mr Thorogood.

Q. Was Mr Thorogood present throughout the procuring of the documentation at the office? – A. Yes.

Q. Was he present with you and the documentation throughout the journey to the police station? – A. I think he drove, yes.

Q. At the police station was the documentation gone through with Mr Rees when he was making his statement in an open office? – A. Yes.

Q. In the presence of other people? – A. Yes.

Q. Was Mr Thorogood around, in and out, while that was going on? – A. Yes. He was two and fro making coffee and that sort of thing.

Q. The court has heard Mr Campbell say that there is no evidence that you in any way tampered with the inquiry. Let me ask you this. So far as that documentation is concerned, did *you have the opportunity to do so? In other words, were you alone with the documentation at any time? – A. The documentation I brought back from Rees's office?*

Q. Yes. – A. It is fair to state I wasn't being overseen.

Q. But were you alone? – A. No. I mean there was always somebody in the office doing something. It was the crime squad office I used.

Q. So far as being medically discharged from the police force is concerned, what was the major contributory factor to the stress condition from which you now suffer? – A. I was in the police force 23 years, or 22 ½ when this happened. I threw myself into the police force. My wife is in court now. The police force came before my family, if the truth is known, for 22 ½ years, and suddenly there is a knock on my door at 6.30 in the morning and I am arrested, and it just threw me, threw me out balance.

Q. Arrest for murder? – A. Yes. Or complicity was the word used. It is hard to imagine, but 22 ½ years, and it did come before my family in many, many instances, and then at 6.30 that morning, I still haven't recovered from it now.

Q. Does it follow that the major factor in your discharge was something that occurred after the murder took place? – A. Yes.

Q. Until you were in fact discharged, did you have any idea that you were going to be? – A. I think towards the end I had an idea that the police force wasn't for me.

Q. At what point did that come about? – A. Quite late on in the proceedings.

Q. What month or what year? – A. I can't say, Sir. I mean, I don't know, maybe Christmas time. I can't put a date on it.

Q. You mean Christmas 1987? – A. Yes.

Sid Fillery informed the Coroner's Court that he had no plans prior to Daniel's murder to leave the police force in anyway and states he first gave consideration to this in or around Christmas of 1987. So, the question is how is it possible that Kevin Lennon made a statement that he had knowledge of this, many months before it was even given consideration or actually occurred.

Kevin Lennon's evidence and allegations of Sergeant Sid Fillery being involved in an alleged plot to murder Daniel Morgan were in conflict and unsubstantiated, before and after the fact.

Sid Fillery remained a person of interest in the police investigations surrounding the murder of Daniel Morgan. It is only fair to say that Sid Fillery has always denied any wrongdoing or having any involvement whatsoever in the murder of Daniel Morgan. There has been no successful prosecution against him regarding any allegations related to the case.

Sergeant Sid Fillery retired from the police service with an exemplary record and was not the subject of any police internal disciplinary action regarding any of these allegations; he attained the police Good Service Conduct Medal and achieved three commendations.

There is however one alarming aspect in character and conduct surrounding Sid Fillery and this came about at the end of 2002. Whilst Fillery was working at Southern Investigations police officers of the anti-corruption squad raided the offices and seized Fillery's computer. What they found on the computer was shocking - a number of indecent images of children.

In October 2003 Sid Fillery faced a criminal prosecution at Bow Street Magistrates Court; District Judge Caroline Tibbs presiding. Fillery pleaded guilty to making indecent images of children. In sentencing him the judge said she had taken into account his admission of guilt and his defence claim that he was of previous good character. The judge gave him a three-year community rehabilitation order, a conviction such as this would also involve his name being added to the sex offenders register.

In February 2017 Sid Fillery is seen in The High Court of Justice. He along with John Rees, Glenn Vian and Garry Vian filed a civil law suit against the Metropolitan Police for malicious prosecution in connection to the Daniel Morgan murder. Sid Fillery's claim was successful and he was awarded substantial damages.

This is an excerpt from the Guardian online dated Friday, 17th February 2017 by Vikram Dodd, Police and Crime Correspondent.

Three men charged with the 1987 murder of Daniel Morgan lost their case that police maliciously tried to get them convicted. Rees, Garry and Glenn Vian were tried for murder the case collapsed in 2011. Sid Fillery was charged with conspiracy to pervert the course of justice; the crown dropped the case against him. At the high court, Mr Justice Mitting ruled against Rees and the Vians, Fillery won part of his claim. A claim of misfeasance in public office went in Fillery's favour. The witness against him was deemed unreliable and had been mishandled by the lead detective.

The police lead Detective referred to in the article was Chief Superintendent Dave Cook and we shall learn more about him in this book. (See Chapter The Daniel Morgan Independent Panel)

△ △ △

Detective Constable Duncan Hanrahan

Detective Constable Duncan Hanrahan was a known friend of John Rees and an acquaintance of Daniel Morgan. He was stationed for a time at Norbury, South London only a couple of miles from Thornton Heath and the offices of Southern Investigations. I find Duncan Hanrahan to be one of the most intriguing witnesses who has ever given evidence in the Daniel Morgan police investigations. I met Hanrahan on a number of occasions at the offices of Southern Investigations and whilst in the company of Daniel and others at pubs in the Thornton Heath area. This is some of his witness testimony at the inquest.

DANIEL MORGAN SOUTHERN INVESTIGATION

This is an excerpt of Day 4, pages 49-53 of the Daniel Morgan Inquest. Detective Constable Duncan Hanrahan is being examined by the Coroner.

Q. *You made a statement on 17th March 1987.* – A. *Yes, I did.*

Q. *In that statement you suggested that you knew Rees and Morgan. How long had you known them at that particular point in time?* – A. *I had known them since 1985. I think it was April 1985 when I was first posted at Norbury.*

Q. *In what capacity during those two years did you know them? Obviously, you were policeman. Did you know them socially as well as knowing them as policemen?* – A. *I knew them more socially than anything else. I met Rees through a solicitor, Mr Goodridge, who has already given evidence, and I met Morgan through Rees.*

Q. *Was there any particular reason that you socialised more with Rees than Morgan?* – A. *He had more contacts with police and people I knew then Morgan did.*

Q. *Were you also conversant about the Belmont Motor Auctions....* – A. *No, I was not.*

Q. *Did you know anything about it?* – A. *I knew about it when Mr Rees was robbed. I was the night duty CID officer at Norbury division at the time.*

Q. *On the night of the robbery?* – A. *Yes, I was.*

THE CORONER: (to the witness). *Were you on duty when that robbery occurred?* – A. *Yes, I was.*

Q. *What can you tell us about the robbery? Were you in charge of the investigation?* – A. *No, I was not. I did the initial investigation. If it had been a more simple matter, I would have dealt with it at the time. I considered it to be more than a straightforward robbery.*

Q. *What bothered you about that robbery?* – A. *Well, to attack somebody outside his house and get £18,000 or at the time it was reported to be in excess of £30,000 you would have to be the luckiest mugger in the world and I felt that either somebody had set Mr Rees up to be robbed ------*

Q. *You say that he would have been the luckiest person in the world. What do you mean by that?* – A. *I felt that somebody had to have some inside knowledge of Mr Rees' movements and the fact that he was going to carry that much money to rob him. He is not the sort of person in my opinion who would in the normal course of events be the target for a street robbery.*

Q. *That is the way you felt about it. When you investigated it, what did you think was odd about that robbery?* – A. *I got the story from a WPC who took the initial report. I then spoke to Mr Rees at the Mayday Hospital, and he confirmed what she had told me about.*

Q. *You may have heard in evidence -- I do not know whether you were here -- that Mr Thorne went to see him in hospital.* – A. *Yes, I did.*

Q. *He was not terribly impressed. He thought there was something odd about the credibility of that story. Is that the way that you felt about it?* – A. *Not initially about Mr Rees' credibility. I felt that it was an inside job.*

Q. *An inside job?* – A. *Certainly somebody who was connected with the car auctions had either set the robbery up or been involved in it.*

Q. You went to the hospital. Somebody suggested that he was in the hospital for six days. Was he in the hospital for six days? – A. I think he was released initially that night and then went back to hospital for a number of days. I know that he was in hospital for a number of days as a result of it.

Q. You went to see him in hospital. – A. Yes, I did.

Q. Did you speak to the sister? – A. Yes, I did.

Q. I have the impression that you were not impressed with the whole set up when you went to the ward because he did not seem to be unduly perturbed about the robbery. Is that right? – A. I was told by the casualty sister at the hospital that Mr Rees was unconcerned by it. That was an opinion that was shared by WPC West - - - - -

Q. Did you say "unconcerned"? – A. Yes.

Q. How much investigation went on about that robbery? Here is a man who has been robbed of £18,000. You think that it might have been an inside job. What went on after that? – A. That night I caused inquiries to be made by the Lee Road police station to check the night safe. They confirmed that the lock in the night safe had been tampered with.

Q. It had been tampered with? – A. Yes. The hospital confirmed that Mr Rees had irritant of one sort or another sprayed in his eyes. Mr Rees did not want to make a statement that night neither did his wife. That was really the extent of my inquiries into it. I did a report for the officers who came on to duty at 9 o'clock in the morning. It was not an investigation that I would have undertook in any case because I was a Norbury officer. Norbury Division covers South Norwood, but South Norwood police station actually investigated that robbery. It was on their ground.

Here we have yet another situation where a serving police officer (Detective Constable Duncan Hanrahan) known to both Rees and Morgan undertook an initial investigation into a crime (street robbery) upon his friend John Rees. The robbery we know of £18,200 being the night's takings on Tuesday the 18th of March 1986 from the Belmont Car Auctions.

The subsequent investigation alerts police about concerns to the possibilities that the robbery might have been an inside job. It is also said that there were reservations of a hospital emergency department sister and investigating WPC West who both formed an opinion that John Rees seemed *"Unconcerned by it"*. Yet we also have Sergeant Sid Fillery telling us that it was John Rees that was initially of the opinion the robbery might have been undertaken by persons known to him.

The situation between the two friends, Rees and Hanrahan, becomes even more convoluted after Daniel was murdered; a time when John Rees did become a suspect in the murder. This is what Detective Constable Duncan Hanrahan had to say at the inquest.

This is an excerpt of Day 4, pages 54–57 of the Daniel Morgan Inquest. Detective Constable Duncan Hanrahan is being examined by the Coroner.

Q. I'm going to put something to you and I would like you to try and explain this to the jury and to the court. After the death of Daniel Morgan am I right in saying that Mr Rees was a suspect? – A. Yes, he was.

Q. Obviously he was arrested and then released. – A. Yes, he was.

Q. Am I also equally right in saying that sometime after this you had an understanding with the Superintendent who is in charge of this case? – A. Yes, that is correct.

Q. Who was it? – A. Superintendent Campbell.

Q. What was the understanding that you had? – A. The understanding we had was that if I met Mr Rees, I would inform him, prior to meeting him, and tell him anything that occurred during the meetings.

Q. Would I be right in saying that you were now to use that Americanism a "plant"? You were going to be friendly with Mr Rees and you are also going to report back to Mr Campbell. – A. That is correct, sir.

Q. From now on you were in a way part of the investigation of Mr Rees. Would you agree? – A. Yes, sir.

Q. I would also like to ask you this. Over the next few months some very odd things happened indeed. – A. Yes, sir, they did.

Q. You tell the court what happened? – A. I had a number of meetings with Mr Rees. One meeting was in a wine bar in Norbury.

Q. Was that with Mr Rees? – A. Yes.

Q. Do you know the date of that? – A. No, Sir. It is in my statement.

Q. Carry on. – A. I had been interviewed by Mr Campbell a few days previously.

Q. Now you were put in the picture, were you not? – A. Yes, I was, sir. He wanted to know what had taken place during the interview, what I had said, what questions I had been asked, and who had interviewed me. I told him that I had made a statement with regard to my dealings with the robbery allegation and I had been interviewed by Mr Jones and Mr Campbell.

Q. You told this to Mr Rees, did you not? – A. Yes, I did.

Q. Before you go any further, did you tell Mr Campbell right at the beginning that you knew them both and you knew them socially? – A. Yes, I did.

Q. Very well. Carry on. – A. I am not sure whether it was this meeting or a previous meeting Mr Rees told me that he had been arrested, he was unhappy with the way he had been treated by the police, that he could point the murder inquiry in certain directions to look for a suspect, but he would no longer cooperate with them.

Q. I would just like this a bit slower. He said that he was unhappy with the way the police were investigating it. Was he unhappy with the way the police were investigating him or generally speaking? – A. Both really. He was particularly unhappy about being arrested.

Q. Can you understand what he meant by that? – A. He just said that he was not going to cooperate with them anymore. He was going to give them no more help. Did he give a reason for that? – A. Just a general reason, that was because of the way he felt he had been arrested and treated as a suspect.

Q. You, of course, made no reference to him that you were going to report this conversation to Mr Campbell? – A. No, I did not.

Q. As far as Mr Rees was concerned, you were the perfect confidant. You had a foot now in both camps. He had you as a friend and presumably you would tell him some story of how the investigation was going. – A. I think that was probably his idea, yes.

Q. What is the next thing that happened? – A. There was a further meeting in a pub in South Norwood. During this meeting he expressed a great desire to harm the reputation certainly of Detective Superintendent Campbell and Detective Inspector Jones.

Q. I would like you to make that very clear. I want you to enlarge on it. – A. He spoke of getting a journalist to write an article about the murder inquiry which would be very critical of police officers, in particular Mr Campbell and Mr Jones. That conversation took place in the wine bar in Norbury, not in a pub in South Norwood.

Q. It was in a wine bar in Norbury. – A. Yes.

Q. What did he want to do? How was he going to discredit the Superintendent in this case? He does not know the Superintendent. The Superintendent was unknown to him. How was he going to do this? – A. He was going to do it by having a journalist write an article that would be very critical of the police.

Q. Did he in actual fact do that? – A. Not to my knowledge, no.

Q. That was one of his ideas, was it not? – A. Yes, it was.

Q. What were his other ideas? – A. He said that part of the article would claim that Mr Jones and Mr Campbell were constantly drunk and not investigating the matter at all.

Q. Did you say that to him that it was totally untrue? – A. I did not.

Q. You did not say that, but you thought that you would go along with him. – A. I went along with virtually everything that he said.

Q. That was part of your job, because you were really taking this back to Mr Campbell. – A. Yes, that is correct, sir.

Q. He wanted to discredit Superintendent Campbell and he wanted to discredit Detective Inspector Jones. – A. Yes, that is correct.

Q. Drunkenness was the first thing. How was he going to do that? – A. He said that he would get a journalist friend of his to write this article. That was as far as it went on that occasion. On another occasion he told me that he was going to have Detective Inspector Jones, as he called it, "fitted up". Whether he was going to do this himself or get other people to do it he did not say.

Q. Now that is an expression which is often used. It is used in American films and it is used in English films. Am I right in saying that "fitted up" means to get him charged with something which is bogus? – A. Certainly, sir, yes. His plan was to have something planted in Mr Jones' car.

Q He was going to have something planted in Mr Jones' car? – A. That is correct.

Q. What sort of thing was he going to plant in Mr Jones' car? – A. He did not say. I got the impression that he was talking about drugs or something like that. He never actually said what it would be.

Q. Did he have any other ideas? He was planting things in Mr Jones' car. What about Superintendent Campbell? – A. He did not actually go any further about Superintendent Campbell.

Q. You must have gone along with this. – A. Yes, I did.

Q. Did you have any more meetings with him? – A. I had other meetings with him, yes.

Q. What other ideas did he have? – A. Basically his main idea was to have Mr Jones and Mr Campbell fitted up. He spoke of making allegations of Mr Jones' behaviour in his personal life.

Hanrahan's testimony informed the Coroner that he was recruited by Superintendent Campbell as a covert plant at a time when John Rees was a suspect and a person of interest in the Daniel Morgan murder investigation. It is understood that DC Duncan Hanrahan had no prior undercover experience. Hanrahan's role was to report any relevant information that might assist the murder investigation. The content of the statements made by Detective Constable Duncan Hanrahan in relation to his conversations and meetings with John Rees were shocking in nature, so much so John Rees' counsel Mr Nutter said the following to the Coroner in the absence of the jury.

This is an excerpt of Day 4, pages 59-61 of the Daniel Morgan Inquest. Detective Constable Duncan Hanrahan is being examined by the Coroner.

MR NUTTER: *Sir, the criticism is that the police have got it into their heads that they have their own idea of who committed this murder and have proceeded to ignore other matters and concentrated on their own innermost conviction or hunch, and even that which Mr Hanrahan has described is not on the basis of covering tracks for Mr Rees, it is on the basis of trying to get the investigation properly conducted.*

THE CORONER: *It seems a very odd way of changing the method of investigation or expressing your dissatisfaction to have drugs planted in a detective inspector's car --- that is a very serious thing --- and then to get a journalist to write an article to say that both police officers are drunks.*

MR NUTTER: *We have not had any evidence of that. All that this is, is evidence of an alleged conversation, the only witness being the officer here. It was not acted upon and the reason for those sentiments being expressed in the first place was apparently, on even that which the officer has to say the honourable one, of trying to see that the investigation was properly carried out, and albeit that these dishonourable means are being suggested, in my respectful submission it is not going to assist this jury in any way to pursue the matter any further.*

MR GOMPERTZ: *All that I would say is that my learned friend Mr Nutter's objection seems to be that this evidence is prejudicial to his client and therefore should not be admitted.*

There is no basis in law of excluding it. I would invite you to continue with your examination of the witness.

MR NUTTER: *Sir, it is your discretion and your discretion is doubtless a matter of relevance. In my respectful submission, this is not relevant to the inquiry that we have here. It is all very interesting and if true is scandalous but it is not really relevant to the questions which the jury have to decide.*

THE CORONER: *I will put it to Mr Hanrahan another way in fairness to the comments that you are making. (To the witness). Was there anything that Mr Rees suggested to you to put the investigation off the track leading towards him? – A. I am sorry; sir, but I do not understand the question.*

Q. So far, we have had comments made to discredit Detective Inspector Jones and Superintendent Campbell. One could feel that he was obviously not very well disposed towards them and wanted to get them back, is the term, I think, you used, but now counsel for Mr Rees has brought this point up. Did he suggest anything to you that you should do or that he was going to do that would divert the investigation away from him? – A. Not directly.

Q. You started off by saying that he had other ideas initially. – A. So that he could point the investigating officers in other directions.

Q. When you say that he could point the investigating officers in other directions, did he mean the direction of being thrown out of the service for being perpetually drunk and having drugs in the car or did he mean that he wanted to point it in a different way? – A. He wanted to give them leads that would take them away from him, but he said he would not do that because he was not going to cooperate with the inquiry any more.

Q. In other words he had links that would take them away from him, but he did not want to cooperate. – A. That is correct, sir.

THE CORONER: *(To the witness). Are you still friendly with Mr Rees? – A. Up to this point I have been, Sir.*

Q. Up to this point you have been? – A. Yes.

Q. Do you think that the friendship will, no doubt, end? – A. I should think so, yes.

Detective Constable Duncan Hanrahan told the court that Rees had said to him that he wanted Campbell and Jones "fitted up" and that one of the ways this was suggested was by way of what he believed to be the planting of drugs in Inspector Jones' car. Mr Nutter, Counsel for John Rees said that Hanrahan's testimony was "*very interesting and if true would be scandalous*".

A simple form of evidence gathering was available to the police investigation, that of a concealed wire. A recording device which could have been worn by Hanrahan to corroborate his testimony by way of audio recording the content of the alleged threats made by John Rees toward both Campbell and Jones.

This is an excerpt of Day 4, page 66 of the Daniel Morgan Inquest. Detective Constable Duncan Hanrahan is cross-examined by Mr Nutter.

Q. There is one very good way that an undercover double agent can protect himself and that is that when he is having a conversation with somebody who is supposed to be his friend and who he thinks he is the friend of the double agent he can turn up nowadays with a suitable set of recording equipment so that that conversation can be recorded. Did that happen on this occasion or any of these occasions? – A. No, it did not.

THE CORONER: *Why were you not wired up? – A. It was not a decision that was in my hands, sir.*

MR NUTTER: *Who was the highest authority who was consulted within the police force to your knowledge to permit you to undertake these covert operations? – A. I do not know, sir. Mr Campbell was aware of them. He may have spoken to officers' senior to him. I do not know.*

Detective Constable Duncan Hanrahan was recruited by Superintendent Campbell because of his friendship with John Rees. He was assigned the task of a double agent in an attempt to obtain any incriminating evidence however he undertakes this role without the aid of a concealed recording device which no doubt would have assisted in corroborating evidence surrounding the allegations and threats Hanrahan says Rees made.

This is an excerpt of Day 4, page 68 of the Daniel Morgan Inquest. Superintendent Campbell is recalled and further examined by the Coroner.

Q. Some comment has been made just now about using an officer in this way to get information from a suspect. Would you like to say something about that? – A. Yes, sir. That was purely my decision and I am entitled within the force's guidelines to make that decision for an officer to obtain information for me. There has been mention that perhaps Detective Constable Hanrahan should have had a concealed tape recorder. Again, that was my decision not to use it. I can explain that if you wish, sir.

Q. It might be a good thing to explain that at this particular stage. I know that some people are wired up and some people are not wired up and so forth, but perhaps you would like to explain because this has been asked so I think we should ask you. – A. Well, very briefly, sir, my decision not to have a concealed tape recorder on Mr Hanrahan was because I felt that possibly Mr Rees in his line of business would have suspected that that might have been used and might have rub down, if you like, Mr Hanrahan to see if he was wearing a concealed tape recorder.

Q. You felt that because he was in that line of business he must be conversant with all methods of detection and so forth which would be stock in trade for him. It was more dangerous for Hanrahan to wear it. I can accept that.

Superintendent Campbell said he thought John Rees, in his line of business, would possibly have suspected Detective Constable Duncan Hanrahan might have been wired with a recording device. Superintendent Campbell did not deny it when the Coroner put to him, *"you felt that John Rees must be conversant with all methods of detection"*.

However, with this knowledge Campbell does mention that his investigation had the ability to use plants to obtain information. Campbell's investigation had the technical know-how in wiring a recording device. This would have included the ability to wire other persons involved in the police investigation. Persons that might have included Ex Detective Inspector Laurie Bucknole and Southern Investigations bookkeeper Kevin Lennon. Recordings of this type would have been invaluable to any prosecution to show evidence existed of any alleged crime or plot actually taking place.

This was not the last that we would learn about Detective Constable Duncan Hanrahan. On leaving the Metropolitan Police Duncan Hanrahan established a business of a private investigator, his friendship with John Rees did not seem to have come to an end as suggested at the inquest. He retained many friends within the police service. Many police officers at that time were Freemasons.

On Friday 19th of March 1999, the retired police officer then private investigator found himself at the Old Bailey Central Criminal Court facing very serious criminal charges.

This is an excerpt from the Guardian online dated Saturday, 20th March 1999 by Duncan Campbell, Crime Correspondent.

A pattern of institutional corruption in the Metropolitan police emerged yesterday as a former police officer who acted as a conduit between the underworld and corrupt detectives was jailed for eight years and four months. Duncan Hanrahan had blown the whistle on former colleagues. At the Old Bailey he pleaded guilty to offences including conspiracy to rob, steal, supply drugs and pervert the course of justice. The judge at the Old Bailey Mr Justice Blofeld said: "The offences strike at the very roots of justice. If society is to have a future, the police force must be above corruption."

If the revelations of character and conduct of Duncan Hanrahan in 1999 and Sid Fillery in 2003 was not scandalous enough even more was yet to come. *Scandalous* was a very precise word used by Mr Nutter, legal counsel for Mr John Rees at the inquest in 1988. In just a few years a chain of events unravelled involving John Rees that would trigger circumstances and establish a tremendous coincidence pertaining to the inquest witness testimony of Duncan Hanrahan.

△ △ △

William Jonathan Rees

Almost from the beginning John Rees has been seen by the police as a person of interest in the Daniel Morgan murder investigation. He was one of the last people to see him alive. Witness testimony has been presented by the police that strongly suggest, to some people in the court of public opinion, that John Rees may have had some involvement in the murder.

In April 1987 Rees was arrested on suspicion of Daniel's murder and subsequently released without charge. In February 1989 Rees is charged with murder and in May of 1989 the charges were dropped due to lack of evidence. In October 2002 John Rees is again arrested in connection to the murder and is bailed. In 2003 evidence for a prosecution fails as the Crown Prosecution Service reports insufficient evidence exists and John Rees who was previously bailed is released.

In April 2008 Rees is arrested on suspicion of the murder; in October 2009 legal argument begins. At the Old Bailey in March 2011 the director of public prosecutions drops the case against him. It is only fair to say John Rees has never been convicted of any offence surrounding the murder of Daniel Morgan. John Rees has always denied any involvement in the murder.

That said it does not mean that Rees has not been prosecuted and found guilty in a criminal court of law pertaining to any other offence unrelated to the murder of Daniel Morgan.

Duncan Hanrahan gave evidence to the Daniel Morgan Inquest regarding conversations he had with John Rees. Particularly in relation to allegations that Hanrahan said Rees made comment to 'fit up' police officers Campbell and Jones by planting incriminating evidence (of what Hanrahan formed the opinion was drugs) in Detective Inspector Jones' car. These were John Rees' responses to the allegations.

This is an excerpt of Day 8, pages 93-94 of the Daniel Morgan Inquest. John Rees is being cross-examined by Miss June Tweedie.

Q. ---- *One further line of questioning, Mr. Rees. Did you hear the evidence of DC Hanrahan?* – A. *Part of it, yes.*

Q. *Is it correct that you had leads which might have helped the police with their inquiries, later last year after the killing of Mr Morgan, but that you were not prepared to cooperate with the police by giving that information?* – A. *No, that is not true.*

Q. *Do you know what he is referring to?* – A. *Yes.*

Q. *Did you give that information to the police?* – A. *The leads? There were no leads.*

Q. *At no time have you had any information that might have led to the killer of Daniel Morgan?* – A. *I have had a discussion. I have the evidence which I have discussed and certain points which I have discussed with Mr Campbell but for some reason they were not pursued.*

Q. *So you did not tell Mr Hanrahan at any time that you had any information that you were not prepared to give to the police?* – A. *No.*

Q. *Did you tell Mr Hanrahan that you are thinking of getting someone to write an article critical of the investigating team?* – A. *No.*

Q. *And that Mr Campbell was constantly drunk?* – A. *No.*

Q. *Did you suggest that you were going to plant something in Mr Jones' car?* – A. *No.*

Q. *And make allegations about his personal life?* – A. *Not at all.*

THE CORONER: *You deny all this?* – A. *I deny all this, sir, yes.*

John Rees absolutely denied the allegations that Hanrahan said he made whilst Hanrahan was acting as a plant on behalf of Superintendent Duncan Campbell.

This is an excerpt of Day 8, pages 95,96,98,99 of the Daniel Morgan Inquest. John Rees is being cross-examined by Mr Nutter.

MISTER NUTTER: - - - - - *Did you murder Daniel Morgan? – A. I did not.*

Q. *Did you arrange for Catford police to murder Daniel Morgan? – A. I did not.*

Q. *Did you arrange for anybody to kill Daniel Morgan? – A. No.*

Q. *Did you have anything to do with his death? – A. No.*

Q. *Did you tell Mr Lennon that you were planning to kill Daniel Morgan? – A. I certainly did not.*

Q. *Did you tell him that you had persuaded friends in the Catford police force to do the job for you? – A. No.*

Q. *Mr Gompertz asked you questions arising out of his concern as to the possibility that it was some sort of random killing, and gave you an opportunity this morning to give any account you could of possible explanations arising on the lines of a random killing. Do you remember being asked those questions? – A. Yes.*

Q. *You heard questions being put on your behalf to certain witnesses, vis a vis, people in the car park. Having reflected upon that is there anything you would like to add about the car park and people who might have used it? – A. Yes. Throughout this inquiry, Sir, throughout the police inquiry there was quite a few allegations that certain officers, and especially Sgt Fillery, were feeding me with information as to the lines of inquiry the police were taking, especially concerning myself. This is absolutely untrue. The only information I have been given from friends in the police force is details about the inquiries not being dealt with and the lines of inquiry that have not been pursued with a vigour that they claim to have done so. I think, Mr Nutter, talking about this particular occasion in the car park, there was information that a drugs deal was being undertaken that very night in the car park.*

THE CORONER: *How do you know that? – A That was information given to me, sir.*

Q. *Did you tell the police? – A. I discussed this with Mr Campbell. He stated that members of his squad had spent some time with the crime squad who was investigating this allegation and that officers had been present when a certain address was raided, but the information that I received was that that certainly was not the case. That very little time or concern was being given to that particular inquiry at all, as to several other inquiries that they were given. Mr Campbell and Mr Jones complained bitterly about the allegations that I have been unwilling to assist them with their inquiries.*

Q. *Have you? – A. No, sir. It is that any information I gave to the police, even on the particular day I talked about having a discussion with Mr Campbell, it was always referred to as "one of their infamous red herrings" but any information I gave was treated as if it was to put them off the scent, so to speak.*

Q. What was the next occasion when anything happened which formed any form of disagreement or dispute between you and the officers investigating the inquiry? – A. It wasn't the officers; it was just one particular officer.

THE CORONER: *Who was the officer? – A. DI Jones, sir. It was prior to our arrest on 3rd April. On numerous occasions I had been interviewed by DI Jones and at no time, as on the night of the murder, did he take any notes, did he take a statement from me, because I found myself being involved in silly arguments about whether I said something or I hadn't said it, or whether he had said it or not said it. I suggested on numerous occasions that I make a statement and a statement be given, and it wasn't.*

Q. What was the next thing after the matter of disagreement with Mr Jones about not writing things down that was the cause of conflict and a disagreement between you? – A. Our arrest.

Q. What was it about your arrest that you did not particularly like? – A. Prior to my arrest I had been available and welcomed the police nearly 7 days a week, long hours, forgone my business so I could spend time with them; I gave them every assistance I could; every item they wanted; any inquiries, answered any question, I was at their beck and call 24 hours a day until 3rd April and then the bombshell hit us. Arrest warrants were issued.

THE CORONER: *That was the 3rd April? – A. Yes, sir.*

Q. What are you actually saying about this arrest? What complaint are you making about it? Are you making the complaint that you should not have been arrested because you had helped the police previously? – A. I am saying, sir, as Miss Tweedie has clearly said during the line of questioning, that I have not been assisting the police with their inquiries. Prior to our arrest on 3rd April I gave every assistance I could, and since. Officers have even since attended my offices. It is just one particular officer.

John Rees told the court he was willing and able to assist the police inquiry however he felt the investigation and any potential leads early on were not being investigated thoroughly. Rees said he continued to assist the police inquiries until his arrest in connection to the murder on the 3rd of April.

A conflict of evidence seems apparent regarding Detective Constable Duncan Hanrahan and Southern Investigations bookkeeper Kevin Lennon whose statements and allegations are denied in their entirety by John Rees. This is further explored as follows.

This is an excerpt of Day 8, pages 102-104 of the Daniel Morgan Inquest. John Rees is cross-examined by Mr Nutter.

Q. You remember the evidence of the officer, Mr Hanrahan. – A. Yes.

Q. Can you give your explanation, your side of the story as regards his double agent activity with you? – A. Yes. I was fully aware of it in the early days of the inquiry. I believe DC Hanrahan was interviewed on a number of occasions by Supt Campbell and DC Hanrahan did inform me that he had been instructed by Mr Campbell and Mr Jones to relate back to him any conversation we had.

THE CORONER: Are you suggesting that Hanrahan was a double- double agent, so to speak? – A. If you want to see it that way, sir, yes.

Q. It gets more and more complicated. Carry on. – A. I have known DC Hanrahan for some time and we were drinking partners. During such sessions of drinking, we have both got a similar sense of humour.

Q. You are not suggesting the things he said about you, getting people fixed up for drink and driving and that sort of thing, was part of a sense of humour? – A. Yes, sir.

Q. Putting drugs in somebody's car? – A. Drugs were not mentioned, sir.

Q. And suggesting the Chief Superintendent was a drunk? – A. No, sir, that wasn't suggested. Drugs, wasn't suggested anyway.

Q. Are you denying these things that were said by officer Hanrahan? – A. Officer Hanrahan came out with quite a few suggestions himself, sir. I suggest that those comments were his, his suggestion.

MR NUTTER: Can you give any account or explanation for why Mr Hanrahan would give false evidence to this court? – A. No. I know that shortly after Daniel's death that Duncan Hanrahan expressed a genuine concern to me that he was a suspect in a robbery.

Q. That was Mr Hanrahan who expressed concern that he himself was a suspect? – A. Yes, a genuine concern.

THE CORONER: In the robbery of Belmont? – A. That is right, sir, yes, because he was one of the investigating officers on that initially.

MR NUTTER: Why might he, a serving police officer of the Metropolitan police, be a suspect in a robbery?

THE CORONER: Here is the question. Do you know any reason why officer Hanrahan should be involved in a robbery which you were involved in to do with the Belmont Auctions?

MR NUTTER: That wasn't the question. Any reason that he might be suspected of involvement in that robbery and I suspect this man might be able to give us a very relevant if surprising answer. – A. I believe -- he was certainly accused, he told me he had been accused by Mr Campbell and Mr Jones of being an informant in the robbery and he was clearly a suspect. I think the stress of that certainly led to Mr Hanrahan's divorce.

THE CORONER: ---- But what we are asking about just now is that you suggested Hanrahan was a suspect in the robbery. Are you suggesting that because he was a suspect in the robbery, that in some way, that had something to do with his role as an agent trying to get information from you? – A. Yes, sir. That is what he told me.

Q. That is what he told you? – A. Yes, and he asked me to supply him with any information, any leads I could get, any theories I had regarding Daniel's death, that I should pass them through him so that it would in some way redeem him with Mr Campbell and Mr Jones.

MR NUTTER: Is it the case that at any stage you have set out to hamper the investigations of those who have been trying to get to the root of the answer to the question "who killed Daniel Morgan"? – A. Absolutely not.

Rees confirmed that conversations took place with Hanrahan and as drinking partners they joked about getting people "fitted up" for drink-driving and this was by way of a sense of humour. Rees said he knew that Hanrahan was a plant for Superintendent Campbell. Rees goes on to say that Hanrahan told him he had genuine concerns about being a suspect in the Belmont Car Auctions robbery of John Rees on the 18th March 1986. However, it is Superintendent Campbell who informed the court that Detective Constable Duncan Hanrahan was never suspected in that robbery whatsoever.

The entire situation left almost everyone in a quandary, yet conjecture and hearsay are admissible and is heard in the Court of the Coroner. However, as I have stated time can sometimes reveal situations to be more accurate or coincidental than first impressions may lead you to believe and this is what transpired involving John Rees a mere 10 years later.

This is an excerpt from the Guardian online Friday the 7th of October 2016 by Lisa O'Carroll and Vikram Dodd.

In the late 1990s police anti-corruption investigators concerned about a private detective agency, Southern Investigations, placed an undercover operative in the firm. Southern was used, among others, by journalists at the News of the World, including Mahmood. The undercover operative, Derek Haslam, told police no later than 2000 that Mahmood was working on stories with two suspects linked to a murder case riddled by police corruption and voiced concerns about Mahmood. Mahmood claimed the evidence from his investigations had helped police secure convictions of more than 100 criminals over 25 years.

Derek Haslam was a police Detective Constable and undercover operative and a known friend of DC Alan 'Taffy' Holmes. Mahmood was a journalist for the News of the World who made claim that his investigations had resulted in successful police prosecutions over many years.

This is an excerpt of the parliamentary statement made by Mr Tom Watson Member of Parliament on the 29th of February 2012. **This document contains parliamentary information licensed under the open parliament licence v3.0.**

As part of the third failed investigation, Operation Nigeria was launched. It included the surveillance of Southern Investigations between May and September 1999 and was run by the Metropolitan police's anti-corruption squad, CIB3. It placed a bug in the offices of Southern Investigations that yielded evidence that convicted Rees for a serious and unrelated crime.

In 1999 Scotland Yard anti-corruption officers concerned that corrupt police officers were selling information of a sensitive nature to Southern Investigations planted a bug, a covert audio listening device, in the offices of Southern Investigations, where Rees and Fillery both worked, in an attempt to obtain any incriminating evidence. Neither Rees nor Fillery had any idea that the offices were bugged and that they were the subject of covert audio surveillance. This operation was headed up by senior police officer Roy Clark.

Operation Nigeria and Operation Two Bridges

Operation Two Bridges was an Investigation into Law and Commercial a private investigation business run by John Rees. (For continuity, Rees operated investigation businesses will continue to be referred to throughout the book as Southern Investigations)

This is an excerpt of The Leveson Inquiry into the Culture Practices and Ethics of the Press. Statement of Robert Quick Dated the 13th of February 2012. *This document contains parliamentary information licensed under the open parliament licence v3.0.*

Operation Nigeria

During 1999, Anti-Corruption Command was conducting an operation, code named Operation Nigeria, which was a covert infiltration of office premises operated by 'Southern Investigations' whose proprietors were two men, Jonathan Rees ("Rees") and Sidney Fillery. Both were suspected of involvement in the murder of a former partner in the company, Daniel Morgan, who was murdered with an axe in a pub car park in Sydenham in 1987. Fillery had been a former police detective and had worked on the original murder investigation. The objective of this operation was to try to advance the investigation into the Morgan murder. During the course of Operation Nigeria, it became clear that, amongst other criminal activities, 'Southern Investigations' was acting as a 'clearing house' for stories for certain newspapers. Many of these stories were being leaked by police officers who were already suspected of corruption or by unknown officers connected to officers suspected of corruption, who were found to have a relationship with 'Southern Investigations'. A number of journalists were identified as having direct relationships with 'Southern Investigations'. To the best of my recollection these included journalists from papers like 'The Sun' and 'News of the World' but may have included other newspapers. My recollection is that one of the journalists suspected was xxxxxxxxxx~an executive with the 'News of the World'. During the operation it became clear that officers were being paid sums of between £500 and £2000 for stories about celebrities, politicians, and the Royal Family, as well as police investigations. I recall one instance where certain officers from the Royalty Protection Branch appeared to have leaked a story in relation to a member of the Royal Family and details of bank accounts. It was often difficult to take direct action against such officers without compromising the covert investigation techniques being used against those connected with 'Southern Investigations', but where possible, action (criminal or discipline) was taken. Matters in Operation Nigeria were brought to a head when evidence emerged that Rees was conspiring with a known criminal to plant cocaine on the criminal's wife in order to have her arrested and prosecuted so as to enable the criminal to win a custody battle over their one-year old child. The Operation Nigeria investigation revealed that this conspiracy involved at least two corrupt Metropolitan Police detectives who were actively involved in attempting to pervert the course of justice in order to ensure the conviction and imprisonment of an innocent woman. These events precipitated the end of Operation Nigeria as police were forced to intervene and arrest those involved, thereby revealing that 'Southern Investigations' had been infiltrated covertly by police. Rees, two known criminals and two detectives were arrested and subsequently convicted and imprisoned for these crimes.

Over time the police heard and became aware of a criminal conspiracy. A wealthy independent businessman, from the London area, Mr Simon James attended the offices of Southern Investigations and met with Rees. James explained to Rees that he was involved in a custody battle with his wife Kim and asked Rees to establish any evidence that his wife was involved in drugs. A situation that if established would offer leverage for the father to obtain sole custody care and control of the estranged couples little boy.

This is an excerpt from the Guardian Online; dated Tuesday the 14th of November 2000 by Keith Perry.

A corrupt detective and a police informer helped frame a model as a cocaine dealer to ensure she lost custody of her child, Kim James, might have been jailed for dealing, if the conspiracy had not been detected. James recruited Rees, the drugs placed in Mrs James's car by, Cook, prosecution said. Warnes, a detective constable, pleaded guilty, allegedly used police informant, Courtney, to persuade a senior officer the information about drugs was genuine. Courtney, James, Rees, Cook, denied the charge. Houlder branded James and Rees as the "heartless instigators", saying James paid Rees large money for "dishonest service".

Rees was unable to establish any evidence whatsoever that Kim James was involved in any activity surrounding drugs yet that did not deter him from hatching a plan with Simon James to 'fit up' Kim by having drugs (cocaine) planted in her car. Then have others tip off police (as to the alleged offence) in an attempt to have her arrested, jailed and discredited as an unfit mother in any custody proceedings allowing Simon James, the father, sole custody of their child. Those alleged to be involved in the plot were Detective Constable Austin Warnes, Registered Police Informant Dave Courtney, John Rees, Simon James and James Cook.

This is an excerpt from the Guardian Online; The Observer dated Sunday the 17th of December 2000 by Tony Thompson, Crime Correspondent.

Warnes played a key role to assist James custody of his son. James hired Rees to plant cocaine in a car belonging to Kim, to get her sent to prison, leaving child in father's care. Warnes, agreed to passing false information to police Kim was involved in cocaine dealing. Plan failed, anti-corruption detectives had been monitoring Rees, following concerns he had been making payments to police in return for information. Bugging devices alerted them. Warnes pleaded guilty, Rees, James were convicted of conspiracy to pervert the course of justice. Both sentenced to six years. Warnes four years. Cook, Courtney acquitted.

During the lengthy period of time the police listening device was in place at the offices of Southern Investigations, it seems from the evidence available to date, no incriminating evidence was heard or recorded that placed Rees, Fillery or anyone else for that matter having any involvement or connection with the murder of Daniel Morgan.

Kevin Lennon's sentence for his fraud crime was an 18-month suspended custodial prison term. At the inquest Lennon said no pressure had been put on him to make any witness statements. The police said (at the inquest) that no deal had been struck with Lennon of any 'assisting by an offender' in their inquiries into the murder investigation of Daniel Morgan as suggested by John Rees. It was my opinion at the time a deal had indeed been struck.

There are other instances in this unsolved homicide where techniques and deals, as suggested by John Rees in 1988, have actually been adopted by the police in much later investigations into Daniel's murder.

Under the 2005 Serious and Organised Crime and Policing Act the term 'assisting offenders' is used to describe criminals who are encouraged to give witness testimony in exchange for preferential treatment by way of sentence adjustment or reduction in giving evidence in pursuit of prosecutions on behalf of the Crown.

I particularly refer to the failed police investigation headed by Detective Chief Superintendent Dave Cook which ultimately saw prosecution charges of murder collapse against Rees, the Vian brothers and James Cook and in the case of Sid Fillery perverting the course of justice, all collapse by March of 2011.

This is an excerpt from the Guardian online dated Wednesday the 29th of February 2012 by Sandra Laville, Crime Correspondent.

The fifth inquiry into the murder collapsed last year and Rees and two other men were acquitted after the judge ruled senior police had coached one of the main supergrasses in the case, and it was revealed that large amounts of evidence had not been disclosed as a result of the vast material gathered over so many years.

I do have my concerns regarding the methods used by the police in the pursuit of evidence in an attempt to secure prosecutions surrounding the Daniel Morgan murder investigations. As much as this may be seen (by some) as a courageous attempt by dedicated police officers to establish a conviction we must not lose sight as to the integrity of the evidence and how it is obtained.

This an excerpt from the Guardian online dated Tuesday the 10th of January 2012 by Sandra Laville, Crime Correspondent.

A former Scotland Yard officer has been bailed by the Independent Police Complaints Commission after his arrest over allegations of unauthorised leaks to a journalist. DCS Dave Cook, 52, was questioned on suspicion of misconduct in a public office after being detained at his Berkshire home. He was arrested after the IPCC was passed information in mid-December by Metropolitan police detectives working on Operation Elveden, which is investigating alleged payments to police officers by newspapers. ---- Cook was criticised by the judge in the Morgan murder trial for misbehaviour in the way he handled a key supergrass witness.

This is the actual online summary findings of the investigation undertaken by the IPCC into the allegations of misconduct that Chief Superintendent Dave Cook was facing dated the 10ᵗʰ of November 2015.

This statement contains public sector information licensed under the Open Government Licence v2.0.

Independent police complaints commission Investigation into unauthorised disclosure of information to journalist by former Metropolitan police service officer.

An IPCC investigation into allegations a former, Metropolitan police service (MPS) officer provided unauthorised disclosure of information to a journalist has found the officer would have had a case to answer for gross misconduct if he was still serving.

The IPCC investigation found evidence to indicate that after his time as a serving MPS officer, the man sent thousands of pages of MPS police documentation to the journalist. The documents included information marked 'sensitive' 'confidential' and 'highly confidential' the majority of which was sent from his work email account to his personal account and then onto the journalist. The former officer was an employee of the Serious Organised Crime Agency (SOCA) at the time but retained an MPS email account in order to complete an investigation. The documentation, which was sent over a three-year period from 2008 to 2011, related to that investigation.

The officer was arrested by the IPCC on 10 January 2012, as the result of information provided by the Metropolitan police team investigating Operation Elveden, on suspicion of misconduct in public office. Data protection act offences were also considered.

A detailed report of the IPCC investigation together with accompanying documentary evidence was passed to the Crown Prosecution Service (CPS). In May 2015 the CPS decided it had sufficient information to make a charging decision. The CPS has now decided it would not be in the public interest to prosecute the former officer for either offence.

IPCC deputy chair Sarah Green said:

"While there was no evidence to indicate that the documents disclosed by the former officer resulted in payment of any kind, the evidence did indicate serious breaches of the trust placed in the officer both by the force itself and by the public. His claim that the information was provided to the journalist as part of a future book collaboration appear to be supported by the evidence but he also accepted that he had not requested nor been given authorisation to disclose the documents. He also acknowledged that sending sensitive and confidential documents to the journalist would never have been authorised. As the officer is now retired, no misconduct proceedings can be instigated."

It is understood that the documents referred to as being sent to the journalist over the three-year period of 2008 to 2011 are related to the Daniel Morgan murder investigation. The IPCC makes mention it will not be publishing its investigation report in its entirety because it contains sensitive personal data relating to the subject officer and others.

This an excerpt from the Guardian online dated Monday the 5th of August 2013 by Duncan Campbell, Crime Correspondent.

In 2011, following a failed Old Bailey prosecution against those alleged to have been involved in the murder, the then acting commissioner, Tim Godwin, apologised. "I am deeply sorry that the Metropolitan Police Service (MPS) has failed to bring to justice those responsible for the murder of Daniel," he said. "The MPS has accepted that police corruption in the original investigation was a significant factor in this failure".

On the 11th of March 2011 the Crown Prosecution Service, Alison Saunders, Chief Crown Prosecutor for CPS London made the following statement. **This statement contains public sector information licensed under the Open Government Licence v2.0.**

CPS stops prosecution for 1987 killing of Daniel Morgan

11/03/2011

The Crown Prosecution Service (CPS) has decided that the prosecution of three men for the killing of private detective Daniel Morgan in 1987 cannot continue.

Alison Saunders, Chief Crown Prosecutor for CPS London, said:

"Daniel Morgan was brutally killed 24 years ago. When we authorised charges against five men in April 2008 in relation to his death, we knew this would be a challenging prosecution because of both the passage of time and the amount of material, more than 750,000 pages, which needed to be considered for disclosure to the defence. Material that could assist the defence or undermine the prosecution must be disclosed.

"We were, until yesterday, satisfied that there was sufficient evidence for a realistic prospect of conviction. However, we must continuously review prosecutions to ensure that it is both fair and appropriate that they continue. We no longer believe this prosecution should continue.

"In December 2009, the police revealed a large amount of material to us that had not been considered for disclosure before. There was then considerable legal argument on whether it was possible for the case to proceed. Officers assured the court that there was no further unconsidered material. The judge was considering this matter when, on Friday 4 March 2011, the police revealed further material that had not been previously considered.

"We have decided that a prosecution cannot continue in these circumstances. We cannot be confident that the defence necessarily have all of the material that they are entitled to. This point would be raised by the defence during any trial, so we are no longer satisfied that there is sufficient evidence for a realistic prospect of conviction.

"This decision has been taken by the CPS with the advice of senior counsel. Daniel Morgan's family was also consulted before this decision was taken. This has been a long and difficult ordeal for the family, and we have offered them our heartfelt sympathies."

One - The CPS authorised charges against five men in April 2008 - a joint charge of murder against William (Jonathan) Rees, Glen Vian, Gary Vian and James Cook and a charge of perverting the course of justice against Sidney Fillery. However, the cases against Cook and Fillery had already been discontinued at an earlier stage in the proceedings.

Two – Three prosecution witnesses were subject to agreements under the Serious Organised Crime and Police Act (SOCPA) 2005.

Three – The case against Sidney Fillery relied entirely upon the evidence of a SOCPA witness that was ruled inadmissible by the court in February 2010. We then offered no evidence against him for perverting the course of justice.

Four – The case against James Cook relied upon the evidence of three witnesses, including the evidence of the SOCPA witness that the court had ruled inadmissible. We carefully considered whether it was possible to continue with the evidence of the other two witnesses, including another SOCPA witness, but decided it was not possible in November 2010.

Five – It emerged in December 2010 that material that could have assisted the defence concerning the prosecution's remaining SOCPA witnesses and should have been disclosed by the police had been lost. Although we could no longer use this witness's evidence against the remaining three defendants, we were satisfied the prosecution could continue.

It is within the remit of the Daniel Morgan Independent Panel to report their findings and the evidence as to what exactly has transpired regarding the entire police involvement and subsequent failed investigations. It is important that we do not lose sight as to what has actually taken place and why. I await the Panel's findings with trepidation.

Chapter 26
Was Danny Afraid

have been asked on many occasions throughout the last 31 years by police, the Coroner, Daniel's family and friends did Danny have any concerns to his personal safety; had he been threatened, did he have any enemies and was he afraid. It is because I spent so much time with him, especially in the latter stages of his life, that I am able to offer some idea to his overall consideration and concerns and this is what I recall.

There were many areas of concern that Daniel and I discussed regarding threats that were made to him. Daniel was not the most tactful person when it came to putting his foot in it. Daniel's attitude in certain matters left a lot to be desired. I am not pulling any punches here. A lot of the threats that Daniel received could well have been of his own making and I believe could and should have been avoided. In the majority of instances as much as he took all of this in his stride, he also accepted that his chosen profession came with occupational hazards.

It was in Danny's personal life with his habitual womanizing where I believe he was courting what could be seen as an inevitable outcome; a disaster waiting to happen. Don't get me wrong, I loved Danny to bits, he was my best mate but the way he went about his life and certain behaviour in business was beyond reckless. Danny was not Captain Scarlett he did not prove to be indestructible. Although Daniel was a brave man, I felt, there were certain times he was definitely afraid.

I recall one particular area of concern that occurred around two years before Daniel was killed.

Daniel and I were driving through southeast London and on reaching the Sydenham area; Daniel said to me, completely out of the blue, that he had been seeing a woman who lived locally and the woman's husband had found out about them. Daniel went on to tell me that he had received a threatening telephone call at home whereby the caller said he was going to *"kill him"*. Amongst the many threats Daniel received this was the one I felt concerned him the most as he took particular action in telling me.

Daniel slowed the car and pointed out an address in the Sydenham area indicating a house in a terrace of houses.

Daniel made me promise him that if he was ever beaten or assaulted and was in hospital that I was to go and see him and he would tell me the entire story of whom and where the person was. Daniel never gave me a name and told me not to tell anybody and to forget about what he had said other than what he had made me promise. I was really taken aback and extremely surprised by this. This was unusual behaviour and completely out of the norm for Danny as he had never mentioned anything quite so concerning to me before.

The very fact that Danny was telling me made me realize he must have been worried. As soon as I learned of Daniel's murder I immediately reported this to the police. However, by the time of the inquest the police had made a decision in how they were treating this information and this is what the Solicitor to the Commissioner of Police actually said.

This is an excerpt of Day 4, pages 16-17 of the Daniel Morgan Inquest. Detective Inspector Jones is further cross-examined by Mr Gompertz

Q. Did I understand you, Mr. Jones, to say that inquiries were made at the address not by yourself but by other officers? Is that right? – A. No, both, sir. I took Mr. Bray round the streets until he indicated to me a certain house. He said: "I believe that was the house that was pointed out to me." He only said he believed it was because it looked similar to the house he was shown before. He was still unsure whether it was the right house. I made some house to house inquiries on both sides of that particular house and got a negative reply as far as I recall now. However, officers then made inquiries at the house that he had pointed out. That was a negative result.

Q. So there is absolutely nothing to connect the occupants of that house with Mr. Morgan? – A. No, and it was not necessarily the right house.

Q. Therefore, although Mr. Nutter may wish to have the address, from your knowledge of the inquiries which have been made, is there the slightest purpose in supplying it? Will it reveal anything? – A. It will reveal nothing, sir.

MR. GOMPERTZ: It is a complete red herring.

THE CORONER: Perhaps you would like to explain this line of reasoning.

MR. NUTTER: There is no red herring at all. If we know what the house looks like, we can conduct our own inquiries at addresses which have a similar description and hopefully we might be able to get to the very root of who killed Daniel Morgan. Sir, that is very important, and it is not to be treated in any way as a red herring. I trust on that basis we will be supplied the information so that the resources at the disposal of my client can be put to work.

THE CORONER: Look up your records, Inspector Jones. – A. Yes.

Further Cross–Examined by Miss Tweedie

Q. Officer, is it right that Mr. Bray told you at the time he had difficulty identifying it because it was perhaps over two years since he had seen the address? – A. I do not remember him qualifying it in that way, but he could not really recall the exact address. The shape of the house was familiar to him and the general area.

THE CORONER: But we are talking about an episode that extends back to 1984. – A. I believe so, yes.

Since day four of the inquest when my evidence was given I have been incensed by the outrageous comment made by Mr Gompertz (Instructed by the Solicitor to the Commissioner of Police) that my testimony regarding a threat that Daniel had told me of in 1984 was in his words, *"a complete red herring"*. Mr. Gompertz was quite specific with his wording. He could have said that the inquires by the police into my evidence had proved unproductive; however, by definition in using the words 'red herring' he makes an absolute conclusion my statement should be discounted.

Before I go any further I would like to explain the definition of 'red herring'. A red herring is a figurative expression referring to a logical fallacy in which a clue or piece of information is or is intended to be misleading or distracting from the actual question.

I find Mr. Gompertz comment contemptuous. To consider the evidence that I gave to the court could be thought of as misleading in any way into Daniel's death is both erroneous and egregious. I have undertaken a long career as a professional witness submitting thousands of affidavits and witness statements of evidence in civil and criminal investigations to all the courts in the land and not once has the accuracy of my content ever been called into question, except at Daniel's inquest. I swore an oath on the bible that my evidence was true. And least not forget as a trained soldier I received a military commendation for highly meritorious service in 1988 from Major General Avery (Lifeguards) Officer Commanding, London District.

My friend was killed in a most violent way and I remember him telling me, *"If anything happens to me remember what I have told you."* I have never forgotten what Daniel told me that day. I explained to police at the time the entire situation however, my memory of the exact address was unsure. But I remain to this day resolute and adamant that my witness testimony was accurate and truthful so much so that I am willing to submit to a polygraph test at any time regarding this matter.

The police have reported they made extensive inquiries yet they found nothing.

I have cause for consideration that on the basis of the statement made by Mr Gompertz it could demonstrate that senior police officers, in the initial Daniel Morgan murder investigation squad, may have completely discounted my witness statements and evidence in this regard. From day one of the murder investigation I never felt that the interviews I had with the police were given the attention or consideration I believed they deserved. I have never felt comfortable that I was asked the right questions or the information I had spoken of was taken seriously or even recorded correctly.

At the end of 2016 I had a meeting, which I requested myself, with the police officers assigned to the Daniel Morgan Independent Panel to confirm the accuracy and integrity of my hand-written witness statements. Transcribed copies of my police statements had found their way into the hands of a very experienced freelance female reporter without my permission. The police gave me an explanation as to when and how this had occurred and that it should not have happened.

I spent more hours in a day with Daniel than most people did in a month. I have expressed my feelings to police regarding this however I feel their response is nothing less than condescending. My response to that is: 31 years later, five police investigations with tens of millions of pounds spent, no one has been convicted for my friend's murder thus allowing a murderer to remain at large.

Danny told me of many other threats and another one in particular comes to mind. It was around Christmas 1986 when Danny's car was broken into outside his home and the stereo was taken. One of his neighbours witnessed the break-in and took the number plate of the car used by the thieves and reported this to police. The youths who had perpetrated the theft were arrested and Daniel's car stereo was found in their possession. The youths were charged and a court case was pending.

This is an excerpt from Day 3, pages 73, 78-79 of the Daniel Morgan Inquest. Michael Goodridge (Solicitor and Friend of Daniel Morgan and John Rees) is examined by the Coroner and then cross-examined by Miss June Tweedie.

Q. ... *"His personality was of a man living on his nerves who could not sit still and quite argumentative. He would certainly threaten anyone who touched his car and I recall that threats were made to Danny and to his wife late one night on the telephone relating to his prosecution witness statement on the theft of his car radio."* – A. *Right.*

Q. *Would it surprise you if you were told that he was very against parking cars because his car had been broken into in the past, especially dark car parks at night? – A. I would not comment either way. I knew that his car had been broken into because I knew the defendant who broke into it.*

Coincidence is a funny thing; as it turned out the alleged perpetrators of the break-in to Danny's car outside his house, whereby his car stereo was stolen, were local and had contacted the law offices of Danny's friend, solicitor Mike Goodridge to seek legal advice.

At the time Daniel began complaining that he was receiving telephone threats at home and he told me he believed that the calls were emanating from the youths who broke into his car.

Sometime after Christmas Danny also mentioned Iris was getting phone calls on the house line from a female saying that Danny was with her last with further content to suggest Daniel was having an affair with her. I remember Iris questioned Danny about this and she was actually laughing.

Iris and Danny briefly discussed the issue and took it as a joke and in fact, Danny told me that he thought it was a girl, in an attempt to 'stir it up', making these calls on behalf of the youths involved in his car break-in outside the house. He never considered that this particular episode could be anything more sinister than that.

Danny would tell me every time he received threatening phone calls and mostly the calls were made by men. Daniel also received threatening calls at the office but in almost all the cases he did not mention the entire content of the threats. He was getting so many that in the end he chose to ignore them and not give them a second thought. It is not normal for one man to receive so many threats.

This is an excerpt from Day 8, page 37-38 of the Daniel Morgan Inquest. John Rees is examined by the Coroner.

Q. Let me put this, another way for you. Are you aware that Daniel had any enemies that would phone him up, threaten him or anything of that nature? – A. Daniel did receive numerous threats, phone call threats towards his life.

Q. He did? – A. He did.

Q. In that recent period around the time of his death? – A. No, this was over a year, two years.

Q. What sort of threats? – A. Some of them were threats to kill.

Q. Why? – A. I don't know. I don't even know who was making the phone calls.

Q. He told you, otherwise how would you know? – A. Yes. I mean some of them I took messages myself.

Q. What did they say? – A. I can't remember word for word.

Q. What was the general tenor about them? Why were they threatening to kill him? – A. I don't know, sir. They didn't explain the reasons behind it. It was part of the messages we got. One I can specifically remember was "Tell the little bastard with the beard that the next time he comes to my house I am going to kill him". I made a note of the voice.

Q. The little bastard with the beard was obviously referring to Daniel Morgan. – A. Yes.

Q. Did Daniel tell you why this man should say that? Your partner, did he turn round and say "I know why because on such an occasion I had to go and take something back, I took a child back", or something of that nature? "I repossessed his house" or whatever the case may be. – A. We didn't know who the person was.

Q. These were anonymous phone calls? – A. Yes.

Q. Were they always anonymous these phone calls, do you remember? – A. Yes. If someone is giving his name and address with threats to kill we would have taken it further.

Q. Would you? Would you have gone to the police? – A. Certainly, yes.

Q. It has been suggested that Daniel Morgan was popular with the ladies. To your knowledge were there any ladies' boyfriends, ladies' husband, and ladies' families that might have rung him up? – A. Not to my knowledge.

Daniel gave out hundreds of business cards and had annual pocket diaries printed containing Southern Investigations business address, telephone numbers and the partner's car phone numbers. Daniel wouldn't think twice about giving out his home phone number if he thought it could be useful or had potential for new business. Daniel was just not that careful to whom he gave his contact information; he was very trusting that way. I am sorry to say but I always thought this was a mistake and a little naïve on Daniel's part.

An office message book was made available to all staff and I believe this was first implemented either by Daniel or Peter. Any messages or calls (this would include verbal threats) for staff members were recorded in a diary format. Diligent record keeping at Southern Investigations was paramount in the day to day running of the business.

This is an excerpt of Day 3, pages 31-32 of the Daniel Morgan Inquest. Peter Newby is being examined by the Coroner.

Q. *"By reference to the office message book John Rees recorded a telephone threat towards Daniel on 5.8.85"* --- *that is going back* – *"and I later took a telephone call on 20.8.85 threatening Daniel. I was of the opinion that the caller I spoke to was a 'nut case' and was unaware at the time of John's earlier call."* – *A. That is true.*

Q. *"Around about September/October 1986 about mid-afternoon, I saw a man going up the stairs to Danny's office. I stopped him and he said: 'Is Morgan in?' I told him 'No' and I think he asked me when he would be back. I said I didn't know. I said to him: 'what's it about?' He said: 'You tell Morgan I'll be back.'"* Was there anything significant about that? You treated the incident as a threat. *"Daniel came back to the office an hour after the chap had left and I told him about it. I treated it as a threat and Daniel went down to the Norbury police station to report it."* – *A. Yes, that is true.*

As soon as I learned of Daniel's murder and its location, The Golden Lion Public House in Sydenham, my heart sank as I immediately recalled what Danny had said to me a couple of years earlier; and the fact he had received a threat of being killed.

I was absolutely shocked and thought to myself, oh my God, could it actually be true? Daniel told me about a threat and now he was dead. I was completely taken aback and for a moment I didn't know what to think.

I composed my thoughts and immediately relayed this information to police, on the 11th of March 1987, making my witness statement pertaining to this threat. At the Daniel Morgan Inquest, the solicitor for the police classed this information as a *"red herring"*.

Is it possible from the threats Daniel received that a motive did indeed exist to his murder?

Chapter 27
The Winds of Change

D aniel Morgan and Southern Investigations employed many casual staff for purposes from building maintenance and vehicle movers to static and mobile security guards; three of these individuals were Glenn Vian, Garry Vian and James Cook. Since the killing these men along with John Rees and Sidney Fillery have been persons of interest in the police investigations into the murder of Daniel Morgan.

This is an excerpt from the Guardian online dated Tuesday 17 January 2017 by Vikram Dodd, Police and Crime Correspondent.

Rees and three other men are suing the Metropolitan Police, alleging officers were so determined to get them that its pursuit was malicious. A high court civil case has allowed the allegations to be aired again. Rees, Vians and others were tried for murder but the case collapsed in 2011 because it relied on a series of informants whose testimony was ruled as inadmissible. The judge criticised the lead detective DCS Cook for mishandling a crucial supergrass witness, it's claimed Cook passed documents about the case to a Sun journalist. In the end prosecutors decided to offer no evidence.

By the time of the 2011 court case, at the Old Bailey in London, all the charges brought against the suspects in the Daniel Morgan murder investigation were dropped. John Rees, Sid Fillery, Glenn Vian, Garry Vian and James Cook were all found not guilty. In January 2017 Rees, Fillery and the Vians filed a civil claim in the high court that the police had acted maliciously in prosecuting them.

This is an excerpt from the Guardian online dated Friday 17 February 2017 by Vikram Dodd, Police and Crime Correspondent.

Three men charged with the 1987 murder of Daniel Morgan lost their case that police maliciously tried to get them convicted. Rees, Garry and Glenn Vian were tried for murder; the case collapsed in 2011. Sid Fillery was charged with conspiracy to pervert the course of justice; the crown dropped the case against him. At the high court, Mr Justice Mitting ruled against Rees and the Vians, Fillery won part of his claim. A claim of misfeasance in public office went in Fillery's favour. The witness against him was deemed unreliable and had been mishandled by the lead detective.

The central criminal court found these men not guilty, however for Rees and the Vians the high court judge Mr Justice Mitting ruled against their claim of malicious prosecution by the police.

I was first introduced to Glenn Vian on a weekend when I visited Daniel's home. Danny was having Glenn undertake some building work on his house. I exchanged pleasantries with Glenn and he seemed a happy enough chap. He spoke mainly about the building work that he had done and seemed quite proud of his achievements. Daniel said that the work Glenn had finished was satisfactory and he expressed that he felt he had received good value for money.

Daniel told me that Glenn was related to John Rees and that he was one of two brothers (the other being Garry) of John's wife Sharon. Daniel said that he gave the construction work to Glenn as a courtesy to his business partner John *"keeping the money in the family"* as Daniel called it.

In the early part of my friendship with Danny I would bump into Glenn and Garry out and about with Daniel in pubs or on the odd occasion when Glenn would attend the office seeking work or visiting. Daniel was kind to Glenn and from time to time Daniel and John would offer the brothers static security guard assignments or other work.

Over the years I only met James Cook on a handful of occasions. Daniel would call upon him to assist in vehicle repossessions or when he needed assistance on larger projects such as entire site repossessions. (See Chapter The Teflon Trail)

It was almost immediately after John was robbed of the Belmont Car Auctions money that Danny had a change of attitude toward all casual staff. As much as no evidence whatsoever existed that any person within Southern Investigations was connected to the robbery; Daniel saw the entire operation as a fiasco and was not impressed. Danny certainly had his doubts as to the circumstances of the robbery and said he liked to keep an open mind. (See Chapter Belmont Car Auctions Robberies)

Daniel's attitude to casual staff undertaking field work assignments significantly changed. He became almost wary of taking on any work that was immediately out of his control and this continued up until around Christmas 1986.

Daniel became very selective as to whom he was giving work and was limiting his availability to casuals for work or social related associations. Casual staff might attend the office on the auspices of obtaining work but failed in meeting Daniel. He deliberately made himself unavailable or difficult to contact; it was obvious from how he was reacting there was a wind of change in Daniel's behaviour. Because of this my workload increased dramatically and Danny said to me, *"Dave, can you handle the extra workload?"* I told Dan I had no concerns as long as I didn't fall behind on time sensitive casework.

James Cook and the Vian brothers were just a few of many casual staff who had undertaken assignments for Southern Investigations. This was as far as my association went with these men, we did not associate outside the confines of that stated.

The 2017 findings of Lord Justice Mitting were however to be tested. Rees and the Vians decided to appeal his decision and hearings took place at the High Court of Justice in the Court of Appeal on the 24th & 25th of April 2018 before Lady Justice King and Lord Justices McCombe and Coulson. Nicholas Bowen QC and David Lemer were legal representation for John Rees and Glenn Vian; Stephen Simblet represented Garry Vian. Jeremy Johnson QC, Charlotte Ventham and Catriona Hodge represented the Respondent-the Commissioner of The Police for the Metropolis.

Legal argument was heard that severely questioned Lord Justice Mitting. The argument was that John Rees and the Vian brothers had been relentlessly pursued by the police for the murder of Daniel Morgan; the investigation culminating against them in prosecution in 2008 which subsequently collapsed in May 2012 with all charged being found not guilty.

It was found that the senior officer in the case Detective Chief Superintendent Dave Cook had persuaded a super-grass witness, Gary Eaton, to falsely claim that he was an eye witness to the murder. In 2017 Lord Justice Mitting found that DCS Cook's behaviour amounted to the offence of perverting the course of justice. However even after coming to this conclusion it was his ruling that three of the four claimants should not be compensated.

Lord Justice Mitting found that Eaton was not present at the scene of the murder at all and that Eaton's account of the events pertaining to the murder was a fabrication. Mitting found that Cook's contact with and the prompting of Eaton made Cook guilty of perverting the course of justice. Even with all this evidence Mitting found that the claims in malicious prosecution and misfeasance failed. In giving his reasons, Justice Mitting was of the opinion that despite this behaviour Cook believed that the claimants were guilty of the murder and felt despite his wrong doing the claimants would have been prosecuted anyway.

On the 5th of July 2018 the Court of Appeal ruled in favour of John Rees, Glenn Vian and Garry Vian. The Court of Appeal handed down a judgement that will now see the claimants receive substantial damages from the Metropolitan Police to compensate them as to the behaviour of one of its senior officers amounting to malicious prosecution and misfeasance in a public office.

The Court of Appeal judgement considered Lord Justice Mitting's decision to deny damages to Rees and the Vians was "negation of the rule of law". The court also said that it "may well appear to be counter-intuitive to any ordinary member of the public" for Lord Justice Mitting to have found that a DCS could be corrupt but find that he was not necessarily acting maliciously.

Lord Justice Coulson, in his findings reported, *"I am in no doubt that Cook acted maliciously...any other finding, on the facts of this case, would be a negation of the rule of law. It would be contrary to basic principle to find, as the judge did, that a senior policeman can pervert the course of justice to create false evidence against the appellants, but not be guilty of malice simply because he personally believed them to be guilty of Daniel Morgan's murder."*

Lady Justice King, in her findings, said this: *"I agree that for the reasons found in the judgments of both McCombe LJ and Coulson LJ this appeal must be allowed. I would endorse, without reservation, the conclusion of McCombe LJ that DSC Cook was a prosecutor who acted maliciously. McCombe LJ observes that any other finding would be a "negation of the rule of law" and Coulson LJ that it would be "contrary to basic principle". I agree that that is undoubtedly the case and, in my view, any other conclusion would, in the eyes of the general public, defy common sense.*

This is a case where no one has been tried or convicted of a particularly brutal murder. It is of importance that where serious and damaging findings of malicious prosecution and of misfeasance in public office are sought against the MPC in such a case, that the public can understand and appreciate the logic of the outcome. With respect to this very experienced judge, the outcome which he reached namely, that although acting corruptly DCS Cook was not also acting maliciously, may well appear to be counterintuitive to any ordinary member of the public.

To say that DCS Cook, a prosecutor guilty of perverting the course of justice by creating false evidence against the appellants, was, on account of his belief in their guilt, not acting maliciously, is rather like saying that Robin Hood was not guilty of theft. One understands the motivation in each case, but any seeming endorsement of such dishonest behaviour, particularly within the police force, leads as McCombe LJ puts it, to a (serious and unacceptable) "negation of the rule of law".

John Rees, Glenn and Garry Vian are now likely to see this matter returned to the High Court of Justice whereby compensation and damages will be determined, it is expected that these damages and costs have the potential to be substantial the entire package could run into a number of millions of pounds. The Commissioner for the police has the ability to seek permission and appeal this decision in the Supreme Court.

Chapter 28
Detective Constable Alan 'Taffy' Holmes

Since the murder of Daniel Morgan on the 10th of March 1987 and the suicide of Alan 'Taffy' Holmes, on the 28th of July 1987, there has been question and speculation that Daniel Morgan and Alan 'Taffy' Holmes may or may not have known each other and/or were in collusion for the purpose of an explosive media expose in the uncovering of organized crime and/or police corruption. The internet is awash with theories and conspiracies regarding this.

Until his suicide Detective Constable Alan 'Taffy' Holmes was a serving police officer. He was a member of Scotland Yard's Serious and Organized Crime Squad and investigated the Brinks-Mat Bullion robbery.

This is an excerpt from the Guardian online dated Monday the 28th of November 1983 by Gareth Parry.

The three tons of gold bullion worth £25 million stolen from the Brinks Mat security warehouse near Heathrow airport at the weekend has probably already been melted down and smuggled out of the country. The 6,800 ingots were individually marked and Commander Frank Cater, head of Scotland Yard's Central Robbery Squad, believes that those responsible for Britain's biggest robbery have already disposed of the loot.

In the time before his death Holmes was involved with an investigation surrounding allegations of serious police corruption in southeast London (Operation Russell and Russia) and the allegations of involvement of Police Commander Ray Adams.

An inquest was held in the Croydon Coroner's Court from the 11th to the 14th of March 1988 which ruled that Alan 'Taffy' Holmes death was a suicide.

This is an excerpt from the Guardian online dated Friday 16th March 2012 by Vikram Dodd.

-----from Operation Russell ----- Adams's close associate, DC Alan "Taffy" Holmes shot himself dead on 27 July, 1987, on the eve of Adams being interviewed by corruption investigators. Holmes had been interviewed twice, and was expected to face further questioning.

It was mid to late summer of 1985 on a Saturday around lunchtime, I was visiting at Daniel's home; we decided to take a short walk to South Norwood Sports Club for a pint. Along the way Daniel brought up the subject of the police investigation of the Brinks-Mat heist. Daniel was enthusiastic talking about it in a way that suggested more than just gossip. I listened to my friend and what was clear to me was he seemed to be quite knowledgeable about the subject.

This was when Daniel first started talking about a Welshman he had met by the name of Alan 'Taffy' Holmes who was a police detective constable. Daniel said that they had a shared interest of rugby and had met in a pub in Croydon. I got the impression that Danny was quite chuffed about this association.

The way Daniel spoke of Taffy led me to believe their association or friendship was established but not to any particular depth. The reason why I remember this conversation was Daniel said what a fantastic source of intelligence Taffy could turn out to be. I formed the opinion from his enthusiasm and from the look in his eyes that Danny was clearly cultivating this idea.

At that time Daniel's sources or contacts with serving police officers were limited if non-existent. Daniel had made a few acquaintances with serving police officers mainly meeting in pubs, restaurants or at social events through John Rees and others. (See Chapter The Best Thing about the Police was Sting)

Daniel said to me that John Rees was already friendly with police officers and it might be a good idea if he started to establish an 'in' with one or two old bill. Daniel had not mentioned to me, at this time, any selling of a potential news story; however, this was about to change.

Daniel started talking about the use of the codename 'Omo' when he received phone calls. Danny would say to me, *"Omo is calling"*. I thought to myself Omo; that's a washing powder. I said to Dan, *"Who is this Omo?"* Daniel told me that was a codename for Alan 'Taffy' Holmes. I said, *"Dan, Omo is a washing powder with a reputation of getting your white wash 'Whiter than White'"*. He said, *"I know that's why we use that name"*. I asked Dan why Holmes needed a codename when he rang and he told me that Holmes was involved in the Serious and Organised Crime Squad and worked out of offices in Barnes and Tottenham Court Road and the codename was used when Taffy called so Daniel knew it was a secure line and safe to communicate. I thought this was a bit unusual as no one else needed a codename when ringing Danny.

It was in the winter prior to his murder when Daniel first started talking about touting and selling a sensational story to the newspapers; he was very vague about its subject and content. I took this to mean it was of a highly sensitive nature. Danny was no stranger to the media and had a few contacts within that industry. Initially Danny talked about a story that may be worth up to 250K until, over time; this figure was established at 40K. Daniel seemed to become almost obsessed and was driven with the idea; talking about it on an almost daily basis. Danny continued to tout the idea of this story until he was murdered.

The touting of the story just so happened to coincide with the time communications with Holmes dramatically started to increase. Danny would often mention wanting to talk to Taffy as a matter of urgency. Danny told me that due to the nature of Taffy's work it was difficult for him to initiate contact and he had to wait for Taffy to contact him; on many occasions making Daniel very impatient and frustrated.

It was a midweek lunchtime prior to our trip to Malta. I was in the offices of Southern Investigations going about my usual duties when Danny arrived. Danny asked me have I had any lunch and I said no. He said, *"I have a meeting at a café in Norbury"*. I said, *"Oh yeah, who you meeting"*, he said *"Taffy Holmes"*. Danny's demeanour was particularly chipper and keen.

We took my car and drove to Norbury, parked and went to a café/burger bar on the main London Road. We sat at a table and after 10 minutes a man joined us whom Daniel introduced to me as Taffy Holmes. He and I shook hands and said hello. Daniel then said to me, *"Taffy and I are just going to sit over there, have a short meeting and then you can come and join us."* I said okay and thought to myself this is a bit cloak and dagger.

After about 15 minutes Daniel called me over to join them. I had not been privy to any of the content of their meeting nor was anything other than civil pleasantries undertaken thereafter. I recall my first impression of Taffy was that he looked like a real hard man however I found Taffy to be a likeable fellow and clearly Welsh. We all ordered something to eat and the entire luncheon took no more than about 45 minutes; we then left with Taffy going his separate way.

During the short drive back to the office Danny was quite preoccupied in thought and told me 'not to spare the horses' as he needed to make some important phone calls. I said to Danny, *"What was all that about"*, he said, *"Dave I can't tell you"*. I said, *"Come on Dan what's going on"*, he looked at me and said, *"Just get us back to the office"*. Danny was rather short with me which was out of character. I backed off and thought when he is ready to tell me he will. Danny's attitude had certainly changed since his meeting with Taffy.

What was clear to me after that meeting, Daniel's relationship with Taffy was more than just that of an acquaintance. Knowing Daniel so well I knew when he was up to something. From what Daniel had previously discussed with me, I formed the opinion that Taffy Holmes may well have established himself as a source of intelligence for Daniel.

It was during the time Daniel was talking about the touting of a story to the newspapers that his car and office were broken into.

I remember that Danny also had a theft from his house. Dan had a big old-fashioned TV set in his lounge, something that would have taken two people to carry. He phoned me in the morning and told me that whilst he was asleep his TV was stolen. I said I would pop round to his house.

On arrival Danny was standing by his front door looking somewhat perplexed. I looked at his front door and could find no sign of forced entry and all the front windows were secure and intact. Danny's front door didn't always close properly and sometimes it seemed to be shut when it actually was not. I said jokingly to him that whoever had nicked the TV had done him a favour and now he would have to buy a modern one.

In the time prior to Daniel's murder he had been receiving threatening phone calls; his house had been entered and his TV stolen, his car had been broken into twice and the offices of Southern Investigations had been burgled. (See Chapter The Office Burglary)

Quite frankly with everything that was going on I was becoming rather concerned for Daniel; he was going on about contacting newspapers and talking big money. I said to him, *"Daniel, the papers don't pay this kind of money for nothing"*. I asked him if he had given consideration that the burglaries, the break-ins and threatening phone calls might in some way be connected. He said nothing but from the look on his face, I formed the opinion he was giving the idea some consideration. I told him he should not get involved whatever it is. Then I said, *"The fact you don't want to share the story's content with me tells me it's dangerous Danny"*. I tried to talk some sense into him but Daniel could be very stubborn. He heard what I was saying but Danny always thought he knew best. In fact, he seemed to become more passionate regarding the whole situation and more determined to establish a buyer for the story.

On the basis of his attitude, demeanour and responses something was troubling him. During a heated discussion between us he let slip that the story he was touting to the newspapers involved police and drugs. That is the most Daniel ever told me.

Daniel did not go into any detail regarding what the story was about and the only reason for that would have been because he believed that my having any knowledge pertaining to the story would place me at potential risk. In all the time I knew Daniel and all the peril involved in our work, there had never been a situation to affect Daniel's behaviour in this way.

I was not the only person that knew Danny was touting a story. Daniel's friend and confidant Bryan Madagan and others have made statements to the police.

DANIEL MORGAN SOUTHERN INVESTIGATION

This is an excerpt from the Guardian online dated Saturday the 11ᵗʰ of March 2017 Vikram Dodd, Police and Crime Correspondent reports the following:

Madagan said: "Morgan was to sell a story to the News of the World, Morgan's contact an Alex Marunchak." Madagan told police Morgan was discussing £40,000 for the story "Daniel would [have] told people of this plan he would not keep quiet about such a deal." "The story was about police corruption and his business as a private investigator." July 1987, Holmes was found shot dead officially declared a suicide. Some in policing are no longer confident of that conclusion. Police source says Holmes told Morgan of the conspiracy involving corrupt officers and criminals to import drugs into the UK.

The police at the time of the initial investigation said that information had come to their attention regarding claims Daniel was touting a news story to the tabloid press prior to his murder.

This is an excerpt of Day 5, pages 60-61 of the Daniel Morgan Inquest. Detective Superintendent Campbell is being cross-examined by Miss June Tweedie.

MISS TWEEDIE: Are you aware of Daniel Morgan having said to anyone before his death, either in the police or outside the police, that he had uncovered a story of police corruption? – A. There was a suggestion of that but we could not confirm it.

Q. Where did that suggestion come from? – A. It came from a man I interviewed.

Q. Was he someone who has given evidence in this court? A. No.

Q. Did you take that information seriously? – A. Yes.

Q. Did you find anything relevant to the demise of Daniel Morgan? – A. I could find no evidence at all. It was a suggestion that he had a story to sell to a newspaper. I spoke to the other person concerned. I even went to the newspaper but if I told you what he was offered you would see it was quite ludicrous. He was alleged to have been offered £250,000 per story.

THE CORONER: You say you looked into that? – A. I can find no evidence of it. This was purely what somebody told me was alleged to have been given to them by Daniel Morgan. We looked at all possible aspects and I could not take it any further.

MISS TWEEDIE: But you did have evidence that Daniel Morgan had told someone that he had uncovered such a story? – A. The person that he told virtually ignored it. He said that Daniel was always talking in that vein.

The person Campbell referred to that Daniel told, was understood to be Daniel's friend Bryan Madagan.

It was around Christmas 1986 or the beginning of the New Year 1987 that I recall a meeting between Daniel and Bryan Madagan. Daniel phoned me and asked if I wanted to go for a drink and a drive. I asked him where we were going and he said, *"We're going out into the sticks to meet Bryan Madagan".* It was a cold winter afternoon, snow on the ground, a white-out in the fields and driving was hazardous. As we ventured further into the countryside the road conditions worsened; yet Daniel was very keen to speak to Bryan so we chanced the risk of accident or breakdown.

The meeting with Bryan was important to Daniel. I don't recall the name of the pub however, it was in Surrey. On our arrival Bryan was already at the bar enjoying a beverage. Daniel ordered our drinks and said to me, *"David, please excuse us for a few moments"*. Danny and Bryan moved to a more private area of the bar and from a distance I watched Daniel speak intensely with his friend. I was not privy to the actual conversation.

It is my opinion from interaction with both men that Bryan Madagan was a trusted confidante and friend; a man Daniel respected. I accompanied Daniel on many occasions when he visited Bryan at different venues to discuss matters that Daniel felt were important or where he wanted to seek advice. The fact that Daniel had ventured out in such very poor weather conditions to meet with his friend informed me that what he had to discuss was important.

Within the space of mere weeks between March and July 1987 both Daniel Morgan and Taffy Holmes would be found dead.

Is it possible that Daniel's friendship with Taffy Holmes and/or the touting of a potential news story or any surrounding events or connection exist that could lead to a possible motive in Danny's murder and/or the suspicious suicide of Alan 'Taffy' Holmes?

Chapter 29
Read All About It

The media has played a significant role in the story of Daniel Morgan and Southern Investigations. I remember when I met Daniel and our friendship began one of the first things he discussed with me was the tabloid press; in which he always showed a tremendous interest.

Daniel was a private investigator however in many ways he saw himself as so much more. I feel Daniel would have preferred to have been a journalist or a story teller. In the course of Daniel's work, he would often come across stories or information that he knew might be valuable to the newspapers. Danny had an understanding that certain stories or information in the journalism industry could have financial benefit for him.

Daniel liked to boast of the contacts he had made with reporters from some of the biggest dailies that were in operation at the time. It excited him that he might have a story that no one else had and that a newspaper might be willing to pay him good money for what he saw as his knowledge. Daniel always seemed to be on the lookout for extra cash and saw the tabloids as a place he could find easy money.

I recall Daniel mentioned to me his fascination and very special interest in Private Eye Magazine. He absolutely adored this publication and would get up early on its day of distribution and obtain his copy from the newsagent. He read the stories intently and took great pleasure and excitement from their subject matter.

In many cases before 8:00 am Danny would have shared with me almost word for word the entire content of the edition. It got to the point I didn't have to read the articles myself; I just let Danny tell me all the stories, he was a truly devoted fan. Daniel had contacts within Private Eye and told me that he previously sold information to the editor.

Back in the 1980s the majority of the daily tabloids were situated on Fleet Street or the surrounding streets of Fetter or New Fetter Lane, London, a time before and during News International moved to Wapping. Fleet Street was in close proximity to the Royal Courts of Justice (RCJ) where both Daniel and I regularly attended to pick up court documents by way of service of legal process.

I was in Daniel's company on a number of occasions when we would walk down The Strand from RCJ to Fleet Street where we would pop into the newspapers. Daniel would ask at reception if he could speak to a particular journalist. Daniel would often ask these individuals if they had time for a chat or if they were available to join him for a drink or a coffee. This was Daniel's way of continuing and growing his established media contacts but also his approach to making new ones within the industry. One journalist in particular that I met on one of these visits whilst in Daniel's company was Anton Antonowich.

There was one particular blonde female journalist in her mid to late thirties whom Daniel and John knew very well. She would attend the offices of Southern Investigations mostly after 6:00 pm on weekday evenings either meeting with John or Daniel. These meetings occurred on a number of occasions and they would only last about 20 to 30 minutes.

I met the journalist on at least two occasions when Daniel had a meeting with her. Daniel would say to me that the meetings were of a confidential nature and the journalist liked to meet in private. On more than one occasion I waited for Daniel in an adjoining office unbeknownst to the journalist that I was in the building.

It is readily reported online and in the media, that both Daniel and John Rees had contacts in the media; a relationship I know from Daniel's point of view was for financial gain. Daniel would tell me that he looked to earn a specific amount of money every month from the tabloid newspapers, money that he actively incorporated in his monthly business turnover. The selling of stories or associated business with the newspapers was so important to Daniel that if he didn't reach his monthly turnover, from this revenue source, he would actually voice his displeasure.

I was not an impressionable young man and I had my own views and opinions of this particular aspect of Daniel's work. I never thought that the relationship Daniel had with the press was healthy. My immediate thoughts were that this is not right, this could have serious repercussions; this attitude to confidential information and sources is dangerous. I voiced my concerns to my mentor and I know he heard me however; he would just shrug it off and felt he knew best.

I never felt comfortable from the first moment Daniel told me that he had involvement in selling stories to the media. Daniel often called me his 'protégé' however I made it clear to Daniel that this area of my training was a mistake.

Chapter 30
My 10th of March 1987

've been asked (on more occasions than I care to remember) what I was doing on the 10th of March 1987; regarding the events that transpired and when was the last time I saw Daniel Morgan.

Daniel and I travelled, worked and played together and if not for work commitments it was likely that I'd have been with Daniel on the night of March 10th 1987. However, that was not the case.

The events which took place that day and evening will remain in my thoughts for the rest of my life.

This is an excerpt of Day 4, pages 3-4 of the Daniel Morgan Inquest. I am being examined by the Coroner.

Q. Did you see Mr. Morgan on the 10th March? – A. Yes, sir, I did.

Q. You tell me in what capacity you saw him on that particular day? – A. On the 10th March, sir, I was at home. It was about quarter to eight in the morning. Danny had given me a bell at home and he said to me: "I've got something I want to talk to you about."

Q. This is at quarter to eight in the morning. – A. Yes, sir.

Q. Where were you coming home from? – A. I was at home and Mr. Morgan rang me there.

Q. Was it unusual for him to ring at quarter to eight? – A. No, basically he would ring me up 24 hours a day if he wanted to talk to me.

Q. I have an impression that he used to ring you almost every day. Sometimes, two to three times a day. – A. Yes, that is correct.

Q. Why would he need to ring you two to three times a day? – A. That was the way he was, sir. We just got on well, and if he wanted to talk to me about anything------

Q. You knew quite a lot about him. – A. To a degree, sir.

Q. Let us go back to 7:45 a.m. He rang you. – A. Danny was at home and he said he was going to the office. He asked me to attend his house, pick up his children, and take them to school and then get down to the office as quick as I could.

Q. Yes, you went down to the office. – A. I went down to the office and Danny was doing a bit of hoovering because we had had a carpenter in the previous evening.

Q. What time did you get to the office? – A. I got to the office around about quarter to nine. Danny never had a chance to speak to me. He said that he wanted to speak to me. As soon as I came in he had finished the hoovering, the telephone started ringing, then I believe Peter Newby came in, and everybody was talking to him so he was getting busy and things were just happening.

Q. Did he tell you what he wanted you for? – A. No, sir, he did not.

Q. What did you do? Did you just hang about the office? – A. I had just got out of bed at quarter to eight and I thought: "You wanted to talk to me about something and now you've been interrupted." I had some work to do, and Peter Newby gave me some work to do. Then I just left the office.

Q. Did you see Mr. Morgan later that day at all? – A. No, sir.

Q. Were you aware that he was going to have a meeting that night at a public house? – A. No, I was not, sir.

Q. Did you hear the public house mentioned? – A. No, sir.

Q. Have you heard of the public house called the Golden ----- --A. Yes, sir, but only in reference to this case.

Q. What is it called? – A. The Golden Lion in Sydenham.

Q. Had you been with Morgan to the Golden Lion in Sydenham? – A. Only on one occasion, but not actually inside the premises. It was outside the premises of the pub.

Q. You saw Mr. Morgan a lot round about that period of time. – A. Yes, sir.

It was around mid-morning on the 10th of March 1987 when I last saw Daniel. He was in the office and was preparing to attend a very important meeting with the Cooperative Wholesale Society (CWS) in Slough, Berkshire. He told me he was to travel by car with Tony Pearce. This was a big meeting for Daniel as CWS was a large land owner and existing client of the business. CWS already instructed Daniel with some very big jobs involving land possession and security and he was hoping to cultivate even more bailiff related work from them.

I could see that Danny had a great deal on his mind but his overall demeanour was nothing out of the ordinary. He did not seem worried about anything and he was his usual self. I had seen Daniel prepare for meetings like this many times before. He changed his clothes in the office and was tidy, suited and looked like the consummate business man. Daniel was quite busy that morning and he never did tell me what he wanted to talk to me about so urgently.

He had ample opportunity during the day to contact me by pager or later by phone whilst I was at home. More likely he was waiting for a moment when he could talk to me in person. Whatever Danny had to tell me he took to the grave.

When I was preparing to leave the office I said to Danny, *"Hey, Dan I am off"*. Danny replied, *"Okay, Dave see you later"*. Unaware these were the last words he would ever speak to me.

I left the office and proceeded to my car and studied some files for the field work I had been designated to undertake that day and evening. I went to a local café for lunch and undertook some enquiries in the southeast London area.

I returned home around 3:00 pm and decided to rest awhile before undertaking my evening work; I awoke around 6:00 pm. I looked out of my window and noticed that traffic was still heavy and the weather wasn't brilliant. My job that evening was to personally serve a witness subpoena upon a gentleman at a private address in the town of Northampton, Northamptonshire; approximately 70 miles north of London; a journey time of approximately two hours by car each way.

Between 6:15 pm and 6:30 pm I telephoned a friend, Steve, who lived in West Norwood and asked if he wanted to accompany me on this journey. He said he had nothing better to do and was happy to go with me. Around 7:00 pm I picked him up and we began our journey to Northampton.

It was cold that night, the journey was uneventful and we arrived at the address of the witness at just gone 9:00 pm. I proceeded to personally serve the legal process (subpoena) upon the witness. We returned to the car leaving Northampton around 9:15 pm; arriving in the West Norwood, London area between 11:00 pm and 11:30 pm.

I got home and into bed around midnight with absolutely no idea of the horrors my friend, Danny, had suffered.

Chapter 31
The Dark Side

Wikipedia defines a Private Investigator as: A private investigator (often abbreviated to PI and informally called a private eye), a private *detective*, or inquiry agent, is a person who can be hired by individuals or groups to undertake investigatory law services. Private detectives/investigators often work for attorneys in civil and criminal cases. (Wikipedia Creative Common's Attribution Share-Alike License)

A *private detective* is not a member of the police, but who is hired by individuals or companies.

A **detective** is somebody who investigates and gathers evidence about crimes or possible wrongdoing, for a police force.

So, who would hire a private investigator and what does he do? You might be thinking what a stupid question. Are you reading this and thinking to yourself what is this bloke going on about; of course, I know what a private detective does and who they might work for.

Well....... let's just see.

I have been a private investigator for a large part of my adult life. Beginning my career (and friendship) with Daniel and Southern Investigations; when I left in 1988, I continued in the industry.

Until 1997 I was an independent investigator; being a full-time field operative specialising in legal process and civil and criminal evidence gathering and fraud investigation. During my career I have acted for some of the largest insurance companies, financial institutions and law firms in the country. My casework has seen me travel to numerous overseas destinations. In 1997 I was needed at home and my workload and involvement in the investigation business changed significantly. Even though I semi-retired I have remained in the capacity of an investigative advisor acting on a case by case basis for over 34 years.

In this book I have dealt with the day to day operations of a legitimate detective agency; activities that are clear cut and work routines that act within lawful process.

However, within this industry there is a more sinister side known to have been undertaken by some private investigators; a very lucrative trade in obtaining and selling many forms of information, in some cases to the highest bidder. These activities are sometimes referred to as 'the dark arts'.

One of the major roles of a private investigator is intelligence gathering; the obtaining of information that is used in many different ways. Information is a commodity and there is an endless supply of buyers and when a commodity is sold it generates wealth.

Everyday information pours into our homes in many different forms. Letters from the bank, DWP, hospital, insurance company, lending institution, the DVLA, etc., even catalogues provide personal information. In all instances these nuggets of information include your name and address; sometimes account numbers, reference numbers, national insurance numbers, D.O.B and other personal and private material. This information about you is a very valuable commodity and should be treated as fine jewellery – to be protected and kept secure.

Let me ask you, where do you store your valuable printed documents and letters? Are you diligent in placing your informational commodity in a safe, secure box or a special hiding place? Do you even realise the value of your personal information? You might think this is an unintelligent question given today's awareness of scams and fraudsters. However, the mid 1980s was a simpler time and no one gave a second thought to discarding these golden nuggets of information in the dustbin; a dustbin outside their home, easily accessible and unsecure to anyone interested in your information. Who do you think that might be? This is what was known in the trade as 'doing the bins'.

The internet is inundated with information that the News of The World and other tabloid newspapers were involved in utilising the services of private investigators.

A private detective with unscrupulous ethics might cultivate a corrupt bank employee for the purpose of a relationship in obtaining and selling private and corporate banking information. The corruption could earn the bank official thousands of pounds per year on top of their legitimate salary paid to them by the financial institution.

A private investigator might recruit a career mole specifically to obtain a position as a paid bank employee. In some cases, the mole working up the banking ladder for the sole purpose of having access to the banking institutions accounts and all the riches this type of intelligence could bring.

Intelligence such as bank account details, bank statement printouts of money transactions, details of mortgages, standing orders, direct debits, savings accounts, pensions and assets; access to the entire institution's account holder portfolio that was registered.

For an unethical investigative research business there would likely have been an infinite number of clients (especially the media) that, through the private investigator, had access to this kind of information.

This river of revenue would have been invaluable to the private investigator; the riches would have kept on coming establishing a monopoly in the sale of private and confidential information.

It wouldn't end there; imagine having an independent source bank employee who might be acting on behalf of a consortium of private investigators and investigative researchers all sharing their sources - like a hub in every conceivable banking institution in the country and even beyond.

Telecommunications would be another significant area where great riches might be sought and again private investigators most likely cultivating bent telecommunications employees on the basis of a relationship in obtaining telecommunications data for profit. Moles acting on behalf of unscrupulous private detectives might become telecommunications staff for the sole purpose of having direct access to ex-directory telephone numbers and data bases of the entire telecommunications network; including landlines and cells gaining access to monthly or quarterly statements of any phone subscriber in the UK. Detailed printouts that could include call times and dates, calls made, calls received, cost charges, address of subscriber and payment details, etc.

Private investigator telecommunication resources might even go as far as to establish bent telephone line engineers who would have the technical ability to place phone tap and recording devices on external telephone lines to eavesdrop or covertly record telecommunications anywhere in the country. This would have been an extremely valued resource of information that could have been sold at a very high price.

A bent source at a telecommunications company could be paid little by the private investigator, per ex-directory telephone number and subscriber details; the end user (client) being charged significantly more. Sums believed to be charged would be plus VAT, (yes, I did say plus VAT) as these cunning individuals would unlikely wish to fall foul of the VAT man. The billing for these services by the investigator to their clients would most likely have been undertaken in a non-descript manner.

Investigators might even negotiate, with their bent sources, a 'bulk discount rate' for their services to reduce the cost to themselves but not the end user (client) making even more money. Some might not think that this could be a lot of profit however, times this between 20 and 40 times a day, per agency, the actual profit would likely have been enormous.

Obtaining an ex-directory telephone number and subscribers address and contract details, from a bent telecommunications source, may well have been as quick as a standard 118 118 call is today.

The Data Protection Act 1987 was established to protect the storage and handling of data. The Act itself only required those handling or using data be registered to comply with the Act and any misuse was likely to be dealt with by way of a slap on the wrist. So, to comply with the Data Protection Act those private investigation businesses dealing with this type of data would have registered immediately when the act came into force.

Many instructing clients of the private investigator are unlikely to have known how the information was obtained; whereas other clients would absolutely know where it came from. For example, if the data was telecommunications print outs it could not have emanated from anywhere else; even if the private investigator had removed any identifying markings from an original printed format.

Over time sources of information are likely to have been established everywhere; where ever a database existed a way to access the storage of information held within would have been found; this would have included all public utilities companies. All accessed either by blaggers or bent sources of the private investigator.

Medical records would have been a tremendous source of information specifically in the area of tracing absconders. Private investigators were likely to have finance houses and banks as clients. The institution's debtors in default in making payments might attempt to cover their tracks knowing they were likely to be pursued for the outstanding monies. However, almost every debtor would not think twice about informing their doctor's surgery, hospital or medical provider as to their actual whereabouts whenever moving or transferring doctor or hospital. Absconders would have thought this was a safe and trusted area; that such information could never be divulged or accessed by any third party.

On a daily basis, financial institutions used the services of private investigators, if not directly then through their legal departments. This was a result driven business. Financial institutions are unlikely to have any idea where the intelligence might have come from and probably they would not have cared; as long as there was a 75 percent plus success rate in locating their absconding debtors.

Some investigative research businesses had large in-house teams of tracing agents that would work on commission or piece work and would use almost any method in obtaining their objectives; working on the basis of no trace of the debtor equals no fee to the agent and no fee from the client. If undertaken legitimately the tracing of persons or assets is not illegal.

Bulk tracing of debtors would have been charged at around £25 to £50 per successful trace. It was unlikely there would be a fee if the trace was unsuccessful. There was no limit to the amount of client instructions these agencies could receive on a daily basis which, might equal many hundreds of traces per week. The cost involved in tracing a debtor would be added to the debtor's outstanding account which the debtor would have agreed to pay at the time of lending and on signing their loan contract.

The accessing of government data bases pertaining to personal and business tax records, VAT, Department of Works and Pensions, etc., is likely to have been common place. Seasoned blaggers may well have had extensive knowledge and understanding in tax coding and departmental language including PAYE and National Insurance contribution.

These blaggers would have been sophisticated and cunning individuals with knowledge of the infrastructure and procedures of the day and there would have been no information that they wouldn't have got their hands on. They would likely train themselves to be as proficient as their counterpart (the actual government official or genuine company representative on the other end of the phone) constantly keeping up on a day to day basis with any governmental or bureaucracy changes; so much so that in-house memos of these changes are likely to have been circulated to all blaggers.

To enhance the façade of their deception these blaggers would likely have telephone land lines set up to answer call back inquiries from any genuine utility or government departmental staff. A system so sophisticated to respond to any authentication inquiry by a legitimate official who might be calling back to relay or authenticate any desired information when questions might arise.

These blaggers would have been exceptionally good at what they did; likely working 40 hours per week Monday to Friday 9:00 am to 5:00 pm shadowing the working times of genuine government utilities and agencies, corporate enterprises staff, etc. These blaggers would have been treated like thoroughbred racehorses with all the perks.

Wherever data was stored someone was likely trying to access it. There was no area in intelligence gathering that would have been left unscathed and that would most likely have included the crown jewel of databases, the Police National Computer (PNC checks). Unscrupulous police officers and support staff were likely to be established and readily available in the obtaining and sharing of some of the most personal and sensitive information that was stored.

This would be a vast area of wealth where some of the greatest financial profits might well be sought. This information could include vehicle registration and criminal records data, intelligence of live police investigations and much more, an area where media clients would have likely showed particular interest. A thirst for this type of information would have been unquenchable.

From confidential and sensitive customs and excise data to the listings of TV License payers to the entire services of local government, data would have been seen as a commodity business.

The use of private detectives was not just for elite businesses; far from it. Career criminals would also have known how useful these services could be.

The unscrupulous private detective was getting fat knowing their actions in the supply of sensitive information might lead to a person suffering a serious assault or even worse. This type of situation is likely to have been 'no questions asked' – just the passing of envelopes - one full of cash.

Intelligence gathering is not illegal if the information is obtained lawfully and used in support of civil or criminal law enforcement or for a genuine lawful purpose.

In handling client instructions moral judgement by an investigator is the most important role they can undertake. Immoral values would lead to a state of anarchy throughout an industry that should conduct itself with honour and respect. The temptation of course is filthy lucre. Back in the day (for some) that was just how it was; and in certain areas may well remain to this day.

With the advances in information technology, phone hacking, telephone scams and cybercrime is it any different or has it just evolved into something else. The commodity however has not changed - information; and information still means money.

This is an excerpt from the Guardian Online Dated Tuesday the 12th of July 2011 by Sam Jones.

An internal Met police report found. Davies notes; "Rees was so useful that News International were put off him neither when he was arrested on suspicion of murdering his business partner (and released without charge), nor when former Scotland Yard detective sergeant Sid Fillery, was convicted of possessing child pornography, nor when he was arrested for plotting to plant cocaine on the estranged wife of a client (for which Rees was sentenced to seven years in prison). News International records show that, even after he emerged from this prison sentence, he was still selling them information, including telephone information.

In the noughties of the new millennium events were to unfold that would bring the actions of some involved in the investigation business to the attention of the authorities sending shock waves through, what was the News of the World.

The following article is an excerpt from Wikipedia (News International Phone Hacking Scandal) Wikipedia: Text of Creative Commons Attribution-Share Alike 3.0.

*The **News International phone-hacking scandal** is a controversy involving the now defunct News of the World and other British newspapers published by News International a subsidiary of News Corporation. Employees of the newspaper were accused of engaging in phone hacking, police bribery, and exercising improper influence in the pursuit of stories. Whilst investigations conducted from 2005 to 2007 appeared to show that the paper's phone hacking activities were limited to celebrities, politicians, and members of the British Royal Family, in July 2011 it was revealed that the phones of murdered schoolgirl Milly Dowler, relatives of* deceased British soldiers, and victims of the 7 July 2005 London bombings had also been hacked. The resulting public outcry against News Corporation and its owner Rupert Murdock led to several high-profile resignations, including that of Murdoch as News Corporation director, Murdoch's son James as executive chairman, Dow Jones chief executive Les Hinton, News International legal manager Tom Crone, and chief executive Rebekah Brooks. The commissioner of London's Metropolitan Police Service, Sir Paul Stephenson, also resigned. Advertiser boycotts led to the closure of the News of the World on 10 July 2011, after 168 years of publication. (Phone-hacking scandal: Timeline. BBC News 12 July 2011. Retrieved 16 July 2011. Public pressure shortly forced *News Corporation to cancel its proposed takeover of the British satellite broadcaster BskyB.*

Operation Nigeria

Private investigators that were illegally providing information to the News of the World were also engaged in a variety of other illegal activities. Between 1999 and 2003, several were convicted for crimes including drug distribution, the theft of drugs, child pornography, planting evidence, corruption, and perverting the course of justice. Jonathan Rees and his partner Sid Fillery, a former police officer, were also under suspicion for the murder of a private investigator named Daniel Morgan. The Met undertook an investigation of Rees, entitled Operation Nigeria, and tapped his telephone. Substantial evidence was accumulated that Rees was purchasing information from improper sources and that, amongst others, Alex Marunchak of the News of the World was paying him up to £150,000 a year for doing so. (Nick Davies, The Guardian 11.03.11 retrieved 18.09.11) Jonathan Rees reportedly bought information from former and serving police officers, Customs officers, a VAT inspector, bank employees, burglars, and from blaggers who would telephone the Inland Revenue, the DVLA, banks and phone companies, and deceive them into releasing confidential information. (Nick Davies, The Guardian 09.06.11 retrieved 19.09.11) Rees then sold the information to the News of the World, the Daily Mirror, the Sunday Mirror and the Sunday Times. (Sam Jones, The Guardian 12.07.11 retrieved 18.09.11)

In June 2002, Fillery had reportedly used his relationship with Alex Marunchak to arrange for private investigator Glenn Mulcaire, then doing work for News of the World, to obtain confidential information about Detective Chief Superintendent David Cook, one of the police officers investigating the murder of Daniel Morgan. Mulcaire obtained Cook's home address, his internal Metropolitan police payroll number, his date of birth and figures for his mortgage payments as well as physically following him and his family. Attempts to access Cook's voicemail and that of his wife, and possibly hack his computer and intercept his post were also suspected. (Nick Davies, The Guardian 06.07.11 retrieved 27.08.11) Documents reportedly held by Scotland Yard show that "Mulcaire did this on the instructions of Greg Miskiw, assistant editor at News of the World and a close friend of Marunchak." The Metropolitan Police Service handled this apparent attempt by agents of the News of the World to interfere with a murder inquiry by having informal discussions with Rebekah Brooks, then editor for the newspaper. "Scotland Yard took no further action, apparently reflecting the desire of Dick Fedorcio, Director of Public Affairs and Internal Communication for the Met who had a close working relationship with Brooks, to avoid unnecessary friction with the newspaper." (Nick Davies, The Guardian 06.07.11 retrieved 27.08.11)

This is an excerpt from the Guardian online dated Wednesday the 6th of July 2011 by Nick Davies.

Brooks confronted evidence her paper's resources had been used on behalf of two murder suspects, to spy on the detective investigating their alleged crime. Brooks was summoned to Scotland Yard she was told, Marunchak, apparently agreed to photographers and vans to run surveillance on behalf of Rees and Fillery, suspected of murdering, Morgan, The Yard saw a possible attempt to pervert the course of justice. Scotland Yard contacted Brooks for explanation. In November 2002 Brooks was confronted by Cook, Commander Baker, and Fedorcio, media relations. Brooks is said to have defended Marunchak. Scotland Yard took no further action.

This news article was compelling stuff but much more was to come in a speech by then Prime Minister David Cameron.

This is an excerpt from the announcement of The Leveson Inquiry which was instigated on the 13th of July 2011 by the then Prime Minister David Cameron to inquire into the culture, practices and ethics of the press by Lord Justice Leveson.

This document contains parliamentary information licensed under the Open Parliament Licence v3.0.

"In recent days, the whole country has been shocked by the revelations of the phone hacking scandal. What this country—and the House—has to confront is an episode that is, frankly, disgraceful: accusations of widespread lawbreaking by parts of our press: alleged corruption by some police officers; and, as we have just discussed, the failure of our political system over many, many years to tackle a problem that has been getting worse. We must at all times keep the real victims at the front and centre of this debate. Relatives of those who died at the hands of terrorism, war heroes and murder victims—people who have already suffered in a way that we can barely imagine—have been made to suffer all over again. I believe that we all want the same thing: press, police and politicians who serve the public. Last night the Deputy Prime Minister and I met the Leader of the Opposition. I also met the Chairs of the Culture, Media and Sport Committee, the Home Affairs Committee and the Justice Committee to discuss the best way forward. Following these consultations, I want to set out today how we intend to proceed: first, on the public inquiry; secondly, on the issues surrounding News International's proposed takeover of BSkyB; and thirdly, on ethics in the police service and its relationship with the press. Before I do that, I will update the House on the current criminal investigation into phone hacking. I met Sir Paul Stephenson last night. He assured me that the investigation is fully resourced. It is one of the largest currently under way in the country, and is being carried out by a completely different team from the one that carried out the original investigation. It is being led by Deputy Assistant Commissioner Sue Akers, who I believe impressed the Home Affairs Committee yesterday. Her team is looking through 11,000 pages containing 3,870 names, and around 4,000 mobile and 5,000 landline phone numbers. The team has contacted 170 people so far, and will contact every single person named in those documents. The commissioner's office

informed me this morning that the team has so far made eight arrests and undertaken numerous interviews. Let me now turn to the action that the Government are taking. Last week in the House I set out our intention to establish an independent public inquiry into phone hacking and other illegal practices in the British press. We have looked carefully at what the nature of the inquiry should be. We want it to be one that is as robust as possible—one that can get to the truth fastest and also get to work the quickest, and, vitally, one that commands the full confidence of the public. Clearly there are two pieces of work that have to be done. First, we need a full investigation into wrongdoing in the press and the police, including the failure of the first police investigation. Secondly, we need a review of regulation of the press. We would like to get on with both those elements as quickly as possible, while being mindful of the ongoing criminal investigations. So,

HC Hansard, 13 July 2011, vol 531, col 311-31

PART A | The Inquiry after listening carefully, we have decided that the best way to proceed is with one inquiry, but in two parts. I can tell the House that the inquiry will be led by one of the most senior judges in the country, Lord Justice Leveson. He will report to both the Home Secretary and the Secretary of State for Culture, Media and Sport. The inquiry will be established under the Inquiries Act 2005, which means that it will have the power to summon witnesses, including newspaper reporters, management, proprietors, policemen and politicians of all parties, to give evidence under oath and in public. …Starting as soon as possible, Lord Justice Leveson, assisted by a panel of senior independent figures with relevant expertise in media, broadcasting, regulation and government will inquire into the culture, practices and ethics of the press; its relationship with the police; the failure of the current system of regulation; the contacts made, and discussions had, between national newspapers and politicians; why previous warnings about press misconduct were not heeded; and the issue of cross-media ownership. He will make recommendations for a new, more effective way of regulating the press—one that supports its freedom, plurality and independence from Government, but which also demands the highest ethical and professional standards. He will also make recommendations about the future conduct of relations between politicians and the press. That part of the inquiry we hope will report within 12 months. The second part of the inquiry will examine the extent of unlawful or improper conduct at the News of the World and other newspapers, and the way in which management failures may have allowed it to happen. That part of the inquiry will also look into the original police investigation and the issue of corrupt payments to police officers, and will consider the implications for the relationships between newspapers and the police. Lord Justice Leveson has agreed to these draft terms of reference. I am placing them in the Library today, and we will send them to the devolved Administrations. No one should be in any doubt of our intention to get to the bottom of the truth and learn the lessons for the future."

1.2

The Terms of Reference were then the subject of further discussion both with the devolved administrations of Scotland, Wales and Northern Ireland and other interested parties.

The Prime Minister returned to the topic on 20 July 2011, when announcing the appointment of the Assessors. He said:

"We have made some significant amendments to the remit of the inquiry. With allegations that the problem of the relationship between the press and the police goes wider than just the Met, we have agreed that other relevant forces will now be within the scope of the inquiry. We have agreed that the inquiry should consider not just the relationship between the press, police and politicians, but their individual conduct too. We have also made it clear that the inquiry should look not just at the press, but at other media organisations, including broadcasters and social media if there is any evidence that they have been involved in criminal activities."

1.3

Thus, the Terms of Reference of the Inquiry, as finally drafted, are:

Part 1

1. To inquire into the culture, practices, and ethics of the press, including:

HC Hansard, 20 July 2011, vol 531, col 919

Chapter 1 | the Announcement

(a) contacts and the relationships between national newspapers and politicians, and the conduct of each;(b) contacts and the relationship between the press and the police, and the conduct of each;(c) the extent to which the current policy and regulatory framework has failed including in relation to data protection; and (d) the extent to which there was a failure to act on previous warnings about media misconduct. 2. To make recommendations:(a) for a new more effective policy and regulatory regime which supports the integrity and freedom of the press, the plurality of the media, and its independence, including from Government, while encouraging the highest ethical and professional standards;(b) for how future concerns about press behaviour, media policy, regulation and cross-media ownership should be dealt with by all the relevant authorities, including Parliament, Government, the prosecuting authorities and the police; (c) the future conduct of relations between politicians and the press; and (d) the future conduct of relations between the police and the press.

Part 2

3. To inquire into the extent of unlawful or improper conduct within News International, other newspaper organisations and, as appropriate, other organisations within the media, and by those responsible for holding personal data. 4. To inquire into the way in which any relevant police force investigated allegations or evidence of unlawful conduct by persons within or connected with News International, the review by the Metropolitan Police of their initial investigation, and the conduct of the prosecuting authorities. 5. To inquire into the extent to which the police received corrupt payments or other inducements, or were otherwise complicit in such misconduct or in suppressing its proper investigation and how this was allowed to happen. 6. To inquire into the extent of corporate governance and management failures at News International and other newspaper organisations, and the role, if any, of politicians, public servants and others in relation to any failure to investigate wrongdoing at News International 7.

In the light of these inquiries, to consider the implications for the relationships between newspaper organisations and the police, prosecuting authorities, and relevant regulatory bodies – and to recommend what actions, if any, should be taken.

1.4

By letter dated 28 July 2011, as responsible Ministers under the Inquiries Act 2005, the Rt Hon Jeremy Hunt MP (then the Secretary of State for Culture Media and Sports) and Baroness Browning (then a Minister of State at the Home Office) appointed me to Chair the Inquiry pursuant to s3(1)(a) of the Act. On the same date, their appointment having previously been announced by the Prime Minister, acting pursuant to s11 (2)(a) of the Act, the Ministers appointed six Assessors with a wide range of professional experience to assist the Inquiry.

PART A | The Inquiry

These were Sir David Bell, Shami Chakrabarti CBE, Lord (David) Currie, Elinor Goodman, George Jones and Sir Paul Scott-Lee.

1.5

From the day of the announcement of my appointment, it was necessary to identify appropriate support. A Director General with a legal background and experience at the Home Office, the Ministry of Justice and the Office of the Deputy Prime Minister, Rowena Collins Rice was an ideal appointment as Secretary to the Inquiry. Kim Brudenell, a senior solicitor from the Treasury Solicitor's office was appointed Solicitor to the Inquiry; Amanda Jeffery (from the Judicial Office) and Rachel Clark (from the Department of Culture, Media and Sport and previously the Department for Business, Innovation and Skills) were appointed as Heads of Administration and Research respectively. With an eye on prudent financial management, suitable civil servants from across Government were recruited to staff the Inquiry and ensure that it could proceed expeditiously and efficiently.

1.6

I also set about appointing counsel. With the assistance of the Treasury Solicitor, I selected Robert Jay QC to be Counsel to the Inquiry; with my approval he nominated David Barr and Carine Patry Hoskins as junior Counsel, later adding Lucinda Boon for Module 2 (concerning the relationship between the press and the police). Counsel were assisted by junior members of the Bar in relation to the necessary research for both preparing the examination of witnesses and the subsequent collation of the evidence.

1.7

At the very beginning of this Report, it is appropriate to record my enormous gratitude to the Assessors, to Counsel and to the entire Inquiry team (whose names are set out in Appendix A to this Report) for their unstinting commitment to the Inquiry and the prodigious effort that has been put into ensuring that it proceeded smoothly, to budget and, most important, was able appropriately to address the Terms of Reference within a time frame that allows early consideration to be given by the Government and Parliament to the way forward.

This is an excerpt of some of the findings of the Leveson Inquiry. The entire content of this statement can be accessed via The UK National Archives.

This document contains parliamentary information licensed under the Open Parliament Licence v3.0.

AN INQUIRY INTO THE CULTURE, PRACTICES, AND ETHICS OF THE PRESS.
EXECUTIVE SUMMARY AND RECOMMENDATIONS.

The Right Honourable Lord Justice Leveson Presented to Parliament pursuant to Section 26 of the Inquiries Act 2005 Ordered by the House of Commons to be printed on 29 November 2012

EXECUTIVE SUMMARY
Introduction

1.

For the seventh time in less than 70 years, a report has been commissioned by the Government which has dealt with concerns about the press.

1

It was sparked by public revulsion about a single action – the hacking of the mobile phone of a murdered teenager. From that beginning, the scope of the Inquiry was expanded to cover the culture, practices and ethics of the press in its relations with the public, with the police, with politicians and, as to the police and politicians, the conduct of each. It carries with it authority provided personally by the Prime Minister. It requires me to consider the extent to which there was a failure to act on previous warnings as to the conduct of the press, the way in which the press has been regulated (if it has) and, in any event, how regulation should work in the future.

The factual background

20.

For many years, there have been complaints that certain parts of the press ride roughshod over others, both individuals and the public at large, without any justifiable public interest. Attempts to take them to task have not been successful. Promises follow other promises. Even changes made following the death of Diana, Princess of Wales, have hardly been enduring. Practices discovered by the Information Commissioner, during Operation Motorman, which led to the publication of two reports to Parliament, revealed that large parts of the press had been engaged in a widespread trade in private and confidential information, apparently with little regard to the public interest. A private detective, Steve Whittamore, had certainly been engaged in wholesale criminal breaches of data protection legislation and, prima facie journalists who engaged his services or used his products (and paid substantial sums for the privilege) must or should have appreciated that the information could not have been obtained lawfully.

21.

None of these revelations led to any newspaper conducting an investigation either into its own practices or into those of other titles. No newspaper sought to discover (let alone expose) whether its journalists had complied with data protection legislation. Some titles promptly forbad the further use of private detectives for data searching; many took some time to take that step and others did not do so at all. When the Information Commissioner sought the support of the Government and then Parliament to increase the penalties available to the courts for criminal breaches of the law, he was met with intense lobbying by the press (and by the Press Complaints Commission) challenging the proposition that breach of the criminal law by journalists, even on a wholesale, industrial basis should ever be capable of being visited with a custodial penalty.

The press and data protection.

102.

One of the areas that I am required to consider is 'the extent to which the current policy and regulatory framework has failed, including in relation to data protection'. This is because of the light that Operation Motorman can shine on the culture, practices and ethics of the press. It is also because the response of the Office of the Information Commissioner (ICO), and its role and functions in relation to the press more generally, is relevant to the adequacy of the regulatory framework.

103.

The Operation Motorman 'treasure trove' constituted evidence of serious and systemic illegality and poor practice in the acquisition and use of personal information which could have spread across the press as a whole. There was a pressing need for a commensurate response from the ICO dealing with all aspects of the personal information problem. It appears that the ICO did not adopt and pursue a sufficiently clear operational strategy to deal with the systemic and practical issues which arose.

104.

None of the journalists named in the Whittamore notebooks was ever investigated or prosecuted for breaches of section 55 of the Data Protection Act 1998 (DPA). This was notwithstanding the strength of the prima facie case across the board; not even the strongest cases were taken forward for criminal investigation, and not a single journalist was so much as interviewed. The ICO did not undertake regulatory investigation or enforcement action of any kind against the press, whether formal or informal, despite the evidence that the press was likely to be holding or using the Motorman information either unlawfully or contrary to standards of good practice. In the circumstances, an opportunity was missed to address problems in the culture, practices and ethics of the press, and to safeguard the position of victims.

105.

The ICO did take significant steps to raise the profile of the issue politically. Two reports were laid before Parliament under section 52 of the DPA, which served an important function of drawing attention to the problem generally. The Information Commissioner also pursued a High-profile strategy: this was to seek to engage with the PCC and to campaign vigorously for legislative change which would broaden the sentencing powers of the criminal courts in relation to data protection breaches. The response to both was unsatisfactory.

107.

The hostile attitude of the press to attempts at law enforcement and improvement of standards goes some way to account for the evident difficulty of the ICO, both past and present, *in engaging operationally with the culture, practices and ethics of the press. Further explanation lies in the legal framework of the DPA, which puts unnecessary and inappropriate barriers in the way of regulatory law enforcement and the protection of victims' rights. I have recommended changes in the law to remove unnecessary procedural red tape and provide for a fairer balance between the public interest in freedom of expression and the public interest in personal information privacy. I have also recommended some extension to the ICO's powers of prosecution.*

This is an excerpt of Deputy Assistant Commissioner of the Police Sue Akers witness statement dated the 31ˢᵗ of October 2012 paragraphs 1, 2, 24 and 25. The entire content of this statement can be accessed via The UK National Archives.

This document contains parliamentary information licensed under the Open Parliament Licence v3.0.

Fourth Witness Statement of: DAC-Sue-Akers.

Statement made on behalf of: The Commissioner of Police of the Metropolis

Exhibits Referred to: None

Date Statement Made: 31 October 2012

The Leveson Inquiry into the Culture Practices and Ethics of the Press

Occupation: Deputy Assistant Commissioner

Address c/o New Scotland Yard Introduction

1.

I have been required by the Inquiry to provide a statement of the current position: regarding Operations Weeting, Elveden and Tuleta – providing as much detail as possible, without naming individuals, as is compatible with the ongoing police investigations; and as to whether the MPS are receiving cooperation with their investigations, with examples of how this is/is not being provided.

2.

I also provide a further update regarding victims of phone hacking. This statement should be read in conjunction with my previous statements dated 11 November 2011, 24 February 2012 and 20 July 2012 and the evidence I gave to this Inquiry on 6 February, 27 February 2012 and 23 July 2012.

Operation Tuleta

24.

Operation Tuleta which began on 2 August 2011 is the operational name given to the assessment and investigation of allegations of the commission of criminal offences by personal data intrusions connected to journalism which fall outside the remits of Operations Weeting and Elveden.

25.

Currently Operation Tuleta is conducting an assessment of 142 complaints of data intrusion, including allegations of phone hacking, computer hacking and improper access to banking, medical and other personal records.

I believe the facts stated in this witness statement are true.

Signed

Dated 31.10.12.

Part one of the Leveson inquiry concluded on the 29th of November 2012. Part two is expected to take place at some time in the future. I personally feel that this is the only realistic way to finally get anywhere near the truth. I recommend, for reference, that the entire transcript of part one of the Leveson Inquiry is accessed online via the UK Government National Archives.

Deputy Commissioner Sue Akers statement was dated the 31st of October 2012 however at the beginning of the month News of the World journalist Alex Marunchak and John Rees find themselves under the gaze of the police.

This is an excerpt from the Guardian online dated Tuesday the 2nd of October 2012 by Vikram Dodd and Jason Deans.

Scotland Yard officers investigating alleged computer hacking have made two further arrests, understood to be former News of the World journalist Alex Marunchak and private investigator Jonathan Rees. The two men were arrested shortly before 7am on Tuesday morning at their homes by police officers working on Operation Kalmyk. Both were arrested for alleged offences under section 3 of the Computer Misuse Act 1990 and sections 1 and 2 of the Regulation of Investigatory Powers Act 2000.

On the 9th of September 2015 almost three and a half years after Marunchak and Rees were arrested in connection to operation Kalmyk, The Crown Prosecution Service, Gregor McGill, Senior Lawyer made the following statement.

This statement contains public sector information licensed under the Open Government Licence v2.0.

Statement in relation to Operation Kalmyk

09/09/2015

Gregor McGill, Senior lawyer at the Crown Prosecution Service said: "The CPS received a full file of evidence from the Metropolitan Police's Operation Kalmyk investigation team in March 2015, after a complex investigation. Having carefully reviewed the evidence in accordance with the Code for Crown Prosecutors, the CPS has concluded that no further action can be taken against any of the suspects involved.

"In total 15 suspects were considered in relation to allegations of 'computer hacking' allegedly carried out between April 2005 and September 2007 against 13 potential victims – some individuals, some corporate.

"The appropriate offence under consideration was unauthorised monitoring of a computer, contrary to section 1 of the Computer Misuse Act. Any potential offending under s1 Computer Misuse Act could not be prosecuted as that offence was time barred due to the age of the allegations. In order to consider other offences, we must be satisfied that any alternative offences would have been preferable had the time-bar not been a barrier to prosecution – for

example that it better illustrated the alleged offending or that it allowed more suitable sentencing powers.

"Accordingly, further consideration was given to potential charges of conspiracy to defraud, other offences under the Computer Misuse Act and also offences under the Fraud Act, Data Protection Act and Regulation of Investigatory Powers Act.

"None were considered appropriate, in particular because any charge under those Acts would have been made to circumvent the time limit which applies to the section 1 offence.

"In one discrete matter it was determined that there was sufficient evidence to charge one suspect with an offence contrary to section 2 of the Fraud Act - fraud by false representation - but we have determined, in accordance with the Code for Crown Prosecutors, that it would not be in the public interest to prosecute that matter due to the age of the allegation and the likelihood that it would result in a nominal penalty only if the suspect were convicted. It is therefore not in the public interest to bring this matter to court now.

"Any decision by the CPS does not imply any finding concerning guilt or criminal conduct; the CPS makes decisions only according to the test set out in the Code for Crown Prosecutors and it is applied in all decisions on whether or not to prosecute.

"Contact has been made with all relevant parties to inform them of the outcome of this case."

It is important to point out that all those that were arrested or interviewed by the police in connection with these offences all received (NFA) no further action.

Chapter 32

The Daniel Morgan Independent Panel

On 29th of February 2012, during a House of Commons adjournment debate, Tom Watson, Labour MP for West Bromwich East made a statement raising the issue of the Daniel Morgan murder and the subsequent failings in the police investigations and concerns of police corruption in support of a judge led inquiry to be considered by then Home Secretary (and subsequent Prime Minister) Theresa May.

This document contains parliamentary information licensed under the Open Parliament Licence v3.0.

This is the transcript of the actual parliamentary statement made by Tom Watson Member of Parliament. This statement was made on the 29th of February 2012.

4.00 pm Mr Tom Watson (West Bromwich East) (Lab)

It is nearly 25 years—10 March 1987—since the son of Isabel and the brother of Alastair, Daniel Morgan, was brutally killed by five blows of an axe to the head. The last blow was probably struck when he was on the ground, because the hilt was embedded in his skull. Alastair is here today representing his family to hear the Minister's response to the family's call for a judge-led inquiry into the five failed investigations into Daniel's murder. All they ask is justice for Daniel.

The five failed inquiries have cost the taxpayer nearly £30 million. I believe that had the murder been investigated adequately a quarter of a century ago, Daniel's killer would have been brought to justice. John Yates said:

"This case is one of the most deplorable episodes in the entire history of the Metropolitan Police Service."

He went on to say that Daniel's family had "been treated disgracefully." I suspect that the Minister will not be able to grant a judge-led inquiry today, but I hope that he will at least keep an open mind, as the Home Secretary has not yet decided whether to grant such an inquiry, which my hon. Friend the Member for Islington South and Finsbury (Emily Thornberry) has also been campaigning for on behalf of her constituents.

I ask the Minister for one thing: please agree to ask his officials and the Metropolitan police a number of searching questions before he and the Home Secretary make their decision. I will put those questions to him at the end of my contribution. Daniel's family categorically do not want another investigation by the Metropolitan police—they have lost trust. Before I raise specific questions for the Minister, I will run through the events that have led to the five failed investigations.

Investigation No. 1 was severely compromised by police corruption. For 20 years the Met failed to admit that, despite the repeated pleas of the Morgan family. Indeed, it was not until 2005 that the Met's then commissioner, Sir Ian Blair, admitted that the first inquiry involving Detective Superintendent Sidney Fillery had been compromised. If that admission had come earlier, the subsequent inquiries might not also have failed.

As part of the first investigation, it is now known that DS Sid Fillery—a member of the original murder squad—failed to reveal to his superiors that he had very close links with Jonathan Rees when he became part of the inquiry. I am told that Fillery took a statement from Rees, but it did not include details that both he and Rees had met Daniel at the Golden Lion pub the night before the murder, nor did it include details of a robbery of Belmont Car Auctions a year earlier. Had those details emerged at the time, they would have revealed that those incidents brought both men into direct conflict with Daniel.

The Belmont Car Auctions story was significant because Jonathan Rees and Daniel had previously agreed that they would not deal with cash-in-transit work. Daniel is known to have been angry when Jonathan Rees took on the job of looking after the takings from the auctions, saying it would, "backfire on them." Rees, who was contracted to carry cash to the bank after a series of auctions, alleged that the bank night-safe had been interfered with, and therefore took the money to his home in March 1986. He alleges that he was attacked outside his house by two masked men who took the £18,000 from him. Belmont Car Auctions then sued Southern Investigations, which resulted in Daniel having to raise £10,000 very quickly for security to the court.

We know that two days before the murder Daniel told a witness, Brian Crush, that he believed that Rees and Fillery had set up the robbery and taken the money themselves. Daniel also told a witness that he was dealing with police corruption and that he did not know whom in the Met he could trust with the information.

It is important that the Minister understands at the outset why the omissions of the meeting at the Golden Lion pub and the auction robbery were so critical to the first investigation being compromised. My source has told me that omissions in the statement gathered by Fillery initially prevented attention being drawn towards Jonathan Rees and, indeed, Fillery himself. Alastair Morgan, Daniel's brother, has also told me how he raised his own suspicions with Fillery about Rees's possible involvement with the Belmont Car Auctions robbery as a possible motive for the murder. Alastair had not known that Fillery had actually recommended Rees to the auction company at the time.

Alastair now believes that it was a mistake to trust Fillery. He tells me that, for example, his information to Fillery later led to a phone call to his sister-in-law in which the family were told directly by Fillery that Alastair should get out of London because he was interfering in the investigation. When Fillery was removed from the team, the investigation quickly focused on those whom the Met believed to be responsible. Fillery, Rees, the two Vian brothers and two other police officers who were closely associated with Southern Investigations were arrested. However, no charges were brought and all six men were released.

At the inquest in April 1988, Kevin Lennon, who worked as a bookkeeper at Southern Investigations, gave evidence that implicated Rees in Daniel's murder. The Guardian newspaper reported that, in evidence to the hearing, Kevin Lennon said Rees wanted Morgan dead after a row. Lennon said:

"John Rees explained that, when or after Daniel Morgan had been killed, he would be replaced by a friend of his who was a serving policeman, Detective Sergeant Sid Fillery."

Lennon also told the inquest that Rees had said to him:

"I've got the perfect solution for Daniel's murder. My mates at Catford nick are going to arrange it."

Lennon added:

"He (Rees) went on to explain to me that if they didn't do it themselves the police would arrange for some person over whom they had some criminal charge pending to carry out Daniel's murder".

In the weeks before his murder, Daniel Morgan had repeatedly expressed concerns over corrupt police officers in south London. The Morgan family also believe that Daniel was about to reveal evidence of corruption.

In the aftermath of the murder and just as predicted by the evidence of Kevin Lennon seven months before at the inquest in 1988, Fillery took early retirement with an enhanced sick pension. Alastair Morgan has also told me how, at the inquest, members of the Met disputed the fact he had ever spoken with Fillery directly as part of the investigation. He believes that they were trying to cover up for Fillery.

Investigation No. 2—an outside inquiry—ordered by the then commissioner, Sir Peter Imbert, following a complaint by the family, was carried out by Hampshire police. It made no attempt whatsoever to address the allegations that Fillery had tried to get Daniel's brother, Alastair, out of London after he had pointed to Rees as a prime suspect in the murder. Had the inquiry done so, it might have found that what Alastair said tallied with the allegations previously made by Kevin Lennon at the inquest in 1988. The inquiry's terms of reference were to investigate "all aspects of police involvement arising from the death of Daniel Morgan".

Unknown to Daniel's family, the remit of the inquiry was secretly changed at a high-level meeting at Scotland Yard in December 1988. The family further believe that the second investigation did not address the statements made at the inquest by serving police officers in which they denied that Alastair Morgan had ever raised his suspicions about Rees with Fillery, directly, as part of investigation No. 1.

In addition, Mr Morgan is frustrated that he offered to provide Hampshire police with a statement after an initial interview, but they refused it—indeed, no further statement was taken until 2000. The inquiry later reported to the Police Complaints Authority that there was

"No evidence whatsoever of police involvement in the murder"

And that the original inquiry had been good.

Understandably, the Morgan family kept up their campaign for justice. In November 1997, they met Sir Paul Condon who promised to review the case—nothing happened until late 1998 when, under the leadership of John Stevens and Roy Clark, the Met launched a third investigation into the murder. That was done without the knowledge of the Morgan family and in secrecy—not including the family was a mistake and the secrecy of the inquiry has deeply troubled them. The secrecy today is still a major issue for the family with the Met. I hope that the Minister understands that he must ask why the family were not kept informed.

As part of investigation No. 3, a covert bug was placed in the office of Southern Investigations. I will return to that later. Yet investigation No. 3 arguably missed its chance to use trigger events to gather further evidence on the murder. After Rees went to jail, the Morgan family had another meeting with Roy Clark. Clark initially said that they would do another investigation. The family ruled that out, as they wanted disclosure of the Hampshire report first. First Clark and then Andy Hayman refused to disclose the report to the family. It was not until the family were forced to go to the High Court that they succeeded. The Morgan's should not have had to do that.

In the interim, the Met conducted a fourth inquiry, led by Detective Chief Superintendent David Cook. However, the fourth investigation, which the family described as the first honest investigation into the murder, gathered insufficient evidence to prosecute Rees, Fillery and three other men for the murder. My right hon. Friend the Member for Salford and Eccles (Hazel Blears) then refused the family's request for a judicial inquiry.

In 2006, a fifth investigation began under Assistant Commissioner John Yates. That happened out of the blue after Alastair Morgan had initially approached the Metropolitan Police Authority chairman, Len Duvall. He had ordered the commissioner to present his own report on the case before that. The family were initially deeply sceptical of the new Yates investigation. Devastatingly, after five years, the case collapsed last year. The Morgan family's solicitors have said that this was "Under the weight of previous corruption".

The accused, Jonathan Rees, Fillery and the Vian brothers were ultimately acquitted because the defence would not have had access to all the documents in the case. The Metropolitan police repeatedly mislaid crates of evidence, owing to the sheer number of documents the case had generated. Mr Justice Maddison also ruled that the super grass witnesses had been mishandled.

I now turn to the situation that the family find themselves in now. Since the collapse of the prosecution, the Met has publicly admitted corruption in the first inquiry. The family believe this corruption had an impact on the second, third, fourth and fifth inquiries. However, what the family did not know during any of the five investigations is the extent to which the relationship between News International, private investigators and the police had an impact on the conduct of the inquiry.

Jonathan Rees and Sid Fillery were at the corrupt nexus of private investigators, police officers and journalists at News of the World. Through the hacking scandal, we now know that Southern Investigations became the hub of a web of police and media contacts involving the illegal theft and disclosure of information obtained through Rees and Fillery's corrupted contacts. Southern Investigations sold information to many newspapers during the 1990s, but we think exclusively to News International after Rees was released from jail in 2005.

The main conduit at News International was Alex Marunchak, chief crime reporter for the News of the World and later the paper's Irish editor. I want to focus the Minister's attention on Marunchak in particular. Rees and Marunchak had a relationship that was so close that they both registered companies at the same address in Thornton Heath. Abbeycover, established by Rees and his colleague from News International, Greg Miskiw, was registered at the same address as Southern Investigations, run by Rees and Fillery. Rees's confirmed links with Marunchak take the murder of Daniel Morgan to a new level.

It is important to remember that, in the days before the murder, Daniel's family believe that he was on the verge of exposing huge police corruption. That was confirmed by Brian Madagan, Daniel's former employer, in a statement in May 1987, in which he said that he believed Daniel was about to sell a story to a newspaper. In a second, later statement, Madagan said he believed that paper to be the News of the World and the contact to be Alex Marunchak who, until recently, still worked for the paper. BBC Radio 4's "Report" programme also confirmed that it has seen evidence suggesting that, a week before the murder, Daniel was about to take a story exposing police corruption to Mr Marunchak and was promised a payment of £40,000. We also know, from the investigative reporting of Nick Davies at The Guardian, that Southern Investigations paid the debts of Alex Marunchak.

As part of the third failed investigation, Operation Nigeria was launched. It included the surveillance of Southern Investigations between May and September 1999 and was run by the Metropolitan police's anti-corruption squad, CIB3. It placed a bug in the offices of Southern Investigations that yielded evidence that convicted Rees for a serious and unrelated crime. Police surveillance shows frequent contact between Rees and Marunchak. I understand that the tapes made by the recording by the bug have not all been transcribed; if they were, they would yield more collusion, perhaps criminal in nature, between News International and Jonathan Rees. I hope the Minister will ask the police if that process is under way.

When Rees came out of jail, he was re-hired by the News of the World, then edited by Andy Coulson. Rees also founded a company called Pure Energy, in which Marunchak was involved. The police hold evidence to suggest that Rees discussed the use of Trojan devices with his associate, Sid Fillery. He was an associate of Philip Campbell Smith, who received a custodial sentence on Monday for a crime related to blagging. Campbell Smith is a former Army *intelligence officer. I will say no more on Campbell Smith, because I do not want to prejudice the Operation Tuleta inquiry. However, I hope that I have demonstrated to the Minister a close association between Rees and Marunchak.*

This is why I think that the Metropolitan police cannot be used in any further investigations: yesterday, the Leveson inquiry heard a startling revelation that Alex Marunchak—a close business associate of Jonathan Rees, then the prime suspect in a murder case—chose to put DCI David Cook and his family under close covert surveillance. The person who was investigating a murder was put under close surveillance by a close business associate of the man he was investigating. That was raised with Rebekah Brooks in 2002, the then editor of the News of the World. I would like the Minister to imagine what his response would have been to that information. A journalist employee tried to undermine the murder investigation of his close associate. Rupert Murdoch claims that News International takes a zero-tolerance approach to wrongdoing. However, far from launching a wide-scale inquiry to investigate wrongdoing, Rebekah Brooks promoted Alex Marunchak to the editor's job at the News of the World in Ireland.

It gets worse. Last year, Mr Cook's then wife, Jacqui Hames, discovered that her records appeared in the evidence file of Glenn Mulcaire. The records show information that she believes could only have been obtained from her private police records. While DCI Cook was investigating a murder, his colleagues in another part of the Met were in receipt of evidence that a close associate of his suspect was illegally targeting him. Did Andy Hayman, the then head of the hacking inquiry, who also happened to be in charge of the fourth investigation into Daniel's murder, ensure that his colleague was informed about this? No. When Andy Hayman retired early from the Met, he became a paid contributor for News International—that is not right. For months, Scotland Yard took no action. Why not? Why was it not willing to pursue what appears to be a clear attempt to interfere with the murder inquiry of Daniel Morgan? The Guardian has reported that the reason why no action was taken by Scotland Yard was not to embarrass the Met with newspapers.

It gets worse. I would like the Minster to request to see all the intelligence reports submitted about Alex Marunchak. I believe the Met is sitting on an intelligence report from late 2002 that claims a police contact overheard Marunchak claim he was paying the relatives of police officers in Cambridgeshire for information about the Soham murders. As far as we know, those allegations have not been investigated. I do not know whether the intelligence reports are accurate, but I do know that Alex Marunchak was involved in writing stories about how the Manchester United tops of those young girls were found. I also believe that at least one of the Soham parents appears in the evidence file of Glenn Mulcaire. The Met police failed to investigate both leads when reported in 2002 and 2006. I think that Rupert Murdoch owes the Morgan family an apology, and I do not think that he has made his last apology to the grieving parents of murdered children.

Daniel's family will never see his murderer brought to justice—corruption at the Metropolitan police has ensured that—but the Minister has it in his power to see that they get an explanation of the failure. He can only do that if the next investigation has their confidence. They seek a judge-led inquiry into the police's handling of the murder, because they have lost confidence in the police. In the circumstances, wouldn't anyone?

4:21 pm The Minister for Policing and Criminal Justice (Nick Herbert)

I congratulate the hon. Member for West Bromwich East (Mr Watson) on securing this debate. I am aware of his interest in this matter and the interest of other hon. Members, including the hon. Member for Islington South and Finsbury (Emily Thornberry).

The Home Secretary and the Government believe that this is a matter of the utmost seriousness, concerning a horrific murder exacerbated by a failure to see those responsible held to account. The Home Secretary is taking a personal and active interest in this issue. She met Daniel Morgan's family and representatives in December last year and listened carefully to what the family had to say to her. She committed to reflect on what she had heard at that meeting and to look into the matters further. At the time, she also made it clear that we do not rule out anything when considering the next steps. She has since spoken to Bernard Hogan-Howe, the Metropolitan Police Commissioner.

There is no doubt that the case of the murder of Daniel Morgan has not been handled properly by the authorities over the years. Although no murder investigation is ever really closed without the perpetrators being brought to justice, the fact is that 25 years on Daniel's murderer remains unconvicted. There has been a failed trial and justice has not been done, or seen to be done. Tim Godwin, as acting commissioner at the time, has apologised for the repeated failure by the Metropolitan Police Service and accepted that

"Corruption had played such a significant part in failing to bring those responsible to justice."

I am sure that hon. Members will agree that none of us can ever begin to comprehend the suffering that the Morgan family has endured over the past years. Our sympathies are with them.

Whatever happens now, the Government, the police and the authorities must do all we can, not just to bring the murderers of Daniel Morgan to justice, if at all possible, but—crucially—to ensure that the wider issues to do with police corruption are identified and addressed. The Metropolitan Police Commissioner has given his personal assurance to the Home Secretary that he is committed to achieving these ends. That is why he has appointed Assistant Commissioner Cressida Dick personally to oversee all aspects of the Morgan case. She is, as hon. Members will be aware, a senior police officer who is currently the assistant commissioner of specialist operations, and she comes to the case and the issues it raises with fresh eyes. It is important to note that she has no previous involvement with the case.

The MPS has also started looking at a full forensic review, which, as hon. Members will recall, was an important factor in the successful prosecutions in the Stephen Lawrence case. The MPS is considering seeking advice from independent counsel on what options are available to it to enable successful prosecutions, in light of the failed trial last year.

Ongoing investigations are relevant, including Operation Weeting and Operation Tuleta, being led by Deputy Assistant Commissioner Sue Akers of the MPS, who, following her evidence to the Home Affairs Committee in July last year, again gave a clear account to the Leveson inquiry earlier this week. Both Operation Weeting, which is looking at the interception of mobile phone messages by journalists and their associates, and Operation Tuleta, which is considering the numerous historical operations that have some bearing on this matter, are ongoing. We must let those investigations run their course, as they have a bearing on the issues raised in the Morgan case. For example, Deputy Assistant Commissioner Akers will be looking at the circumstances surrounding the surveillance by News of the World journalists of David Cook, the former senior investigating officer in the murder inquiry. I take seriously these allegations, repeated in the evidence of Jacqui Hames to the Leveson inquiry yesterday.

I appreciate the concerns of Daniel Morgan's family about further investigation by the police. However, I do not believe that the police service is incapable of investigating itself. The investigations led by DAC Akers have led to the arrests of police officers. There are many examples of corrupt and criminal officers having been removed from their force and brought to justice. In addition, the Independent Police Complaints Commission is a robust, independent body that can always oversee on referral or call in any such investigation. So, there are strong checks and balances over the police in such matters, too.

Hon. Members will note that the Home Secretary has recently appointed Dame Anne Owers as the new chair of the IPCC. Dame Anne, former chief inspector of prisons, has a formidable public reputation, not only as an expert in criminal justice matters, but for her integrity and independence from the Government.

The MPS and the Crown Prosecution Service are jointly reviewing the reasons for the collapse of last year's trial of five suspects relating to this case. This review is focusing specifically on the methodology, decisions and tactics adopted by the prosecution team, including any omissions in relation to disclosure and the use of the assisting offender provisions in the Serious Organised Crime and Police Act 2005. I realise that this review will not answer all the issues that might be raised in a judicial inquiry, which remains the Morgan family's preferred outcome. However, it might have a bearing on how we could frame any judicial inquiry, should that be the way forward. It would also help the MPS and the CPS consider what options would be available to them, were they to look to prosecute those responsible in future. This report has been much delayed, partly because the MPS and the CPS have been considering the forensics aspects, but I understand that it will be completed shortly. The MPS has offered to brief the family and their representatives on the findings.

Jacqui Hames's evidence to the Leveson inquiry has brought these issues into even sharper focus this week. That inquiry has now turned from considering press practices alone to focusing on the relationship between the press and the police, whether those relations were inappropriate or indeed corrupt, and what bearing they might have on how the police conducted their investigations into phone hacking.

The detailed investigation of specific cases, such as the Morgan case, might be considered to be more a matter for this second part of the inquiry, although it is clearly a matter for Lord Justice Leveson himself to decide how far he wants to investigate specific cases, such as this part of the inquiry.

Given all this ongoing work, it is important to consider what options are now available to identify and address police corruption and bring those responsible for Daniel's murder to justice. As I have mentioned, the Morgan family has called for a judicial inquiry and this call has been endorsed by the Metropolitan Police Authority. However, such an inquiry is unlikely to be quick—a key concern for Daniel Morgan's mother—and it cannot directly lead to prosecutions. Any such prosecutions based on what the inquiry may unearth would need to follow further police investigations. I recognise that this would satisfy the Morgan family's demands and we are considering carefully whether this is the right way forward. The Home Secretary and I have not ruled out ordering a judicial inquiry at this stage. The Home Secretary wrote to the Morgan family's solicitors yesterday and will do so again shortly with her decision on the way forward.

Any decision will need to take into account whether the MPS might invite another police force to conduct a police investigation, particularly focusing on the allegations of corruption in this case. There may yet be value in this course, involving officers with no connection to the MPS investigating allegations of police corruption, because even now aspects of the alleged corruption have not been properly investigated. The MPS has not ruled out this option.

Were such an investigation to proceed, any judicial inquiry would be limited in what work it could do alongside these investigations. An alternative might be for the Government to ask a Queen's Counsel to supervise the investigation of the corruption aspects of the Morgan case, again by an outside force, involving police officers with no connection to the MPS. This option would most likely be quicker, with a QC providing the integrity and independence required.

In conclusion, I reiterate the Government's commitment to seeing that all that can be done is done to bring justice for Daniel Morgan and his family. Similarly, the MPS is also fully committed to seeing that justice is done. The Home Secretary continues to take a personal and active interest in this matter. The hon. Gentleman asked that we remain open-minded about this matter. I assure him that we do. I am committed, as he is, to making sure that we get to the bottom of this matter, in one way or another. (See Chapter The Dark Side)

This was most enthralling as the Chamber listened intently to what Tom Watson and then Nick Herbert had to say; a story told with allegations almost as shocking as it was unfathomable. But with the resolve of a seasoned campaigner it seems that Tom Watson may well have done more in 20 minutes than could be achieved in 25 years - a request for an independent judge led investigation. However, before the ink on the document to the home secretary was dry the journalist who had an association with John Rees and the News of the World, Alex Marunchak, would respond to these allegations and this is what he said.

DANIEL MORGAN SOUTHERN INVESTIGATION

With kind permission of The Press Gazette: this is the Press Gazette news article, dated the 1ˢᵗ of March 2012 by Dominic Ponsford, Editor.

March 1, 2012

Marunchak: Tom Watson allegations 'absolutely untrue'

Yesterday, Tom Watson MP made a series of allegations about former News of the World journalist Alex Marunchak, the News of the World and the murder of private investigator Daniel Morgan in 1987.

During a Commons adjournment debate he claimed that Daniel Morgan went to Marunchak with a story making allegations about police corruption a week before he died, that he was offered £40,000 for the story and that Marunchak also paid the relatives of police officers for information about the Soham murders in 2002.

Watson said that two of the men arrested on suspicion of the Morgan murder were part of a 'corrupt nexus of private investigators, police officers and journalists at the News of the World".

On Tuesday, former policewoman Jacqui Hames alleged that Marunchak commissioned surveillance of Met police detective Dave Cook in 2002 to 'subvert' a new inquiry into the Morgan murder.

Press Gazette put the following questions to Alex Marunchak today:

Did Daniel Morgan go to you, or someone else at the News of the World, with a story about police corruption the week before he died?

Was he offered £40,000 for it?

Did you, or anyone else at the News of the World, do anything which could have tipped off the police or Daniel's then partner at Southern Investigations Jonathan Rees about what he was said to be alleging?

Was the News of the World's surveillance of detective chief superintendent Dave Cook in 2002 linked in any way to his involvement in the Daniel Morgan murder inquiry?

The general innuendo from what Watson said appears to be that the murder of Daniel Morgan was linked in some way to corrupt relationships involving the News of the World, the police and Morgan's former company Southern Investigations. What is your response to this?

Here is Marunchak's written response:

"Mercifully I didn't see Tom Watson's performance but regret it came slightly too late for him to be an also-ran at the Oscar ceremony.

No related posts.

It astonishes me an MP can abuse parliamentary privilege and waste everybody's time by peddling untruths in this way.

I have never met Watson, nor talked or communicated with him in any way.

Perhaps I should make this clear at the outset — lest he be found crucified on a hill overlooking Jerusalem and I am held, in some way, to be responsible.

The Daniel Morgan murder:

Watson's comments about my professional dealings with murder victim Daniel Morgan are absolutely untrue.

I do not doubt that Morgan's family now believe he was on the verge of exposing police corruption before he died.

If that was indeed a motive for his death — then I know nothing about it.

The reason is that I never heard of Daniel Morgan or Southern Investigations until after his murder.

He never phoned me, contacted or met me, neither directly nor through a third party, by telephone or letter or by any other method.

Nor did he leave graffiti sprayed on walls for me to spot on the way to work which asked me to contact him.

But, I admit, for all I know, he may even have employed someone claiming to have ESP powers to contact me.

Sadly, for Mr Watson, I did not receive any ESP messages either.

Perhaps he should look into this as the basis for his next parliamentary diatribe on the topic?

I was told to cover the Morgan murder story as the News of the World's crime reporter.

Then news editor Bob Warren told me: 'Find out who this man is for a start. We've never heard of him."

Neither I, nor anyone else at the News of the World, offered Morgan £40,000 for his story.

Nor did we offer £100,000.

In fact, we never knew he even existed prior to his murder.

The Soham murders:

I was promoted to associate editor of the News of the World in 1997 after 10 years on the News of the World news desk.

My primary job was to edit the Irish News of the World in Dublin.

At about this time I was also offered the post of head of news at the Sunday Mirror by the Trinity Mirror director, Kelvin Mackenzie, an offer which I turned down.

I never worked on stories about the Soham murders [which happened in 2002], never wrote copy, nor interviewed anyone.

I did not pay any relatives of police officers involved in the Soham murders.

Instead, I carried on with the task of editing the Irish News of the World and commuted between Dublin and London.

Watson said in parliament he had been told a police informant claimed he overheard me boasting I had paid relatives of police officers in Cambridgeshire for information about the

Soham murders. He also claimed I had written Soham stories. For the avoidance of any doubt – what Watson said is completely untrue.

In the unlikely event an experienced Fleet Street hack like myself, based in Dublin, were paying relatives of police officers in Cambridgeshire, would he be stupid enough to blurt it out in front of strangers, one of whom was a police informer? Er, no. I don't think so.

The simple fact is that I was not involved in the Soham story. It was an English story run by the London news desk. I was in charge of the Irish News of the World and had no role whatsoever in the Soham story.

Jacqui Hames and NOTW surveillance of Dave Cook in 2002:

I received information from a source that then minor BBC Crimewatch personality Jacqui Hames was having an affair with a senior officer who was appearing on her TV show.

For the avoidance of doubt, I did nothing to check this, because it was of no interest to me.

I did not look at cuttings, because I had no time, and I was editing the Irish News of the World. But I passed the tittle-tattle on to the London news desk as a bit of gossip, which had been passed on to me, and left it to them to deal with as they saw fit.

I do not know to this day what checks they carried out, if any at all, or indeed if they did anything about the information. Nor did I ask them to keep me posted with progress or developments. End of story.

But I do know that I did nothing more than have a 30 second conversation passing on the rumour to the London news desk and that was the end of my involvement.

Marunchak had a registered company based at the same address as Southern Investigations:

As part of my master-plan to escape Fleet Street and become a multi-millionaire I registered a limited company at Companies House in London through a chartered accountant. I believe he registered numerous companies at the same address which is the office from which he worked and rented. My name and home address were readily available from Companies House records.

The master plan was to import vodka into Britain and become so incredibly wealthy I could afford to stick two fingers up at Fleet Street. Sadly, the best laid plans of mice and men oft go awry, and the vodka company never traded. Not once. It did not take one single penny, nor import a single drop of vodka, let alone a whole bottle-full.

Instead, I was so busy carrying out my work for the paper I never had time to turn my attention to anything else. After a couple of years on the shelf and not trading I had the firm wound up after receiving threatening letters from Companies House for not filing accounts – of which there were none to file.

The allegation Southern Investigations paid Marunchak's debts:

I have a signed, witnessed, dated statement of truth from the then bursar of the school attended by my sons that no one except myself ever paid school fees. These were gratefully received because they were never paid on time or in full.

Eventually these were finally settled in total after I had left the employ of the News of the World and only after the threat of legal action against me and two years after my youngest son finished university. That's five years after he left the school.

But should anyone be interested, then I am happy to give tips to anyone interested in knowing how I managed to achieve this incredible feat and avoid paying school fees for so long. Ditto for my credit cards.

My responses to Watson's childish and infantile accusations, which have no basis in fact whatsoever, have been repeated ad infinitum whenever he mischievously makes them.

But he persists in doing so, for whatever motives he has conjured up for himself. After all, he didn't get to where he is on the Labour back benches by being stupid."

Alex Marunchak has stated that he never knew Daniel Morgan. However, in statements made by Bryan Madagan, Daniel's friend and confidant he said, *"I can confirm I believe this paper to be the News of the World and Daniel Morgan's contact was a Mr Alex Marunchak".*

Another witness in the Daniel Morgan murder investigation was Marjorie Williams. I first met her when she came to work at the offices of Southern Investigations shortly after Daniel's murder as a part-time bookkeeper.

I found her to be a nice and genuine lady who just got on with her job. I recall she generated my P45 when I left Southern Investigations in 1988. One afternoon Marjorie Williams asked me to deliver some Southern Investigations invoices she had generated. They were placed in a large manila envelope which required being hand delivered to an individual at a tabloid newspaper; that newspaper was the News of the World and the delivery was for the attention of Alex Marunchak.

Initially I was to undertake the delivery however for some reason John Rees intervened saying that he would deliver the parcel himself. I recall this because it was odd that John insisted on making the delivery. This was the first time a delivery of a parcel was not undertaken by me which would have been one of my duties.

What Tom Watson achieved for the Morgan family and the friends of Daniel Morgan on the 29th February 2012 is set forth below in a statement made on the 10th of May 2013 by then Home Secretary (and subsequent Prime Minister) Theresa May and this is what she said.

This document contains parliamentary information licensed under the Open Parliament Licence v3.0.

This is the transcript of the actual parliamentary statement made by The Secretary of State for the Home Department Theresa May on the 10th of May 2013.

The Secretary of State for the Home Department (Mrs Theresa May)

Daniel Morgan, a private investigator, was found murdered in a pub car park in south-east London on 10 March 1987. It is one of the country's most notorious unsolved murder cases.

DANIEL MORGAN SOUTHERN INVESTIGATION

After numerous separate police investigations into the case between 1987 and 2002, the Crown Prosecution Service discontinued the final attempted prosecution against five suspects in 2011.

The Metropolitan Police (MPS) have indicated that there is no likelihood of any successful prosecutions being brought in the foreseeable future. They have also admitted that police corruption was a "debilitating factor" in the original investigation. This has led to calls for an inquiry from Mr Morgan's family, who have waged a long campaign for those responsible for his murder to be brought to justice. I have met the family and, after further serious consideration with them and their representatives, I am today announcing the creation of the Daniel Morgan independent panel.

Importantly, the panel's work will put Mr Morgan's family at the centre of the process and the approach to this issue has the support of the MPS Commissioner and the Independent Police Complaints Commission.

The panel will utilise learning from the Hillsborough independent panel process in addressing how to approach its work. The panel will be chaired by Sir Stanley Burnton, a retired Lord Justice of the Court of Appeal. The appointment of other members of the panel will take place over the coming weeks and will be announced as soon as possible.

The remit of the panel will be to shine a light on the circumstances of Daniel Morgan's murder, its background and the handling of the case over the period since 1987. In doing so, the panel will seek to address the questions arising, including those relating to:

Police involvement in the murder;

The role played by police corruption in protecting those responsible for the murder from being brought to justice and the failure to confront that corruption.

The incidence of connections between private investigators, police officers and journalists at the News of the World and other parts of the media and alleged corruption involved in the linkages between them.

The panel will ensure maximum possible disclosure of all relevant documentation, including information held by all relevant Government Departments and agencies and by the police and other investigative and prosecuting authorities. There is a serious and considerable public interest in having an independent panel look at this case, as part of the Government's commitment to identifying, exposing and addressing corruption.

Recognising the volume of material that must be catalogued, analysed and preserved, the panel will seek to complete its work within a year of the documentation being made available.

A copy of the full terms of reference of the Daniel Morgan independent panel has been placed in the Library of the House.

The panel was initially chaired by Sir Stanley Burnton however he stepped down. The panel is now chaired by former Northern Ireland Police Ombudsman, Baroness Nuala O'Loan.

The Daniel Morgan Independent Panel has made a public appeal for help from anyone who has information about Daniel's murder to contact the panel or the police.

The failed police investigations and prosecutions together with what could be seen as parts of the media in collusion with private investigation businesses and a culture of police and media corruption over three decades is shocking; along with the admission by senior police officers that corruption played a heavy hand in certain aspects of this case.

I find the most significant part that the panel will undertake is the three key related areas of concern, one, police involvement in the murder; two, police corruption and any attempts in shielding or protecting those responsible for the murder from being brought to justice and the failings in dealing with that corruption; three, the connections between police officers, private investigators and journalists of the News of the World and allegations and associated links of other media where alleged corruption may exist.

The limitations of the panel are that it cannot impose any criminal liability, but it is hoped the panel may expose corruption and failings allowing for accountability for wrongs having been done. Justice is all that is asked and it should never have come to this, for without justice all we are left with is anarchy.

We have a 31-year quest into the death of my friend leading to the Home Secretary and subsequent Prime Minister, Theresa May, ordering the Daniel Morgan Independent Panel inquiry in May 2013; the findings of which are expected to be announced sometime in 2018 or thereafter.

I personally feel it is most important that no conclusions are made until the findings of the panel's report are fully published and available for scrutiny.

We can only hope the panel have been assisted in the supply of the full criteria of evidence from all sources, (which I have my concerns) have studied it and are able to make a real difference in their recommendations surrounding Daniel's murder.

Chapter 33

It's About Time

This book has mainly concentrated on the years and events that Daniel and I shared together and my recollections of what took place.

Listed here in summary are important dates from the 18th of March 1986 to the present day. These dates include: police investigations, legal hearings, and persons of interest surrounding the police investigations into Danny's murder.

18 March 1986 Robbery of John Rees, Belmont Car Auctions: On Tuesday 18th March 1986, John Rees was robbed (outside his home) of £18,200 this being the nights takings from the Belmont Car Auctions. (Crime unsolved by the police)

10 March 1987 Murder of Daniel Morgan: Daniel Morgan was murdered in the car park of the Golden Lion public house, Sydenham in south London. He was attacked with an axe. His death was a result of multiple head injuries. The Metropolitan Police Service (MPS) commenced a murder investigation. (Crime unsolved by the police)

3 April 1987 First arrests: Six men, some who were police officers, were arrested in connection with the murder. There was insufficient evidence to charge any person and they were all released. (See Chapter Belmont Car Auctions Robberies)

12 April 1987 Operation Russell / Russia: Allegations of police corruption in South East London and the investigation of Commander Ray Adams involving Alan 'Taffy' Holmes. Two years into the investigation Commander Adams is cleared.

28 July 1987 Alan Holmes Death: The body of Alan 'Taffy' Holmes is found in his back garden having been shot in the chest with a shotgun. His death ruled a suicide. (See Chapter Detective Constable Alan 'Taffy' Holmes)

August 1987 Daniel's Funeral: Danny's body is released by the Coroner and is interned at Elmers End cemetery.

11 – 25 April 1988 Inquest held: An inquest was held at Southwark Coroner's Court by Coroner Sir Montague Levine. A verdict of 'unlawful killing' was delivered. (See Chapter Sir Monty and the Inquisition)

24 June 1988 Concerns received from Daniel Morgan's family: Following concerns expressed by members of Daniel Morgan's family, the investigation was referred by the MPS to the Police Complaints Authority (PCA) and the next month a review, conducted by a team from Hampshire Constabulary, commenced. Entitled 'Operation Drake' its terms of reference were: 'To investigate allegations that police were involved in the murder of Daniel Morgan and any other matters arising'.

31 January 1989 Arrests: Three people were arrested and charged by Hampshire Constabulary – two for murder and one for perverting the course of justice.

11 May 1989 Proceedings discontinued: The Director of Public Prosecutions discontinued proceedings due to a lack of sufficient evidence.

9 June 1989 IPCC Report: The Independent Police Complaints Commission inquiry stops because no evidence is produced to support any allegation of criminal wrong doing by the Metropolitan police officers.

January 1999 Operation Two Bridges: Operation Two Bridges is underway and a covert investigation into Law and Commercial (previously known as Southern Investigations) establishes relevant findings to the case. The investigation establishes an unrelated matter and police charges are brought against John Rees, Austin Warnes, Simon James, James Cooke and Dave Courtney. (See Chapter The Teflon Trail)

May to September 1999: Part of the third failed police investigation was Operation Nigeria/Operation Two Bridges. This included the surveillance of Law and Commercial (previously known as Southern Investigations) and was run by the Metropolitan police's anti-corruption squad, CIB3. It placed a bug in the offices of Law and Commercial and it was this that yielded evidence that convicted Rees. Police surveillance showed frequent contact between Rees and Marunchak. (See Chapter The Teflon Trail)

October 2001 Murder Review Group examination: The MPS Murder Review Group examined the investigation files. New investigative opportunities were identified and a recommendation was made that the case should be re-investigated.

May 2002 Operation Abelard: The MPS launched a new covert investigation into the murder. The following month it was extended to encompass an overt investigation of the murder (Operation Morgan II). An appeal seeking new witnesses was made on the BBC television programme *Crimewatch*.

October 2002 – Jan 2003 Further arrests: Eight arrests were made in connection with the investigation. All those arrested were released on bail pending the receipt of advice from the CPS. In September 2003 the CPS determined that there was insufficient evidence to prosecute anyone and all eight suspects were discharged.

March 2003 CPS Reviews Evidence: The Crown Prosecution Service receives evidence for consideration from the Metropolitan Police in connection to the eight arrests mentioned above.

September 2003 CPS Reports Insufficient Evidence: Evidence for a prosecution fails as the CPS reports insufficient evidence exists and all those previously bailed are released. The Metropolitan murder review group receives another referral from the CPS stating its conclusions and all lines of inquiry have been extensively researched and are exhausted.

2003 Operation Glade: An investigation conducted by the Metropolitan Police into the corruption of officials who provided private investigators with personal data. (Information Commissioner's Office)

2003 Operation Motorman: A 2003 investigation by the Information Commissioner's Office into allegations of offences under the Data Protection Act by the British press.

27 October 2005 MPA commissioned report: Following a meeting with members of Daniel Morgan's family, the Metropolitan Police Authority (MPA) commissioned a report by the MPS on the murder, pursuant to s.22(3) of the Police Act 1966.

March 2006 Operation Abelard II: The MPS commenced a further investigation into the murder.

August to September 2006 Arrests: Three men were arrested in connection with the murder. All were bailed pending further inquiries.

April 2008 Charges laid: The three men answered their bail and were charged with murder. Two further men were arrested, one was charged with murder and the other man, a former police officer involved in the original investigation in 1987, was charged with perverting the course of justice. A sixth man, a serving police constable, was arrested on suspicion of misconduct in a public office and bailed pending inquiries; in September 2008 a decision was taken not to prosecute him but the officer, who had been suspended from duty, subsequently resigned from the MPS.

December 2008 Further arrest: A seventh man was arrested on suspicion of attempting to pervert the course of justice.

June 2009 Further arrest: A woman was arrested on suspicion of conspiracy to murder and bailed. Subsequently, a decision was taken not to prosecute her.

March 2010 to March 2011 Pre-trial Hearings: Legal argument prior to the trial of the remaining defendants took place. As a result of this the prosecution decided to offer no evidence and all the men were formally acquitted.

The Acting Commissioner of the MPS, Tim Godwin, made a public statement that police corruption in the original investigation was a significant factor in the failure to bring to justice those responsible for the murder. He also stated that members of Daniel Morgan's family were entitled to an apology for the repeated failure by the police to acknowledge this corruption.

26 January 2011 Operation Weeting: An investigation under the Specialist Crime Directorate of the Metropolitan Police Service into allegations of phone hacking in the News of the World phone hacking affair the operation is being conducted alongside Operation Elveden, an investigation into allegations of inappropriate payments to police by those involved with phone hacking, and Operation Tuleta, an investigation into alleged computer hacking for the News of the World. All three operations are led by Deputy Assistant Commissioner Sue Akers Head of Organised Crime & Criminal Networks within the Specialist Crime Directorate.

10 July 2011 News of the World: Advertiser boycotts lead to the closure of the News of the World on 10 July 2011, after 168 years of publication. (Phone-hacking scandal: Timeline BBC News 12 July 2011) Retrieved 16 07 2011.

13 July 2011 The Leveson Inquiry: Part one of the inquiry was instigated on 13th of July 2011 by the then Prime Minister Mr David Cameron to inquire into the culture, practices and ethics of the press by Lord Justice Leveson.

10 January 2012 Arrest of DCS Dave Cook: This an excerpt from the Guardian online dated Tuesday the 10th of January 2012 by Sandra Laville, Crime Correspondent. *A former Scotland Yard officer has been bailed by the Independent Police Complaints Commission after his arrest over allegations of unauthorised leaks to a journalist. DCS Dave Cook, 52, was questioned on suspicion of misconduct in a public office after being detained at his Berkshire home. He was arrested after the IPCC was passed information in mid-December by Metropolitan police detectives working on Operation Elveden, which is investigating alleged payments to police officers by newspapers. ---- Cook was criticised by the judge in the Morgan murder trial for misbehaviour in the way he handled a key supergrass witness.* (See Chapter The Teflon Trail)

May 2012 Trial Collapse: Blame is placed firmly at the feet of the police and the CPS in a report regarding the collapse of the trial. The report states that potential evidence failed to be presented and that witnesses in the case for the prosecution were mishandled. (See Chapter The Teflon Trail)

2 October 2012 Operation Kalmyk arrest of Rees and Marunchak: This is an excerpt from the Guardian online dated Tuesday the 2nd of October 2012 by Vikram Dodd and Jason Deans. *Scotland Yard officers investigating alleged computer hacking have made two further arrests, understood to be former News of the World journalist Alex Marunchak and private investigator Jonathan Rees. The two men were arrested shortly before 7am on Tuesday morning at their homes by police officers working on Operation Kalmyk. Both were arrested for alleged offences under section 3 of the Computer Misuse Act 1990 and sections 1 and 2 of the Regulation of Investigatory Powers Act 2000.*

29 November 2012 The Leveson inquiry: Part 1 concluded on the 29th of November 2012. Part 2 has no scheduled time frame to take place at any time soon in the future

10 May 2013 Establishment of the Daniel Morgan Independent Panel: Following sustained pressure from members of Daniel Morgan's family from the time of his death in 1987, the Home Secretary announced that an Independent Panel was being set up to report on the circumstances of Daniel Morgan's murder, its background and the handling of the case over the whole period since March 1987. Sir Stanley Burnton, a retired Lord Justice of Appeal, chaired the independent panel until November 2013 when he resigned for personal reasons and was replaced in July 2014 by Baroness Nuala O'Loan, the former Police Ombudsman of Northern Ireland.

9 September 2015 Operation Kalmyk Report No Further Action: Almost three and a half years after Marunchak and Rees were arrested in connection to operation Kalmyk, The Crown Prosecution Service, Gregor McGill Senior Lawyer made the following statement. *"The CPS received a full file of evidence from the Metropolitan Police's Operation Kalmyk investigation team in March 2015, after a complex investigation. Having carefully reviewed the evidence in accordance with the Code for Crown Prosecutors, the CPS has concluded that no further action can be taken against any of the suspects involved."* In total 15 suspects were considered in relation to allegations of 'computer hacking' allegedly carried out between April 2005 and September 2007 against 13 potential victims - some individuals, some corporate. *"Contact has been made with all relevant parties to inform them of the outcome of this case."*

10 November 2015 DCS Dave Cook No Further Action: The officer was arrested by the IPCC on 10 January 2012, as the result of information provided by the Metropolitan police team investigating Operation Elveden, on suspicion of misconduct in public office. Data protection act offences were also considered. A detailed report of the IPCC investigation together with accompanying documentary evidence was passed to the Crown Prosecution Service (CPS). In May 2015 the CPS decided it had sufficient information to make a charging decision. The CPS has now decided it would not be in the public interest to prosecute the former officer for either offence.

17 February 2017 Rees and The Vians Lose Civil Claim for Malicious Prosecution by the Police. Fillery Wins Part of His Claim: This is an excerpt from the Guardian online dated Friday the 17th of February 2017 by Vikram Dodd, Police and Crime Correspondent. *Three men charged with the 1987 murder of Daniel Morgan lost their case that police maliciously tried to get them convicted. Rees, Garry and Glenn Vian were tried for murder the case collapsed in 2011. Sid Fillery was charged with conspiracy to pervert the course of justice; the crown dropped the case against him. At the high court, Mr Justice Mitting ruled against Rees and the Vians, Fillery won part of his claim. A claim of misfeasance in public office went in Fillery's favour. The witness against him was deemed unreliable and had been mishandled by the lead detective.*

23 November 2017 Daniel's mother Isobel Hulsmann dies aged 89 years. Isobel passed away never seeing justice of the murder of her beloved son.

24 & 25 April 2018 The High Court of Justice in the Court of Appeal (Civil Division) hear an application of appeal by Rees and the Vians for Malicious Prosecution and Misfeasance in Public Office by the Police pertaining to the judgement of Justice Mitting dated 17 February 2017.

5 July 2018 The High Court of Justice in the Court of Appeal (Civil Division) before Lady Justice King and Lord Justice's McCombe and Coulson overturn Justice Mitting and find in favour of Rees and The Vians that the Metropolitan Police undertook Malicious Prosecution and Misfeasance in Public Office. The matter is now to be returned to the High Court for the claimant's damages to be determined. The claimants expect to receive substantial payments in compensation and costs which could run into a number of millions. The Commissioner for the Police has the ability to seek permission by way of appeal to the Supreme Court.

References used in the creation of this timeline include the following licenses:

Daniel Morgan Independent Panel official website.

Wikipedia: Text of Creative Commons Attribution-Share Alike 3.0 License.

This Document of Statement Contains public sector information licensed under the Open Government Licence v2.0.

This document contains parliamentary information licensed under the Open Parliament Licence v3.0.

IN CLOSING

n writing this book I have relived a great deal of the past. You may be forgiven in thinking the content of this book reads like fiction unfortunately a good man died for this book to be written.

Friends and a family suffered the loss of a loved one and this must never be forgotten.

I bear no malice to anyone who I have spoken of and I believe I have represented the events as accurately and as fairly as I remember them taking place.

It must also be remembered that a number of individuals have been arrested and charges as to the murder and other matters surrounding the murder investigation have been made. However, with many police investigations and operations and a tremendous amount of money spent the evidence against those persons was not sufficient (by the police authority and the courts) to find any of these persons guilty of the murder or any other matter surrounding the police investigation into the murder; and therefore, they are not guilty.

The objective in writing this book was for you to have much more information into the life of Daniel Morgan. It is my sincere hope that you have enjoyed getting to know my friend, Danny. I hope that you have a more comprehensive understanding of the man he was and the work he undertook. At times he acted recklessly; was naïve and foolish in many ways but aren't we all at some stage in our lives, however he absolutely did not deserve what happened to him.

To this day I still miss him and am happy for the time I did know him.

"Rest in peace my friend; I'll see you again, on the other side."

This is not the end of the story as far as the case and I am concerned. At a time in the future the Daniel Morgan Independent Panel will be submitting its findings and a second book project is planned to study and comment on the panel's report. So, if you wish to continue the journey with me, be on the lookout for my next publication titled:

"Daniel Morgan Southern Investigation. The Daniel Morgan Independent Panel
– A Review of the Report."

ACKNOWLEDGEMENTS

Writing a book is not a solitary venture – it takes a village to produce a well written publication.

Thank you to Maher Naziri of Southwark Coroner's Court for your patience and perseverance in administration of court documentation.

Thank you to the Southwark Deputy Coroner Phillip Barlow.

To Marion Lawrence, thank you for taking the time to visit and confirm the location of Daniel's memorial on my behalf.

Thanks to Russell Campbell for your consideration in development and marketing.

Thank you to Victoria Simon-Shore for your legal representation, advice and kind words.

Sincere thanks to Malcolm, Pauline and Debbie D'Mello for the generous gift of your time in reading and editing and your honest opinions.

Last but by far from least, Ms Joan Kayajanian.

Without Ms Kayajanian this project would not have been possible. She has managed this project tirelessly with a level of skill and devotion which I will never be able to repay in gratitude. My most heartfelt thanks and appreciation to Joan for her infinite patience, thought, consideration and input. Joan is a gifted individual in heart and mind and has been absorbed in the creation and development of this story.

"Well done Ms Kayajanian".

GLOSSARY

Bairns
Children
Beggars belief
To appear implausible or unbelievable
Bell (to give someone a bell)
To telephone someone
Bent
Dishonest or corrupt in behaviour
Bird
Woman or girl
Blagg / Blaggers of Information
Obtain information by lying, by deception or by stealing
Bloody Minded
Obstinate or stubborn
Bonnet
Hood of a car
Bugger
Something that causes dismay
Captain Scarlett
An animated puppet character known to be indestructible
Casual Staff
Part time employee with no benefits
cc
Engine cubic capacity
CCTV
Closed Circuit Television
Cheeky
Playfully disrespectful
Chuffed
Very pleased or satisfied, delighted
Coshed

Hit on the head
CPS
Crown Prosecution Service
Crown
The government

DC
Detective Constable
DS
Detective Sergeant
DSI
Detective Superintendent
Dustbin
Garbage/trash can
DVLA
Driver and Vehicle Licensing Agency
DWP
Department of Works and Pensions
Effing and Blinding
Swearing and using offensive language
Fall Out
Disagreement/parting of the ways
Fitted Up
Conspire to incriminate falsely a presumably innocent person
Flash
To flaunt or display in a showy manner
Fortnight
A period of 14 days; two weeks
Gents
A men's room, a lavatory intended for use by men
Hospital Sister
A senior or supervisory nurse
Hostelry
Establishment used as a public house or inn
HP-Hire Purchase
A method of purchasing an item, where the buyer pays regular instalments
In Stitches
Laughing vigorously, very amused
IPCC

Independent Police Complaints Commission
Jam Jar
Cockney rhyming slang for motorcar
JCB
An earthmoving machine

Job
A police operation
Keen
Intense, vehement
Kick Off
To be overcome with anger, to start an argument or a fight
Lemming
Any member of a group given to conformity, especially a group poised to follow a leader off a cliff
Lorry/Lorries
A motor vehicle for transporting goods/a truck
Mate
Friend
Mews
A street where there are or were stables; a passage
MPS
Metropolitan Police Service
Mug
Easily fooled or gullible individual
Nick
Police station
Nicking
Stealing
Non-Molestation Court Order
Restraining Order
Not to spare the horses
Drive quickly
Off License
A shop selling alcohol for consumption only off the premises
Old Bill
Police officer
On His Toes
To walk away
Over the Moon

To be delighted, thrilled
PAYE
Pay As You Earn (taxes)
Penny beginning to drop
Finally understand what someone is saying

Pong
A stench, a bad smell
Pram
A small vehicle, usually covered, in which a new-born baby is pushed around in a lying position
Queue
A line of people waiting
Quid
Pound sterling
Sacked
To be fired from employment
Shady
Not trustworthy; disreputable
Shagging
Vulgar slang for sexual intercourse
Stone
A unit of mass equal to 14 pounds
Swift Half
Half a pint of larger
Take the Mickey
To tease, ridicule or mock
Taking the Piss
To subject those present to teasing, ridicule or mockery
Torch
A portable light source powered by electricity; a flashlight
Twit
A foolish or annoying person
VAT
Value Added Tax/sales tax
Wicked
Slang for excellent; awesome; masterful
Wind Up
To play a prank
WPC

Woman Police Constable
Y Fronts
Man's underpants

Certain definitions provided by Wikidictionary – Attribution–Share Alike 3.0 Licence.

Printed in Great Britain
by Amazon

63649635R00196